A Practical Guide to Implementing School-Based Interventions for Adolescents with ADHD

Brandon K. Schultz • Steven W. Evans

A Practical Guide to Implementing School-Based Interventions for Adolescents with ADHD

Brandon K. Schultz
Department of Psychology
East Carolina University
Greenville
NC
USA

Steven W. Evans
Department of Psychology
Ohio University
Athens
OH
USA

ISBN 978-1-4939-2676-3 ISBN 978-1-4939-2677-0 (eBook)
DOI 10.1007/978-1-4939-2677-0

Library of Congress Control Number: 2015937728

Springer New York Heidelberg Dordrecht London

Printed on acid-free paper

Springer New York is part of Springer Science+Business Media (www.springer.com)

To our wives, Debbie and Judy

Preface

Most children who are diagnosed with attention-deficit hyperactivity disorder (ADHD)—roughly 70–80%—exhibit persistent academic difficulties in middle and high schools. Oppositional and antisocial behaviors also emerge at a disproportionally high rate for adolescents with ADHD over the same timeframe. Such problems strain families, schools, and even the juvenile justice system; but it is unclear how counselors, therapists, social workers, psychologists, psychiatrists, school support personnel, and other helping professionals can effectively intervene. Several books have been devoted to late-stage, tertiary interventions for serious conduct problems, particularly when intensive family or multisystemic interventions are warranted, but relatively fewer volumes have focused exclusively on adolescents with ADHD who are at risk for serious problems, but who do not yet require the most intense treatments. We find that there is an important distinction between adolescents who are at risk for conduct problems and those who exhibit serious delinquent behaviors, such as chronic violence, sexual aggression, or substance abuse disorders. The treatments described in this book are intended for the former and not necessarily the latter.

Our aim is twofold: (1) to describe the Challenging Horizons Program (CHP)—a school-based, psychosocial treatment program that has been the subject of extensive research over the past 15 years; and (2) to discuss how to implement the CHP effectively in school-based settings (with implications for clinic-based settings). To achieve these goals, we present materials from the treatment manuals we have used to train parents, students, teachers, and paraprofessionals in the techniques implemented in the CHP, as well as share case examples and verbatim transcripts taken directly from those interactions. Such information is rarely provided in the same source. On the one hand, the counseling literature is generally *process*-focused, meaning that materials written by and for counselors do not necessarily discuss specific disorders, but rather the therapeutic interactions between client and counselor, often exemplified by case vignettes and client-therapist dialogues. In our view, the vignettes in this literature are often implausibly expedient, with client responses so favorable that we often wonder where to find such motivated and insightful clients! On the other hand, the psychiatry and research-outcome literatures are generally *treatment*-focused, rarely delving into counseling process and instead focusing on group-level outcomes and successful treatment protocols. Unfortunately, these discussions are often too abstract to be of immediate use to most practitioners. The treatment outcomes literature points to the promise of various techniques, but the restrictive format of research articles (and even some treatment manuals) leave out important details needed for implementation. In this book, we hope to avoid these limitations by presenting both the lessons of group-level research outcomes and process-level strategies for successful psychosocial intervention.

We begin Chap. 1 by discussing the persistent research-practice gap in our field and then in Chap. 2 we summarize the research to date on ADHD that is most useful to practitioners. Beginning Chap. 3, we start to present the CHP as we have implemented it through several clinical trials. We support this information with actual client-counselor session transcripts—complete with stammers, false starts, and mistakes—so that our readers get an accurate feel for the "three-steps-forward-and-two-steps-back" process of real-life counseling work with adolescents. At the same time, we provide *modules* taken from our treatment manuals to give readers a useful reference guide for the interventions that have shown promise in our research. Our hope is that the chapters covering the CHP—Chaps. 3–7—will be both an interesting read and a user-friendly, quick reference guide for the busy practitioner.

Our discussion is informed by our experience designing and testing various iterations of the CHP at James Madison University and Ohio University, as well as the research of our colleagues who have tested variations of the CHP at Lehigh University, University of Cincinnati, the University of South Carolina, and the University of Pittsburgh Medical Center. Collectively, we have trained and supervised hundreds of graduate students, undergraduate students, and paraprofessionals to provide direct psychosocial interventions for middle and high school students diagnosed with ADHD and related disorders. In addition, we have trained and consulted with hundreds of middle and high school teachers and school counselors to implement school-based interventions to address academic and social impairments associated with the target disorders. Although, we are committed to school-based mental health and believe it to be the most promising route for intervention—a topic we will return to at several points—we discuss both school- and community-based professionals in the hope of informing practice across both settings.

Brandon K. Schultz, EdD
Steven W. Evans, PhD

A Note on Terminology

Readers should be aware that we use the terms *intervention* and *treatment* interchangeably, whereas other sources often make a distinction between the two. Readers should also be aware that we use the terms *counseling* and *psychotherapy* interchangeably, whereas in some other sources the latter term is often used to describe so-called depth therapies (e.g., psychoanalysis), but we make no such distinction here. Thus, when we refer to 'therapists' or 'counselors,' we are referencing a wide range of professionals who might implement the interventions we describe herein, including school psychologists, school counselors, social workers, clinical psychologists, or psychiatrists. Similarly, we use the terms 'adolescent' and 'student' somewhat interchangeably because so much of our work has occurred in secondary schools. Unless otherwise specified, we use the term 'student' to refer to middle and high school-aged adolescents.

In terms of specific diagnostic labels, we refer to the current Diagnostic and Statistical Manual of Mental Disorders (DSM-5; American Psychiatric Association 2013) and assume that our readers are familiar with those criteria. Although the conceptualizations have changed slightly (see Chap. 2), we use the phrase "disruptive behaviors" to refer to ADHD, oppositional defiant disorder (ODD), and conduct disorder (CD), and the phrase "conduct problems" to refer to just ODD and CD. We recognize that school-based practitioners may be more familiar with the Individuals with Disabilities Education Act (IDEA) rather than the DSM, but the IDEA speaks mostly about how schools allocate and manage educational resources rather than to how practitioners select specific interventions. For this reason we base our discussions mainly on the DSM conceptualization of these disorders and the relevant research.

Acknowledgments by Steven W. Evans

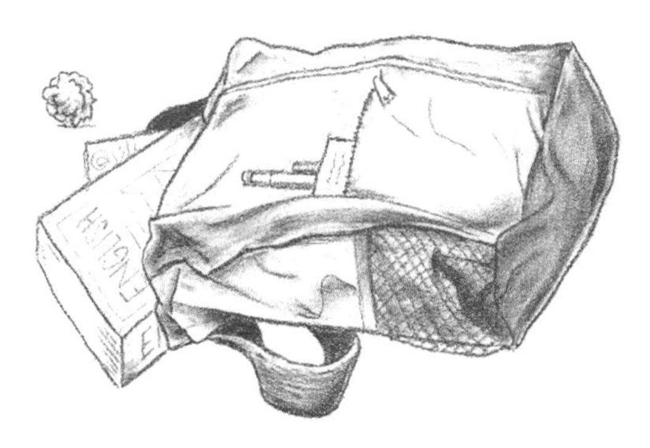

The approach and strategies described in this book form the basis for the CHP, a secondary school-based treatment program I designed for adolescents with ADHD. Some of the CHP strategies were originally based on the extensive research on the Summer Treatment Program (STP) model, designed by William Pelham and his colleagues at the Florida International University, and the Bridges for Education Program at Western Psychiatric Institute and Clinic, which I directed in the 1990s. In addition to Dr. Brandon Schultz's many contributions, I would also like to acknowledge several colleagues who have helped to design and test the CHP through its many versions, including George DuPaul, Kate Flory, Erin Girio-Herrera, Josh Langberg, Brooke Molina, Julie Owens, Zewe Serpell, and Aaron Vaughn. I also would like to thank the many graduate students and paraprofessionals who have participated in the demanding process of testing the CHP in school settings, including Shannon Achey, Jennifer Axelrod, Ruth Brown, Mateja Holter, Steve Marshall, Sheryle Moore, Margaret Nemeth, Alyssa Poskarbiewicz, Veronica Raggi, Jennifer Sapia, Maggie Sibley, Kathryn Van Eck, Casey White, Jeff Williams, Joanna Sadler Yost, and Allison Zoromski. Financial support for some of the research and development work on the CHP has come from the Center for Intervention Research in Schools at Ohio University, the Alvin V. Baird Attention and Learning Disabilities Center at James Madison University, as well as research grants from the National Institute of Mental Health, the Institute for Educational Sciences, and the Virginia Tobacco Settlement Foundation.

S. Evans

Contents

About the Authors

Brandon K. Schultz is an assistant Professor in the Department of Psychology at East Carolina University (ECU). Dr. Schultz has a background in school counseling, receiving a Master's in Education from Frostburg State University in Maryland, before attaining a doctorate in school psychology from Indiana University of Pennsylvania. From 2002–2013, Dr. Schultz provided school psychological services and clinical supervision during several research projects examining the Challenging Horizons Program, first at James Madison University and then at Ohio University. Currently, Dr. Schultz teaches in the pediatric school psychology doctoral program at ECU and directs the School Behavior Consultation Lab. His current research focuses on evidence-based program implementation strategies in secondary schools.

Steven W. Evans is the co-director of the Center for Intervention Research in Schools at Ohio University and professor of psychology. Dr. Evans graduated from Case Western University with a PhD in clinical psychology and then completed a clinical internship and post-doctoral fellowship at Western Psychiatric Institute & Clinic (WPIC). Following his fellowship he joined the faculty at WPIC for 8 years prior to going to James Madison University and then Ohio University. Before earning his doctoral degree he was a special education teacher in a public elementary school. Service to national organizations includes having been a member of the Professional Advisory Board of CHADD and a member of the advisory board of the Center for School Mental Health Assistance. Dr. Evans is a fellow in the American Psychological Association and the CHP is listed as an evidence-based program on SAMHSA's National Registry of Evidence-based Programs and Practices. Dr. Evans is the founding editor of the journal School Mental Health: A Multidisciplinary Research and Practice Journal (Springer Publishing).

Part I
Research on Attention Deficit Hyperactivity Disorder

Chapter 1
Prologue

Nobody would dream of justifying the validity of a logical inference, or of defending it against doubts, by writing beside it in the margin the following protocol sentence. "Protocol: In checking this chain of inferences today, I experienced an acute feeling of conviction."
Sir Karl Popper, from *The Empirical Basis* (1934)

At about the time we started pilot studies of the Challenging Horizons Program (CHP), surveyors conducting the national stigma study—children (NSS-C) asked participants, "Should children be given counseling for attention deficit hyperactivity disorder (ADHD)?" Of the 906 adults who responded, a strong majority—more than 4 out of every 5 (84 %)—indicated that counseling was an appropriate treatment (Davis et al. 2007, p. 1211). However, counseling for ADHD is a dubious prescription; in part because it is unclear what the NSS-C respondents hoped would be accomplished. Imagine, for example, a middle school student with ADHD who is falling behind his peers in the classroom curriculum. He is socially withdrawn at school and argumentative with his mother most evenings over homework and chores. Would the goal of counseling be to improve academic achievement by addressing the student's motivation for school? Should the counselor attempt to improve the child's social connectedness by encouraging greater involvement in positive social activities? Perhaps the purpose of counseling should be to reduce arguments and fighting in the home through parent training or anger management? Or maybe a counselor should address all of these concerns? Unfortunately, it is imposible to know the NSS-C respondents' goals for counseling or their understanding of counseling styles or strategies. "Counseling" can include behavior therapy, play therapy, cognitive-behavioral therapy, nondirective client-centered therapy, psychoanalysis, or any of the hundreds of other specific therapies—each with theories and techniques designed to bring about client change. Which approach (if any) did the survey respondents have in mind?

Although the answers to these questions are unclear, the overwhelming approval of counseling for ADHD suggests that most adults generally find psychosocial in-

B. K. Schultz, S. W. Evans, *A Practical Guide to Implementing School-Based Interventions for Adolescents with ADHD*, DOI 10.1007/978-1-4939-2677-0_1

terventions for childhood attention and behavior problems appropriate. So, it seems safe to conclude that counseling is widely accepted. But is counseling *effective* for children and adolescents with ADHD and other disruptive behaviors? And if so, how? Part 1 of this book addresses these questions, based in part on the research we have conducted on secondary school-based interventions. Research offers preliminary answers to our questions and points to new and exciting avenues of inquiry; however, there are disagreements about how mental health research is best interpreted and applied. Although it is beyond the scope of this book to reconcile all competing views on these questions, the intervention models we describe in Part 2 require some basic understanding of the strengths and limits of the research, so some initial remarks are in order. In this chapter, we shall briefly describe the contentious debates in applied psychology and offer recommendations for practitioners to make sense of the growing—and often equivocal—research literature. As part of our training practices for clinical and school psychologists, we discuss this topic in depth to prepare our students to be both effective clinicians and consumers of research. We hope to replicate those discussions here.

The Research–Practice Debate

Even a glance at the research literature on interventions for ADHD and other disruptive behavior disorders would suggest that there is no universally correct answer to the NSS-C survey item regarding the appropriateness of counseling. At the core of this uncertainty is a debate concerning the presumptive key ingredients necessary for successful intervention. Although there is a consensus among researchers that, in general, counseling is effective for most clients regardless of their initial complaints (Lambert 1992), what counselors should do in those sessions is vehemently debated. So, what is the debate? On the one hand, the evidence-based practice movement, which came to prominence in the 1990s, is an attempt to identify useful psychotherapies for mental health conditions through clinical trials. Proponents of the movement argue that the specific *techniques* used by counselors (i.e., activities) are the key ingredient to successful therapy and that these techniques can be empirically evaluated. Thus, the gold standard method to uncover vital technique is the randomized control trial (RCT), where one group of adolescents might be randomly assigned to an experimental therapy (with experimental techniques) and a second group to a control condition consisting of a traditional therapy or no treatment at all (i.e., placebo condition). After some time, these two groups are compared to see if the experimental therapy led to better outcomes on average than in the control group. Ideally, once techniques are shown to be effective in multiple, independent RCTs, the treatment protocols are disseminated for use in everyday clinical practice, usually in the form of treatment manuals. In this way, evidence-based treatments (EBTs) are established.[1] So in response to the NSS-C survey item discussed

[1] In truth, there are competing definitions of evidence-based practice, but all definitions generally require high-quality trials that are replicated.

at the top of this chapter, proponents of the evidence-based practice movement might conclude that counseling can be effective for ADHD only when the counselor competently adheres to a treatment protocol with a proven track record of success, spanning several rigorous research trials.

On the other hand, many practitioners and researchers argue that individual techniques are not the most important components of counseling. Rather, according to this argument (hereafter *humanistic perspective*[2]), the client–counselor alliance and other situational factors, such as client resources and motivation, explain the largest proportion of client change. Hence, counseling outcomes depend mostly on elements that are nonspecific to any one theory or practice, nor easy to examine in isolation. So in contrast to the evidence-based practice movement, proponents of the humanistic perspective see two main methodological problems with the "gold standard" RCT approach: First, there is typically a careful screening process when recruiting potential participants for clinical trials, often using specific diagnostic criteria that the researchers believe are amenable to the techniques in question. Screening of this kind is unlike clinical settings where clients often have multiple concerns that complicate treatment, so the results of clinical trials speak to the potential *efficacy* of specific interventions, but not necessarily the *effectiveness* of those interventions in actual clinical settings (Addis et al. 1999). Second, the treatment manuals and treatment protocols used in RCTs often prescribe counseling techniques in a rigid session-by-session manner, without adequate regard for individual client needs. Proponents of the humanistic perspective argue that an overreliance on manualized procedures could potentially undermine the clinical judgment of practitioners who might otherwise design an effective therapeutic experience for a client based on her individual needs. So again, clinical trials appear to have limited bearing on actual practice, and attempts to alter practice based on these findings could have a negative impact on client outcomes in real-world clinical settings. In a managed care environment, for example, where practitioners are reimbursed by third-party insurers, manualized EBTs might proffer an unrealistically simple treatment option. Insurers who demand low-cost, circumscribed interventions might then unfairly prioritize EBTs over idiosyncratic[3] therapy using reimbursement policies that are essentially discriminatory (Fox 2000). Proponents of the humanistic perspective fear that, over time, the evidence-based practice movement and the managed care environment will ultimately constrain practitioners to inflexible procedures, even if mental health services suffer as a result (Reed and Eisman 2006). As an alternative, some proponents of the humanistic perspective advocate a qualitative approach to

[2] We recognize that the term humanistic perspective might be construed as overly simplistic to describe all criticisms of the evidence-based practice movement, especially considering that some criticisms come from parts of the field that are not "humanistic" in the traditional sense; however, we will use this term for conciseness, with an implicit recognition of the heterogeneity of these arguments.

[3] We are using the term "idiosyncratic" to mean individualized treatment planning and implementation, similar to Manuchin et al. (2006). We are by no means suggesting this practice is less organized or less thoughtful than manualized therapies.

research (e.g., ethnography, narrative analysis)[4] that acknowledges the uniqueness of each therapeutic encounter (Maione and Chenail 1999) and allows for a more suitable analysis of counseling that is tailored for each client. So, when answering the NSS-C item, proponents of the humanistic perspective might conclude that counseling for ADHD is warranted, but only when there are individualized goals based on the client's specific needs and context, particularly if similar approaches have been supported by qualitative studies.

Regardless of the merits of either argument, the research-practice debate appears to contribute to a profound and persistent gap between the research literature and actual clinical practice. For instance, only a fraction of children and adolescents (<22 %) with mental health needs receive any services (Kataoka et al. 2002), and when services are provided, practitioners do not prioritize research-supported therapies (Addis et al. 1999; Nelson and Steele 2008; Weisz et al. 1995). Rather, mental health services appear largely dependent on local resources and practitioner judgment. In other words, practitioners typically use idiosyncratic approaches, and these practices do not necessarily follow treatment protocols, manuals, or other resources and techniques tested in the research literature.

Of course, applied psychology is no stranger to controversial issues that fracture the field into ideological camps (cf. Henriques 2004; Kimble 1984), but the questions surrounding the research literature have implications for the future of all mental health services. Which side of the research–practice debate is most influential? In terms of training, the humanistic perspective may be dominant because many graduate training programs prepare the next generation of practitioners in an idiosyncratic manner.[5] For example, in a survey conducted well after the evidence-based practice movement came to prominence, psychology graduate students reported that they were less likely to receive training in EBTs for childhood conduct problems than other students had reported in the past (Woody et al. 2005). Perhaps, students in scientist-practitioner training programs are skeptical of clinical trial research; most appear to confuse the basic definition of evidence-based practice and report that they are unlikely to consult the literature to inform their practice, even though the research-practitioner model was designed to wed research and practice (Luebbe et al. 2007). Such trends persist even though clients who receive therapy at training clinics exhibit better outcomes when those clinics switch from idiosyn-

[4] Since the initial report of the American Psychological Association (APA) Task Force on Promotion and Dissemination of Psychological Procedures, which first attempted to define well-established and probably efficacious psychotherapies (Chambless 1993), several professional organizations have offered alternative definitions. Mostly, these alternatives have challenged the vaulted status of the RCT. For instance, some organizations have argued that other research designs can be more easily used and as informative as the RCT in certain situations. For its part, the APA has revisited these questions and the Presidential Task Force on evidence-based practice has acknowledged the value of several alternative research designs, but still refers to the RCT as "the standard for drawing causal inferences about the effects of interventions" (APA Presidential Task Force on Evidence-Based Practice, 2006, p. 274). Still, disagreements regarding the merits of competing research designs persist.

[5] Readers are encouraged to read the excellent discussion by Baker et al. (2008), as well as the thoughtful framework for how EBPs might be best integrated into clinical training by Hershenberg et al. (2012).

cratic to EBTs (e.g., Cukrowicz et al. 2011). When these facts are juxtaposed with federal research expenditures—the National Institute of Mental Health provided $917 million in research project grants in 2014 alone (National Institute of Mental Health n.d.)—it is unclear whether practitioner ambivalence toward research belies such large public investments. Or, from our perspective as researchers, we wonder when the findings from clinical trials will impact training and dissemination efforts at a level commensurate with the investment.[6]

Comparing EBTs and Treatment-As-Usual: Three Meta-Analyses

The gap between research and practice persists in part because of legitimate questions regarding the relative effectiveness of EBTs when compared to typical clinical practice. Conceptually, idiosyncratic therapies can be *as* or even *more* effective than research-supported treatments in bringing about desired client outcomes. In fact, some researchers argue that virtually any systematic approach to counseling results in equally positive outcomes—a point often made by proponents of the humanistic perspective because it seemingly confirms that the active ingredient is *not* a specific technique, but rather the nonspecific elements of the client–counselor relationship and other contextual factors. If psychotherapies based on contradicting theories and using dissimilar techniques can lay claim to similar outcomes, then conceivably the specific elements of the therapies are less important than the factors that all have in common. Several researchers have contemplated this possibility, beginning with Rosenweig (1936) who attributed counseling outcomes primarily to the counselor's relationship with the client—an element that is universal to all schools of therapy. Since that time, these so-called *common factors* of counseling have been enumerated in varying ways, but generally are thought to include:

- Empathy
- Acceptance
- Warmth
- Positive regard
- Genuineness
- Trust[7]

[6] The majority of the treatment evaluation research project grants funded by the NIMH are awarded to RCT designs. Thus, in addition to altering practice to reflect research, as we suggest here, the research–practice gap can also be closed by shifting research funding to modified versions of the RCT that better reflect practice, and this shift has been occurring at NIMH and other federal funding agencies.

[7] For a contemporary discussion of the research on common factors, we recommend Norcross and Wampold (2011).

The common factors set the groundwork for the therapeutic alliance between client and counselor, and the strength of this relationship appears to predict client outcomes, with stronger alliances leading to the most positive outcomes (Lambert 1992). So, despite a history of competition between the various schools of psychotherapy, it has been argued that as long as counselors establish the common factors, most approaches to counseling will be equally successful. This hypothesis has been referred to as the "Dodo bird conjecture," named after the *Alice in Wonderland* character who proclaims all participants in a chaotic race winners (Carroll, cited in Wampold et al. 1997, p. 203).

In recent decades, a series of meta-analyses have been conducted to quantitatively determine whether the Dodo bird conjecture is accurate. In a widely cited study, Wampold and colleagues (1997) conducted a meta-analysis of 114 treatment studies, published between 1970 and 1995 inclusive, comparing "bona fide" therapies in head-to-head trials across a wide range of client problems. Bona fide psychotherapies were defined as: (1) requiring a master's level or higher clinician in face-to-face meetings with clients, and (2) targeting client concerns that would typically be addressed in clinical settings. Further, the authors ensured that the psychotherapies under investigation were either based on previous research or theories, or systematically delivered, such as through the use of written procedures. Based on their meta-analysis, Wampold and colleagues' concluded that almost all therapies were equally beneficial. Meaningful differences between competing psychotherapies occurred very rarely, and only at a rate that would be expected by chance. So in short, all psychotherapies won in head-to-head comparisons, presumably because all bona fide therapies embrace the common factors.

But, of course, no study is flawless, and critics have questioned Wampold and colleagues' methodology. Perhaps the most pertinent criticism involves the manner in which the authors computed and interpreted the between-therapy effect sizes (see Box 1.1 for a brief explanation of effect size). The authors examined between-therapy effects two ways: First, due to the fact that effect size calculation requires the effect of one therapy to be subtracted from the second therapy, the direction (i.e., sign) of the effect size is arbitrary, depending on which therapy is entered into the calculation first. To address this problem, Wampold and colleagues randomly assigned either a negative or positive sign to the effect size estimates. Using these data, the authors then examined whether the effect sizes were homogenously distributed around zero—the midpoint representing no difference between therapies. The authors found no evidence of significant spread (i.e., platykurtosis) in this distribution—the effect sizes clumped closely around zero consistent with the Dodo bird conjecture. Second, the authors calculated an overall estimate of between-therapy difference by adding the absolute values of all observed effect sizes and dividing by the number of observations, which resulted in a statistically significant overall difference between competing therapies ($d = 0.19$). However, Wampold and colleagues concluded that this latter estimate was overly generous and represented "an upper bound" of the true effect that was not strong enough to reject the Dodo bird conjecture (p. 209). Critics point to this conclusion and argue that the second analysis is actually the more accurate of the two (e.g., Howard et al. 1997). Based on Wampold and colleagues' own effect size estimate, it would be predicted that 94 out of every 1000 clients differentially benefit from receiving one therapy over another, suggesting that the average between-therapy effect was meaningful, despite the authors' conclusions (Hunsley and Di Giulio 2002).

Box 1.1

What Exactly Is an Effect Size?

An effect size is an estimate of change in one group relative to a comparison group; or alternatively, it is an estimate of change within individuals before and after an intervention is attempted. Thanks to a long tradition in statistics, we are obligated to say that effect sizes tell us "how much bang we get for our buck" when testing interventions. Perhaps the simplest of the many formulas for estimating an effect size is to subtract the average performance of one group (M_1) on a measure of interest from the same of a second group (M_2), and then divide by the pooled standard deviation (SD):

Formula 1.1: Effect Size

$$\frac{M_1 - M_2}{\text{Pooled}\,SD}$$

If we are comparing a treatment and control group, for example, we would subtract the average performance of the control group (e.g., 100) from that of the treatment group (e.g., 115), and then divide by the pooled SD (e.g., 15), giving us an effect size of 1.0, which tells us that the treatment group did the equivalent of one standard deviation better on the outcome of interest than the control group. Unlike approaches that examine statistical significance, effect size estimates offer a standardized estimate of how much impact the treatment had, rather than whether the two groups were unusually divergent. Of course, there are many approaches to estimating effect sizes depending on the research design and how the researchers compare experimental conditions; so, effect sizes are not always as straightforward as our example. Odds ratios and correlations are estimates of effect size in some instances. Thankfully, statisticians have offered general rules of thumb for interpreting effect sizes depending on what type of effect size is used. In Fig. 1.1, the effect sizes are calculated in a manner similar to the formula above, which is known as Cohen's *d*. In these instances, effect sizes can be interpreted using the following scale (Cohen 1988):

>.80	Large
.70	
.60	
.50	Medium
.40	
.30	
.20	Small
.10	
.00	*Nil*

Using Cohen's guidelines, the results of the meta-analyses summarized in Fig. 1.1 suggest that although the Wampold studies found average effect sizes approaching the "small" range, the meta-analysis conducted by Weisz and colleagues suggests that the between-therapy effects fall between the "small" and "medium" range. (Note that the three effect size estimates in Fig. 1.1 were adjusted based on sample sizes, allowing for unbiased comparisons across the three studies.)

From our standpoint, the other important limitation of Wampold and colleagues' study is that adult and child therapies were not analyzed separately. A review of the titles included in their meta-analysis suggests that very few studies focused exclusively on children or adolescents. In a follow-up meta-analysis, Miller and colleagues (2008) examined only child and adolescent psychotherapies using roughly the same techniques. The distribution of effect sizes from 23 studies was significantly platykurtic, suggesting that an unexpectedly high number of studies found meaningful between-therapy differences. However, the average between-therapy effect size ($d = 0.22$) was "small" (p. 11), and the authors argue that these differences can be explained by differential researcher allegiances to therapies. In other words, the authors attributed the observed differences between child therapies to the degree to which researchers were personally invested in the techniques under investigation. In head-to-head trials, the therapies preferred by the researchers most often fared better—a phenomenon sometimes referred to as the *allegiance effect* (Luborsky et al. 1999). So, in Miller and colleagues' judgment, the Dodo bird conjecture cannot be rejected because biased researchers unfairly resource their preferred therapies. Assuming this is correct, the inference is that the fairest comparison between competing psychotherapies would require that each is delivered by separate groups of practitioners with equally vested interests in the outcomes.

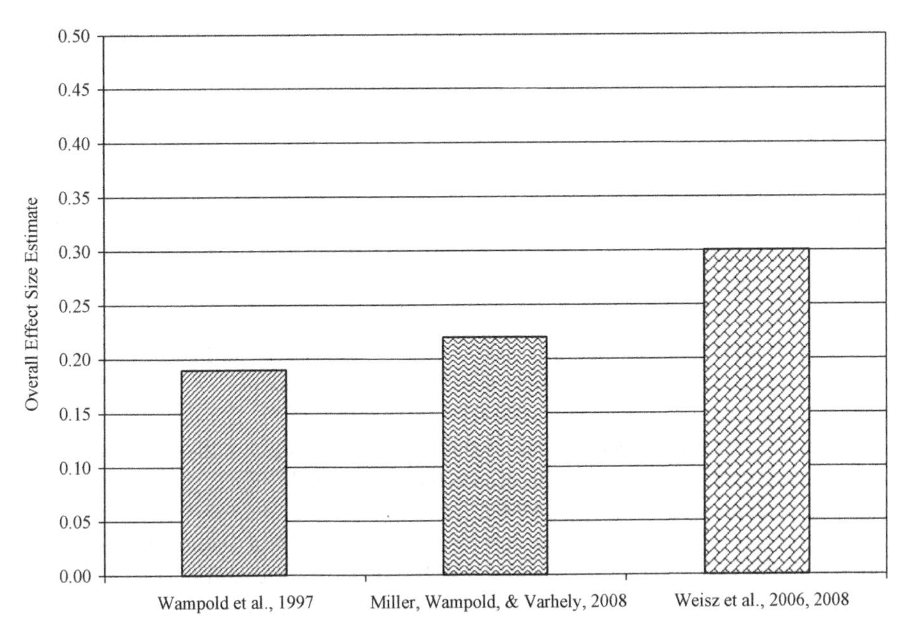

Fig. 1.1 Comparison of between-therapy effect size estimates across three related meta-analyses

Weisz and colleagues (Weisz and Gray 2008; Weisz et al. 2006) have examined psychotherapy outcomes for children and adolescents by summarizing the results of 32 studies that directly compared EBTs to treatment-as-usual control conditions, spanning the years from 1973 to 2004. The authors included only those studies where researchers randomly assigned participants to either an EBT or typical clinical services. The participants in the typical clinic conditions most commonly received outpatient therapy, case management, or juvenile justice services.[8] In this way, Weisz and colleagues' research speaks directly to the research–practice debate for child and adolescent psychotherapies, while avoiding the potential confound of allegiance effects. In this design, all practitioners were committed to ensuring that the treatments were as effective as possible. The results of the meta-analysis suggest that EBTs have a moderate overall advantage over treatments-as-usual ($d = 0.30$; see Fig. 1.1). Thus, it appeared that the average child or adolescent who received an EBT fared better than 62% of children receiving treatment-as-usual at post-treatment analysis (Weisz et al. 2006).

[8] Although community control and treatment-as-usual control groups are common in RCTs, most researchers simply encourage participants in these groups to seek out services of their choice. Weisz and colleagues (2006) were careful to include only those studies where the researchers reported specific attempts to ensure that control participants actually received services "intended to have beneficial effects" (p. 684).

Although Weisz and colleagues' results are remarkable, it is important to note that not all comparative studies found that EBTs outperformed treatment-as-usual. Of the 39 direct comparisons examined, four outcomes favored typical clinical practice. The exceptions where usual clinical practice outperformed EBTs are revealing: Two were derived from a single dissertation comparing the social and behavioral outcomes of 18 children with conduct problems who received evidence-based anger and problem-solving programs versus traditional day treatment (Guarton 1992); another exception was observed in a dissertation that compared outcomes for 26 aggressive adolescent boys who received either an evidence-based problem-solving intervention or typical residential care (Grant 1988); and the final exception was observed in a peer-reviewed study that examined the impact of behavioral family systems therapy compared to typical (i.e., eclectic) outpatient therapy for 19 children with conduct problems and no ADHD (Luk et al. 1998). The first three exceptions are not necessarily surprising because dissertations generally result in more conservative estimates of treatment effects than published studies, possibly because doctoral students design and implement less potent treatments and have fewer resources on average than seasoned researchers (McLeod and Weisz 2004). In the study conducted by Luk and colleagues (1998), however, the results are difficult to interpret. Here, all treatments under investigation resulted in positive benefits for participants, reminiscent of the Dodo bird conjecture; but notably, participants in the family therapy condition attended fewer sessxions on an average than did the participants in the treatment-as-usual condition (5.1 versus 5.6, respectively). At the beginning of the study, the researchers planned to schedule 12 sessions over 24 weeks, so client attendance was clearly a concern. We interpret the exceptions in Weisz and colleagues' study to suggest that EBTs are somewhat less likely to outperform treatment-as-usual when poorly resourced or not implemented as intended, but clearly there may be other explanations that only further research can elucidate. Still, the majority of studies demonstrate an advantage for EBTs designed for child and adolescent clients.

The Ingredients of Counseling

Even though the evidence suggests modest differences between competing counseling strategies for children and adolescents, it is still unclear whether these differences are attributable to specific techniques. For example, clients might *expect* that their experience in a "new" or "innovative" therapy will be positive, thereby improving outcomes in clinical trials simply on the basis of hope or wishful thinking. Or children and adolescents who participate in clinical trials may differ from those who do not in ways that make generalization to other populations unwise; for example, it is possible that the parents who consent to clinical trials have greater support systems and resources at home that allow them to take advantage of new treatments, whereas less advantaged families might not. Such questions have caused researchers to carefully consider the active ingredients of successful therapy, beyond just the specific counseling techniques and the common factors. Clearly, there are multiple components to counseling, including client expectations and family resources, and each of these components has a differential impact on client outcomes.

One of the most widely cited models of counseling outcome is offered by Lambert (1992). Lambert proposes four main ingredients in psychotherapy and their relative proportional influence in eliciting client change:

- Extratherapeutic change (40 %)
- Common factors (30 %)
- Expectancy effects (15 %)
- Specific techniques (15 %)

The largest factor is what Lambert refers to as extratherapeutic change, which is largely outside the control of the client or the counselor, and includes client resources, resiliency, and social support systems. The estimated proportion of extratherapeutic influence is based on research examining the phenomenon of spontaneous improvement, which is the likelihood that clients will recover from their symptoms with minimal or no intervention. Although these estimates vary widely depending on the presenting problem, Lambert estimates that the median spontaneous remission rate across studies is 40 %.

In terms of the common factors, research supports the notion that a proportion of treatment outcome is attributable to the elements common to all schools of therapy. Most studies of this relationship cite correlations between client or counselor ratings of the therapeutic alliance and treatment outcomes and as mentioned above, this research suggests that stronger alliances are associated with more positive client outcomes. Again, the estimates of this association in the literature vary widely, but of the studies reviewed by Lambert, the median correlation suggests that roughly 30 % of the variance in outcomes is attributable to the client–counselor interpersonal dynamic.[9] As for Lambert's estimates of the influence of client expectancy factors (i.e., placebo effect) and specific techniques, no explicit rationales are provided.

When interpreting these conclusions, several caveats should be noted. First and perhaps most important, Lambert came to this conclusion based entirely on adult psychotherapy research. Beyond any doubt, counseling with children and adolescents presents concerns that are not shared in adult therapies, including the fact that very few children or adolescents seek counseling voluntarily; most are referred by parents, teachers, courts, or other concerned adults. Thus, it is likely that when compared to adults, children and adolescents generally enter therapy with a lower expectation for positive outcome. Second, child and adolescent therapies must take into account shifting developmental concerns, including cognitive and emotional development that impacts the client's ability to understand and benefit from some counseling strategies. Third, mental health concerns in childhood and adolescence generally have a poorer prognosis than concerns that do not emerge until adulthood. For example, childhood depression is often predictive of severe illness in adulthood, leading to more frequent and persistent depressive episodes when com-

[9] We are assuming that Lambert makes his estimate (30 %) based on the ranges he reports from his review of the literature. In a summary table, Lambert (2003) reports estimates that range from 0 to 57 % (p. 107).

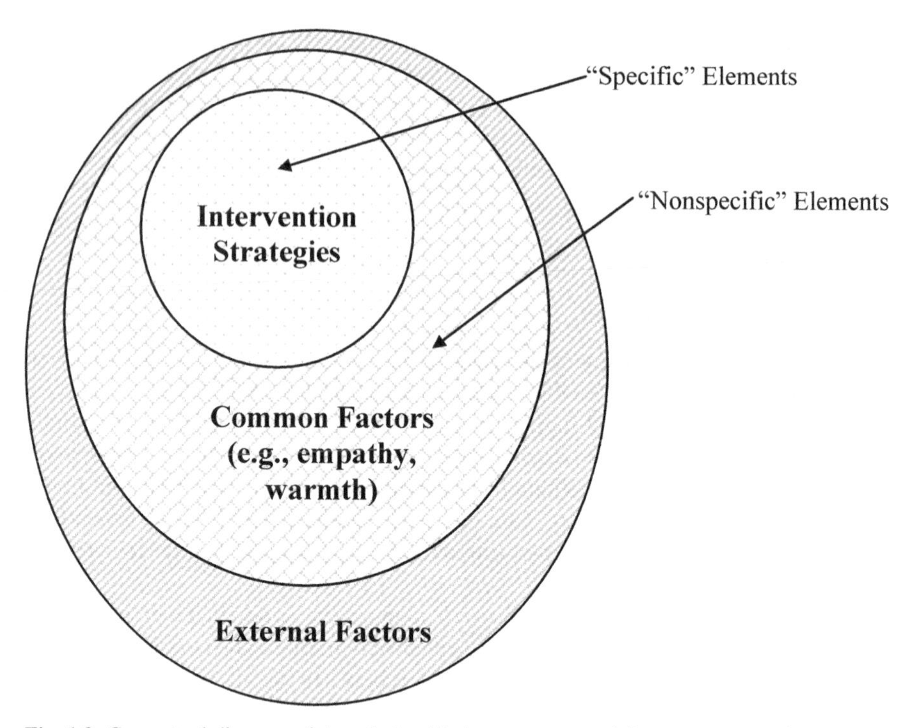

Fig. 1.2 Conceptual diagram of the relationship between external factors, common factors, and intervention strategies

pared to individuals whose first depressive episode occurs in adulthood (Weissman et al. 1999). Thus, it seems safe to assume that childhood mental health concerns will have a lower spontaneous improvement rate than adult-onset concerns, and the true rate will vary as a function of the presenting problem. As we shall see in Chap. 2, the spontaneous recovery rate for individuals with ADHD is well below Lambert's estimate of 40%. Fourth, the relationship between the components of therapeutic change is clearly more complicated than Lambert's model suggests. It is conceivable, for example, that there is an interaction between therapist factors and therapeutic technique, such that the same technique has differential effectiveness depending on which therapist uses it. For example, some therapists appear better than others when helping clients get the most benefit from complementary treatments (Wampold and Brown 2005). Given such complexities, it is still unclear what proportions of client outcomes are attributable to common versus specific factors.

When preparing staff to implement the Challenging Horizons Program (CHP), we offer an alternative model of therapeutic change (see Fig. 1.2). In our view, the components of counseling are interrelated, beginning with the extratherapeutic factors (referred to in Fig. 1.2 simply as external factors). Undoubtedly, counseling outcomes are largely dictated by the unique situations that clients find themselves in before entering counseling. Once counseling is started, the relationship between the counselor and client is vital to achieving desired outcomes, but the strength of those outcomes is also influenced by external factors, including the manner in which adults in the child's life support and encourage change. When the counselor implements specific, technique-driven interventions, the outcome is then a product of technique, the therapeutic alliance, and the external factors. It is therefore difficult to calculate the unique contributions of the external factors, common factors, or specific interventions because these elements cannot be easily examined in isolation, as all three overlap and are essentially co-articulated. However, we might think of these elements as multiplicative: If any one factor equals "zero"—for example, a complete lack of parental support, an inability to establish a therapeutic relationship, or the absence of technique—there is no therapeutic change beyond what would occur without intervention. The result is a failed intervention.

Consequences of the Research–Practice Debate

Despite evidence that, in our view, shows rather convincingly that certain counseling techniques outperform others in child and adolescent therapies, these insights are largely lost in the din of the research–practice debate. Currently, researchers can safely assume that treatment studies published within the professional literature are likely to be read by other committed researchers, but not as widely read by practitioners. Even when studies reach a broad audience there seems to be a tendency for consumers to selectively attend to the aspects that support their preexisting convictions and ignore those that do not, regardless of the strength or relevancy of the research design. After all, if a wide variety of research designs warrant equal merit, then how do we decide which treatment studies are most compelling? In this confusing environment it is not unusual for supporters of "Therapy X" to overstate supportive studies, even when those studies have inadequate sample sizes, fail to control for obvious confounds, fail to explore alternative interpretations, bypass the peer-review process, or fail to be replicated. To illustrate this point, we encourage readers to search the Internet for information on the Feingold Diet for ADHD or the original Drug Abuse Resistance Education (DARE) program for substance use disorders. In both cases there appears to be broad support for these interventions, yet overwhelming empirical evidence shows that neither is likely to be meaningfully effective for most children (cf. Rowe and Rowe 1994; West and Neal 2004). It appears that the research–practice debate has created false equivalencies in the minds of many regarding "evidence," and the result has been unwarranted attention to poorly supported therapies over those that have stood up to rigorous testing. Weak findings are trumpeted while strong findings go unheeded.[10] Of course, this is not

[10] The tendency to prefer and defend evidence that confirms rather than challenges personal belief systems would likely persist despite the research-practice debate. Social psychologists refer to this phenomenon as "attitude polarization" (Lord et al. 1979). However, we argue that the research-practice gap and ongoing debates regarding "evidence" in psychotherapy has exacerbated attitude polarization among practitioners and other research consumers, to the detriment of the field at large.

a new observation. Lambert and colleagues (1986) noted, "Advocates of different positions have tended to set up a double standard of judgment regarding data in the literature by which evidence favorable to their therapy is interpreted flexibly despite a variety of defects, while contrary data are either ignored or treated to a methodological hatchet job that makes the original findings unrecognizable" (p. 158). Lambert and colleagues were referring to the stark divisions between schools of psychotherapy at that time, but it seems that the research–practice debate renewed such partisanship, only with redefined battle lines.

Another unfortunate consequence of the research–practice debate has been weak advocacy and dissemination of effective psychological treatments. For example, what proportion of adults in the NSS-C survey described at the top of this chapter would have identified *behavior modification, behavioral parent training*, or *classroom contingency management* as effective "counseling" interventions for ADHD (Evans et al. 2014; Farmer et al. 2002)? Based on our experience working with families of adolescents with disruptive behavior disorders, the answer is probably very few. Many parents hope that by sending their child to a counselor—regardless of which psychotherapeutic strategies are used—behavior at home and school will somehow improve. Some practitioners refer to such unrealistic expectations as the "garage mechanic" view of counseling: Parents simply drop off children for a "tune up" and pick them up again at 5:00 p.m. But we know from research that traditional, one-to-one counseling that does not simultaneously include behavior management strategies at home or school (or both) is not likely to be meaningfully effective for children with disruptive behaviors—a point we examine at length in the next chapter. We argue that the disagreements about evidence within the field have contributed to disorganized and poorly funded treatment dissemination attempts, and this helps to explain why many parents are uninformed consumers of mental health services.

Finally, the research–practice debate appears to have led some practitioners to conclude that if therapies are equally beneficial, as posited by the Dodo bird conjecture, then all therapies are equally free of unwanted side effects. Although this is not often stated outright, it is inferred whenever practitioners suggest that it is always better to do some psychosocial intervention rather than no psychosocial intervention. We have heard it said that a light touch is better than no touch; but we could not disagree more. It is crucial to acknowledge that specific techniques can be counterproductive, even when common factors are achieved. Logically, *any* intervention that has the potential to produce positive client change also has the potential to cause harm; otherwise, it is therapeutically impotent. The side effects are most often subtle, but still problematic. For example, parents who receive parent training but are unsuccessful can become skeptical of professional counseling and, in frustration, avoid assistance for future concerns. The time spent in the unsuccessful therapy alone can be considered an *opportunity cost* because that time might have otherwise been spent in an effective treatment. Another example is the mother who constructs a behavior contract with her son and, after some success with punishment, over-relies on restrictions rather than rewards. Ultimately, this leads to withholding basketball practice, even though the team represents one of the few positive connections her son has with his school. In such instances, the outcomes are clearly unintended and potentially worse than if no psychosocial interventions had been attempted (Evans et al. 2008).

Moving Beyond the Debate

Counselors must look beyond the research–practice debate to truly understand best practice therapeutic approaches for children with mental health needs. To start, it is important to acknowledge that EBTs are generally advantageous over idiosyncratic practice when interventions are properly resourced and implemented as intended. Weisz and Gray (2008) conclude that, "Ideally, priority would be given to specific EBT protocols that have been shown to outperform the forms of usual care that prevail in the setting where the change is contemplated" (p. 61). Taken into context with the exceptions noted above and the findings regarding the sources of therapeutic change, research suggests that practitioners should consider EBTs as first line treatments, and idiosyncratic therapies should be reserved for situations where

1. There are insufficient data to prioritize one specific intervention over another, given the client's primary presenting problem(s);
2. EBTs are somehow precluded or infeasible (e.g., client and counselor do not achieve an effective alliance; client refuses a specific technique; attendance requirements prove unrealistic); or
3. EBTs are implemented in the manner intended but fail to bring about the desired outcomes.

These general conclusions make clear that there are overlaps between the two sides of the research–practice debate, pointing the way to a potential synthesis. Although it has been convenient so far to treat the evidence-based and humanistic perspectives as mutually exclusive, readers should be aware that most mental health professionals—practitioners and researchers alike—typically voice positions that fall somewhere along a continuum between the two ideological extremes. Indeed, the research–practice debate has not undermined a broad commitment among professional organizations to improve services. Many professional mental health organizations advocate an accountability system that examines treatment outcomes and adjusts best practice guidelines based on those results. Many mental health professionals also seem to agree that the system of research and feedback should ultimately be conducted within real-world environments and include as many experimental controls as possible to ensure that outcomes are due to the therapies under investigation and not alternative explanations (Van Eck et al. 2007). Thus, the ongoing debate does not suggest that some professionals are *pro-evidence* and others are *anti-evidence*. Rather, the research–practice debate is rooted in an epistemological question concerning how research is interpreted, and reasonable people can certainly disagree on the details. The challenge moving forward is finding ways to inform practice through research while taking into account the criticisms and limitations we have alluded to in this chapter.

In our opinion, so-called *modular therapies* represent a promising strategy to synthesize the literature. Chorpita and colleagues (Chorpita et al. 2007; Chorpita et al. 2005) recommend that practitioners focus their efforts on the individual intervention techniques that span several well-researched program treatment manuals, with an emphasis on those that are used most often (e.g., token systems, overcorrection). These elements are *distilled* into modules that can be used as standalone sessions or therapeutic activities.[11] Therapists then construct treatments based on these modules, using clinical judgment to select modules based on client needs. In this manner, practitioners are free to design individualized treatment plans, while at the same time using techniques for which there is widespread empirical support. In a fascinating effectiveness trial, Weisz and colleagues (2012) found that modular therapies outperformed both standard treatment manual and usual care conditions on parent ratings of behavior outcomes, and most of these differences were maintained 1-year after treatment (Chorpita et al. 2013). The apparent advantage of modular therapy seems to have been the flexibility afforded to practitioners when determining the sequence of elements because the content largely overlapped the standard, manualized treatments. Whether or not such developments provide a meaningful solution to the research–practice divide is unclear, but we are hopeful that attempts to synthesize the literature will lead to increasingly effective treatments in the near future.

Conclusion

In this chapter, we have examined an ongoing debate in the field of applied psychology regarding how psychosocial treatment research should be conducted and interpreted. When training new clinicians to implement the CHP, we often open our early discussions with the epistemological arguments raised by both the proponents of the evidence-based practice movement as well as the counterarguments offered by the proponents of what we have termed the "humanistic perspective." It is important for practitioners to understand both sides of this debate, but we point out that several published meta-analyses provide compelling evidence that EBTs offer some advantages over treatment-as-usual for child and adolescent clients. Contrary to the assumption of parity across competing models of therapy, it appears that some techniques outperform others in certain circumstances. Of course, this is not to say that the common factors have no impact on client outcomes because interventions occur within the context of, and are clearly impacted by, the client–counselor

[11] Throughout this book, we use Chorpita and colleagues' (2013) recommendations for the layout of modules when presenting elements from the CHP treatment manuals. We selected the elements of the manuals that have been used most consistently across the studies we and our colleagues have conducted since 1999.

relationship (Horvath and Symonds 1991). However, we believe that the evidence indicates that the common factors are insufficient alone to bring about change for many children and adolescent clients, given the nature of the referral questions and the relative lack of client autonomy when compared to adult clients. We cannot assume, for example, that children will come into counseling with high hopes for success or an ability to spontaneously recover from mental illnesses. Similarly, it would be highly unlikely that an adolescent with ADHD would change his behaviors on the basis of client-centered interactions alone. Rather, we would anticipate that he would passively chat with the therapist and return to his previous behaviors upon leaving the room. Research on the effectiveness of standalone client-centered therapies offers some support for this conclusion, as such strategies appear comparable to no-treatment control groups (e.g., Kazdin et al. 1987). Thus, we try to impress upon our trainees that psychosocial interventions require both the common factors of psychotherapy as well as specific intervention techniques; and when choosing techniques, practitioners have a duty to use techniques that have been shown to be safe and effective.

Some of the criticism of the evidence-based practice movement seems to assume that EBTs skip the common factors and naively implement techniques without regard for the therapeutic alliance. Clearly, this too would be a mistake. As Addis and colleagues (1999) explain, "The common conception that manual-based treatments turn therapists into technicians rather than genuine human beings, suggests that training programs and psychotherapy researchers have not succeeded in conveying the importance of the therapeutic relationship in these treatments" (p. 432). Manual-based treatments and the common factors are not hopelessly at odds, even though some of the research literature admittedly does a poor job of recognizing the role of common factors in study outcomes. Whether in the clinic or in a research study, clients enter therapy with varying degrees of readiness for change (Prochaska et al. 1992), and attempting to move directly to techniques without adequate attention to the therapeutic alliance can result in client resistance and possibly dropout (overtly or covertly). When a counselor starts a specific intervention, client resistance, missed sessions, and treatment dropout are the likely outcomes when a therapeutic relationship is strained or underdeveloped. Adequate attention has to be paid to the quality of the common factors because without these elements, even the most carefully designed intervention is likely to fail.

References

Addis, M. E., Wade, W. A., & Hatgis, C. (1999). Barriers to dissemination of evidence-based practices: Addressing practitioners' concerns about manual-based psychotherapies. *Clinical Psychology: Science and Practice, 6,* 430–441.

Alexander, J. F., & Parsons, B. (1982). *Functional family therapy*. Monterey: Brooks/Cole.

American Psychiatric Association. (2000). *Diagnostic and statistical manual of mental disorders* (4th ed., text revision). Washington DC: Author.

American Psychiatric Association. (2013). *Diagnostic and statistical manual of mental disorders* (5th edn.). Washington DC: Author.
APA Presidential Task Force on Evidence-Based Practice. (2006). Evidence-based practice in psychology. *American Psychologist, 61,* 271–285.
Baker, T. B., McFall, R. M., & Shoham, V. (2008). Current status and future prospects of clinical psychology: Toward a scientifically principled approach to mental and behavioral health care. *Psychological Science in the Public Interest, 9,* 67–103.
Chambless, D. L. (1993). *Task force on promotion and dissemination of psychological procedures: A report adopted by the Division 12 board.* Washington, DC: Division 12 of the American Psychological Association. Available at http://www.apa.org/divisions/Div12/est/chamble2.pdf.
Chorpita, B. F., Becker, K. D., & Daleiden, E. L. (2007). Understanding the common elements of evidence-based practice: Misconceptions and clinical examples. *Journal of the American Academic of Child and Adolescent Psychiatry, 46,* 647–652.
Chorpita, B. F., Daleiden, E. R., & Weisz, J. R. (2005). Identifying and selecting the common elements of evidence based interventions: A distillation and matching model. *Mental Health Services Research, 7,* 5–20.
Chorpita, B. F., Weisz, J. R., Daleiden, E. L., Schoenwald, S. K., Palinkas, L. A., Miranda, J... Research Network on Youth Mental Health. (2013). Long-term outcomes for the child STEPs randomized effectiveness trial: A comparison of modular and standard treatment designs with usual care. *Journal of Consulting and Clinical Psychology, 81,* 999–1009.
Cohen, J. (1988). *Statistical power for the behavioral sciences* (2nd edn.). Hillsdale: Erlbaum.
Cukrowicz, K. C., Timmons, K. A., Sawyer, K., Caron, K. M., Gummelt, H. D., & Joiner, T. E. (2011). Improved treatment outcome associated with the shift to empirically supported treatments in an outpatient clinic is maintained over a ten-year period. *Professional Psychology: Research and Practice, 42,* 145–152.
Davis, J. A., Smith, T. W., & Marsden, P. V. (2007). *General social surveys, 1972–2006 cumulative codebook.* Chicago: National Opinion Research Center.
Evans, S. W., Owens, J. S., & Bunford, N. (2014). Evidence-based psychosocial treatments for children and adolescents with attention-deficit/hyperactivity disorder. *Journal of Clinical Child and Adolescent Psychology, 43*(4), 527–551.
Evans, S. W., Schultz, B. K., & Sadler, J. M. (2008). Safety and efficacy of psychosocial interventions used to treat children with attention-deficit/hyperactivity disorder. *Psychiatric Annals, 38,* 58–65.
Farmer, E. M., Compton, S. N., Burns, B. J., & Robertson, E. (2002). Review of the evidence base for treatment of childhood psychopathology: Externalizing disorders. *Journal of Consulting and Clinical Psychology, 70,* 1267–1302.
Fox, R. E. (2000). The dark side of evidence-based treatment. *APA Practitioner Focus, 12*(2), 5.
Grant, J. E. (1988). A problem solving intervention for aggressive adolescent males: A preliminary investigation (Doctoral dissertation, Syracuse University, 1988). *Dissertation Abstracts International, 49,* 912.
Greene, R. W., & Ablon, S. (2005). *Treating explosive kids: The collaborative problem solving approach.* New York: Guilford Press.
Guarton, D. H. (1992). Anger control training and social problem solving training: Effects on social competence and problem behaviors (Doctoral dissertation, Hofstra University, 1993). *Dissertation Abstracts International, 53,* 3477.
Henggeler, S. W., Schoenwald, S. K., Borduin, C. M., Rowland, M. D., & Cunningham, P. B. (1998). *Multisystemic treatment of antisocial behavior in children and adolescents.* New York: Guilford Press.
Henriques, G. R. (2004). Psychology defined. *Journal of Clinical Psychology, 60,* 1207–1221.
Hershenberg, R., Drabick, D. A., & Vivian, D. (2012). An opportunity to bridge the gap between clinical research and clinical practice: Implications for clinical training. *Psychotherapy, 49,* 123–134.
Horvath, A. O., & Symonds, B. D. (1991). Barriers to dissemination of evidence-based practices: Addressing practitioners' concerns about manual-based psychotherapies. *Clinical Psychology: Science and Practice, 6,* 430–441.

Howard, K. I., Krause, M. S., Saunders, S. M., & Kopta, S. M. (1997). Trials and tribulations in the meta-analysis of treatment differences: Comment on Wampold et al. (1997). *Psychological Bulletin, 122,* 221–225.

Hunsley, J., & Di Guilio, G. (2002). Dodo bird, phoenix, or urban legend? The question of psychotherapy equivalence. *The Scientific Review of Mental Health Practice, 1,* 11–22.

Kataoka, S. H., Zhang, L., & Wells, K. B. (2002). Unmet need for mental health care among U.S. children: Variation by ethnicity and insurance status. *American Journal of Psychiatry, 159,* 1548–1555.

Kazdin, A. E., Esveldt-Dawson, K., French, N. H., & Unis, A. S. (1987). Problem-solving skills training and relationship therapy in the treatment of antisocial child behavior. *Journal of Consulting and Clinical Psychology, 55,* 76–85.

Kimble, G. A. (1984). Psychology's two cultures. *American Psychologist, 39,* 833–839.

Lambert, M. J. (1992). Implications for outcome research for psychotherapy integration. In J. C. Norcross & M. R. Goldstein (Eds.), *Handbook of psychotherapy integration* (pp. 94–129). New York: Basic Books.

Lambert, M. J. (2003). Psychotherapy outcome research: Implications for integrative and eclectic therapists. In J. C. Norcross & M. R. Goldfried (Eds.), *Handbook of Psychotherapy Integration* (2nd edn., pp. 94–129). New York: Oxford.

Lambert, M. J., Shapiro, D. A., & Bergin, A. E. (1986). The effectiveness of psychotherapy. In S. L. Garfield & A. E. Bergin (Eds.), *Handbook of psychotherapy and change* (3rd edn., pp. 157–211). New York: Wiley.

Lord, C. G., Ross, L., & Lepper, M. R. (1979). Biased assimilation and attitude polarization: The effects of prior theories on subsequently considered evidence. *Journal of Personality and Social Psychology, 37,* 2098–2109.

Luborsky, L., Diguer, L., Seligman, D. A., Rosenthal, R., Krause, E. D., Johnson, S., et al. (1999). The researcher's own therapy allegiance: A "wild card" in comparisons of treatment efficacy. *Clinical Psychology: Science and Practice, 6,* 95–106.

Luebbe, A. M., Radcliffe, A. M., Callands, T. A., Green, D., & Thorn, B. E. (2007). Evidence-based practice in psychology: Perceptions of graduate students in scientist-practitioner programs. *Journal of Clinical Psychology, 63,* 643–655.

Luk, E. S. L., Staiger, P., Mathai, J., Field, D., & Adler, R. (1998). Comparison of treatments of persistent conduct problems in primary school children: A preliminary evaluation of a modified cognitive-behavioural approach. *Australian and New Zealand Journal of Psychiatry, 32,* 379–386.

Manuchin, S., Lee, W., & Simon, G. M. (2006). *Mastering family therapy: Journeys of growth and transformation* (2nd edn.). Hoboken: Wiley.

McLeod, B. D., & Weisz, J. R. (2004). Using dissertations to examine potential bias in child and adolescent clinical trials. *Journal of Consulting and Clinical Psychology, 72,* 235–251.

Miller, S., Wampold, B., & Varheley, K. (2008). Direct comparisons of treatment modalities for youth disorders: A meta-analysis. *Psychotherapy Research, 18,* 5–14.

Murphy, J. J. (1997). *Solution-focused counseling in middle and high schools.* Alexandria, VA: American Counseling Association.

Murphy, J. J. (2008). *Solution-focused counseling in schools* (2nd edn.). Alexandria: American Counseling Association.

National Institute of Mental Health. (n.d.). *Congressional justification by fiscal year.* http://www.nimh.nih.gov/about/budget/cj2016_final_149031.pdf. Accessed 11 May 2015.

Nelson, T. D., & Steele, R. G. (2008). Influences on practitioner treatment selection: Best research evidence and other considerations. *Journal of Behavioral Health Services and Research, 35,* 170–178.

Norcross, J. C., & Wampold, B. E. (2011). Evidence-based therapy relationships: Research conclusions and clinical practices. *Psychotherapy, 48,* 98–102.

Popper, K. (1934). The empirical basis. In D. W. Miller (Ed.), *Popper Selections* (pp. 152–161). Princeton: Princeton University Press.

Prochaska, J. O., DiClemente, C. C., & Norcross, J. C. (1992). In search of how people change: Applications to addictive behaviors. *American Psychologist, 47,* 1102–1114.

Reed, G. M., & Eisman, E. J. (2006). Uses and misuses of evidence: Managed care, treatment guidelines, and outcomes measurement in professional practice. In C. D. Goodheart, A. E. Kazdin & R. J. Sternberg (Eds.), *Evidence-based psychotherapy: Where practice and research meet* (pp. 13–35). Washington, DC: American Psychological Association.

Rosenweig, S. (1936). Some implicit common factors in diverse methods of psychotherapy. *American Journal of Orthopsychiatry, 6,* 412–415.

Rowe, K. S., & Rowe, K. J. (1994). Synthetic food coloring and behavior: A dose-response effect in a double-blind, placebo-controlled, repeated-measures study. *Journal of Pediatrics, 125,* 691–698.

Van Eck, K., Evans, S. W., & Ulmer, L. J. (2007). From evidence-based to best practices: What does it mean? *Report on Emotional and Behavioral Disorders in Youth, 7,* 35–40.

Wampold, B. E., & Brown, G. S. (2005). Estimating variability on outcomes attributable to therapists: A naturalistic study of outcomes in managed care. *Journal of Consulting and Clinical Psychology, 73,* 914–923.

Wampold, B. E., Mondin, G. W., Moody, M., Stich, F., Benson, K., & Ahn, H. (1997). A meta-analysis of outcome studies comparing bona fide psychotherapies: Empirically, "all must have prizes.". *Psychological Bulletin, 122,* 203–215.

Weissman, M. M., Wolk, S., Goldstein, R. B., Moreau, D., Adams, P., Greenwald, S., Wickramaratne, , P (1999). Depressed adolescents grown up. *Journal of the American Medical Association, 281,* 1701–1713.

Weisz, J. R., Chorpita, B. F., Palinkas, L. A., Schoenwald, S. K., Miranda, J., Bearman, S. K., … Research Network on Youth Mental Health. (2012). Testing standard and modular designs for psychotherapy treating depression, anxiety, and conduct problems in youth: A randomized effectiveness trial. *Archives of General Psychiatry, 69,* 274–282.

Weisz, J. R., Donenberg, G. R., Han. S. S., & Weiss, B. (1995). Bridging the gap between laboratory and clinic in child and adolescent psychotherapy. *Journal of Consulting and Clinical Psychology, 63,* 688–701.

Weisz, J. R., & Gray, S. (2008). Evidence-based psychotherapy for children and adolescents: Data from the present and a model for the future. *Child and Adolescents Mental Health, 13*(2), 54–65.

Weisz, J. R., Jenson-Doss, A., & Hawley, K. M. (2006). Evidence-based youth psychotherapies versus usual clinical care. *American Psychologist, 61,* 671–689.

West, S. L., & Neal, K. K. (2004). Project D.A.R.E. outcome effectiveness revisited. *American Journal of Public Health, 94,* 1027–1029.

Woody, S. R., Weisz, J. R., & McLean, C. (2005). Empirically supported treatments: Ten years later. *The Clinical Psychologist, 58,* 5–11.

Chapter 2
Lessons from the Literature

...if we have memorized a maxim and observed it, we may begin to be modified by the natural consequences.
B. F. Skinner, from *About Behaviorism (1974)*

In this chapter, we review the current conceptualization of behavior problems in childhood and adolescence. Specifically, we will examine a class of disorders that was previously referred to as the "disruptive behavior disorders" (DBDs) in the Diagnostic and Statistical Manual of Mental Disorders, Fourth Edition (DSM-IV; American Psychiatric Association [APA] 2000). The DBDs were comprised of three constituent disorders: attention deficit hyperactivity disorder (ADHD), oppositional defiant disorder (ODD), and conduct disorder (CD). The definitions of these disorders have changed somewhat in the DSM-5 (APA 2013), and ADHD is now categorized as a neurodevelopmental disorder, while ODD and CD are classified in a separate section addressing "disruptive, impulse control, and CDs." These diagnostic criteria will continue to change over time, so we will consider the DSM as well as the epidemiological, psychosocial, and academic facets of childhood behavior disorders discussed in the research literature. Much of this research has focused on ADHD, and it is important for practitioners who work with at-risk adolescents to understand this research and its implications for treatment. Perhaps most importantly, there appears to be a common developmental trajectory that begins with ADHD symptoms in early childhood and leads to comorbid ODD or CD in later childhood or adolescence. We explore this issue and then turn our attention to the research on treatments for these disorders, including the landmark Multimodal Treatment Study of Children with ADHD. We then conclude this chapter with an overview of the research we and our colleagues have conducted on the Challenging Horizons Program (CHP).

B. K. Schultz, S. W. Evans, *A Practical Guide to Implementing School-Based Interventions for Adolescents with ADHD*, DOI 10.1007/978-1-4939-2677-0_2

Attention Deficit Hyperactivity Disorder

ADHD is one of the most researched childhood-onset psychiatric disorders, with more than 6000 peer-reviewed articles published to date (Barkley 2006). The cardinal symptoms of ADHD are marked and persistent impairment in attention or regulating one's activity level (i.e., hyperactivity and impulsivity), as compared to other individuals of the same developmental level. To be diagnosed with ADHD, individuals must exhibit clinical levels of inattention or hyperactivity-impulsivity beginning prior to age 12 and lasting for longer than 6 months, with several symptoms spanning two or more settings (e.g., home and school), leading to impairment in social, familial, vocational, or academic functioning (APA 2013).

To illustrate how ADHD affects children and adolescents, consider a hypothetical high school. According to the US Department of Education (2010), the average high school has 752 students, which we will round up to 1000 for simplicity,[1] and then divide by the four grades resulting in hypothetical class cohorts of 250. So imagine an incoming class of high school freshmen at the start of the school year. Because ADHD is thought to affect 3–7% of all school-aged children (APA 2013),[2] we would predict that up to 18 students in our freshman class would exhibit behaviors and impairments consistent with, and attributable to, ADHD. We would also predict that within this group, there would be 12 boys and 6 girls, based on the lowest sex ratio estimated by the DSM-5 (2:1; APA 2013).[3]

In truth, these estimates are difficult to ascertain in practice because there would be many students who would exhibit ADHD-like behaviors but *not* have the disorder. For example, depressed students would appear distractible, inattentive, and perhaps fidgety, but if their symptoms are better explained by a mood disorder, then the diagnosis of ADHD would be inappropriate. The same might be true for some children with anxiety disorders, as anxiety is often a better explanation for inattention or overactivity than ADHD. Similarly, some children with intellectual disabilities can exhibit attention-related difficulties,[4] or in other instances, head injuries or central nervous system damage can mimic ADHD. At the other end of the intellectual spectrum, gifted children can be misdiagnosed with ADHD due to academic boredom (e.g., daydreaming and off-task behavior), or alternatively, gifted

[1] High schools consisting of about 1000 students are the norm in states such as CA, NY, RI, NC, and SC.

[2] Prevalence rates of ADHD vary considerably across studies and locations within the USA, with most researchers noting an increase in diagnoses over time. For ease, we use the DSM estimates in our example.

[3] There is some suggestion that, beginning with the DSM-IV, the diagnostic criteria led to identification of more girls than the previous DSM-III-R criteria (e.g., Lahey et al. 1994), so we are assuming the lowest estimated sex ratio here in our example.

[4] Although the DSM allows for children with intellectual disabilities to be diagnosed with ADHD, the attention problems or overactivity must be deemed excessive given the child's mental age. Some research suggests that a lower IQ threshold should be established to *exclude* behaviors attributable to severe forms of intellectual deficits (Barkley 2006), but the DSM-5 allows dual diagnosis in instances where inattention or hyperactivity-impulsivity is excessive.

children with ADHD may not be diagnosed because adults cherish their intellectual strengths and willfully overlook disorganization or overactivity (Webb et al. 2005). Given the similarities among these conditions, the diagnosis of ADHD requires careful screening of similar psychiatric conditions to determine whether there are comorbidities or potentially better explanations for the symptoms. Still, even with a careful diagnosis that rules out all unrelated disorders, we would expect roughly 18 "true" cases of ADHD within our hypothetical freshman class of 250 students.

Presentation Specifiers

Now imagine that the school counselor at our hypothetical high school would like to work with the freshmen with ADHD, and she is able to identify, consent, and schedule counseling sessions for the entire group. Would it be reasonable to expect that the 18 freshmen would present with similar concerns? Despite their shared diagnosis, we would expect great variation within the group because ADHD manifests in myriad ways. Some of the group members would be well known among the school administrators due to frequent discipline referrals, and others would rarely (if ever) come to the administrators' attention. Some would seem gregarious, outgoing, or even overbearing, while others would seem quiet, reserved, and withdrawn. In short, the 18 freshmen would appear an unlikely grouping, and this is partly because the current conceptualization of ADHD posits three presentation specifiers (formerly referred to as "subtypes"): predominately inattentive (ADHD-PI), predominately hyperactive-impulsive (ADHD-HI), or combined subtype (ADHD-C).[5] In other words, some children in our group will mostly have problems of inattention, others will mostly have problems of hyperactivity and impulsivity, and still others will have both problems. Of course, when all potential comorbidities and contextual factors are taken into account, there are as many manifestations of ADHD as there are cases, so any subtyping scheme is insufficient to describe the extreme heterogeneity of this population; but as we will see, the specifier distinctions offers a useful starting point for understanding the various risks associated with this disorder.

For two decades, studies have supported a distinction between symptoms of inattention and hyperactivity-impulsivity. For example, mothers' ratings of the two factors were consistently distinct from early childhood through adolescence (Burns et al. 2001). Similar distinctions have been made among teacher ratings (DuPaul et al. 1997; Evans et al. 2013), in both European and American samples, and across rural and urban settings (Wolraich et al. 2003). These findings suggest that inattention is related to, but meaningfully different from, problems of hyperactivity and impulsivity. On the contrary, hyperactivity and impulsivity are rated in very similar ways, such that children and adolescents who are hyperactive are almost always

[5] In the DSM-III-R, ADHD was described as a unitary disorder without subtypes. However, this conceptualization did not seem to comport with the research or prevailing clinical wisdom that recognized the diversity of concerns among children with ADHD.

impulsive, and vice versa.[6] Distinctions between inattention and hyperactivity-impulsivity are furthered by research that shows that these symptom clusters lead to different impairments, and this is where the research has meaningful implication for intervention. Specifically, inattention appears to be associated with academic impairment, whereas hyperactivity-impulsivity is related to global impairments that include both academic and social problems (Lahey et al. 1994).

Other research on ADHD suggests a third subset of symptoms that closely mimic inattention, including increased daydreaming, mental torpidity, tendency toward confusion, and physical hypoactivity. Collectively, these symptoms have been termed "Sluggish Cognitive Tempo" (SCT; Barkley 2006). Field trials for the DSM-IV found that although SCT symptoms were correlated with the PI subtype, most children with ADHD did not experience these symptoms. Hence, SCT criteria have not been included as diagnostic criteria in the DSM (Hartman et al. 2004), but it is clear that a minority of cases fit this general description and may have unique implications that are still unclear.

Gender Differences

As mentioned at the beginning of this chapter, ADHD is disproportionally diagnosed among boys (APA 2000), which might reflect true biological differences in the population, referral biases, or some combination of the two. A meta-analysis of gender differences found that, in general, girls are less likely to exhibit hyperactivity, conduct problems, or externalizing behavior problems than boys; however, among clinic-referred samples, girls exhibit unusually high levels of intellectual impairments and inattention (Gaub and Carlson 1997). In other words, girls referred to clinics tend to be the most severe cases, and studying only clinic-based cases may provide a skewed picture of girls with ADHD in the community. This phenomenon has been referred to as the "paradoxical gender effect" (Waschbusch 2002, p. 120). In community samples, it is clear that boys exhibit more HI symptoms (Gaub and Carlson 1997) and inattention combined with hyperactivity-impulsivity when compared to girls (Hartung et al. 2002). Not surprisingly, adult raters generally perceive overactivity as more disruptive than inattention alone (Sciutto et al. 2004), which may explain some of the differential referral rates between boys and girls. Boys with HI symptoms have a more difficult time "flying under the radar" than do inattentive girls.

Even though symptom expression appears to vary between boys and girls, partly explaining differential referral rates, boys are more often referred for assessment and treatment *regardless* of symptoms. This is commonly referred to as a referral bias. Sciutto and colleagues (2004) found that when teachers were asked to rate fictional scenarios of children, teachers were more likely to refer boys than girls

[6] Impulsive symptoms appear to load on a separate factor in some samples (Amador-Campos et al. 2006), but the conditions that produce a three-factor solution are unclear. Other research suggests that impulsivity may uniquely predict some long-term outcomes, such as conduct problems and antisocial behavior (White et al. 1994), but this possibility is also unclear.

despite identical symptom descriptions. Specifically, teachers—men and women alike—were 1.5 times more likely to refer a hyperactive boy than a hyperactive girl. The referral bias further helps to explain the higher number of referrals for boys as compared to girls. It may also suggest that many girls with the disorder are undiagnosed and untreated (Waschbusch and King 2006).

Functional Impairment

In our hypothetical freshmen cohort of 250, there would likely be some adolescents with ADHD-consistent behaviors who do not experience academic or social problems. In these instances, a mental health diagnosis of any kind would be inappropriate because of the lack of harmful or unwanted consequences. So if inattentive and HI symptoms do not result in significant impairment, a diagnosis of ADHD is unwarranted. According to parent and teacher reports, the impairments most commonly associated with ADHD include social difficulties, academic underachievement, and disrupted relationships with adults (Kent et al. 2011). Interestingly, these impairments appear to predict long-term outcomes better than ADHD symptoms alone (Pelham et al. 2005); so in our view, counselors and other interventionists are wise to focus their efforts on impairment, and not necessarily the symptoms that define the disorder. Educators generally adhere to the same standards when determining eligibility for special education, focusing on whether functional impairments caused by the disorder (e.g., academic underachievement) require targeted intervention.

Social Difficulties Over time, the professional literature has increasingly recognized social problems as a serious issue for many children with ADHD (Landau and Moore 1991), especially among children with HI symptoms (Gadow et al. 2004; Lahey et al. 1994) or aggression (Bagwell et al. 2001; Hinshaw et al. 1997). Children who mainly experience attention problems can also exhibit social impairments, but are more likely than HI children to be withdrawn or shy (Hodgens et al. 2000). Interestingly, significant social problems can occur even in the absence of comorbid disorders. For example, ADHD appears to uniquely contribute to peer rejection even in the absence of more serious delinquent or antisocial behaviors (Bagwell et al. 2001).

Children with ADHD exhibit communication problems, including dysfluent (e.g., shifting and non sequitur) conversation patterns. When our hypothetical school counselor interviews the group of 18 freshmen with ADHD, she will find that many will have difficulties staying on topic, and their conversations will jump from one topic to the next. Children with ADHD are also likely to have deficient social problem-solving skills, and are more likely than their undiagnosed peers to anticipate desirable consequences for aggressive behavior (King & Waschbusch 2010). So, in interviews with a counselor, adolescents with ADHD may describe recent problems with peers, but show difficulties in generating realistic solutions for those problems. Moreover, their solutions are likely to be more aggressive or vindictive than those generated by same-age peers without the disorder.

Unlike children with developmental disorders and autism spectrum disorder where social learning is impeded, children and adolescents with ADHD largely understand social expectations, but are unable to perform them effectively at appropriate times. As a result, the social problems associated with ADHD are inconsistent because performance is adversely impacted by situation-specific behavioral excesses (Wheeler and Carlson 1994). We might find, for example, that a boy in our hypothetical group can calmly tell a counselor several appropriate ways to establish new friendships, but when this same young adolescent is observed in social situations, he appears excitable, sidetracked, and unable to implement the skills he previously described. Thus, the relevant literature draws a distinction between social skill deficits and social *performance* deficits, with ADHD associated mostly with the latter. In social interactions, performance deficits commonly lead to two primary negative outcomes: First, children with ADHD are often actively rejected by their peers, and this can be observed in settings where unfamiliar children are allowed to create their own impressions of one another. Social rejection can occur quickly, even within the first day that children meet one another (Erhardt and Hinshaw 1994). In fact, when children without ADHD are told that they will soon meet a peer who exhibits ADHD-consistent behavior (e.g., talkativeness and disruptiveness), the quality of subsequent social interactions is negatively impacted. Such expectations result in less reciprocal play and more disagreements (Harris et al. 1990). Unfortunately, when reputation biases are formed they appear highly persistent, even when intense efforts are made to remediate ADHD symptoms through behavioral or pharmacological interventions (Hoza et al. 2005). In fact, reputation biases can worsen with time, especially when children stay with the same class of peers through elementary and secondary school.

Second, many children with ADHD (especially boys) appear to have unrealistically positive self-appraisals of their social skills as compared to the appraisals of their peers (Diener and Milich 1997; Ohan and Johnson 2002; Owens et al. 2007) and teachers (Hoza et al. 2005)—a phenomenon that has been referred to as the *positive illusory bias* (PIB). Overly generous self-appraisals may serve to protect self-esteem, but often complicate intervention efforts. For example, when children with ADHD are given positive feedback on their social interactions, the result can be a counterintuitive increase in the child's self-criticism. So it is not unusual to find that attempts to encourage a child with positive feedback can unexpectedly undermine his confidence. One interpretation of these findings is that children with ADHD are motivated mostly to avoid appearing socially incompetent, and when this concern is assuaged by positive feedback, the self-protective PIB is removed (Hoza et al. 2005; Diener and Milich 1997). More research on the PIB is clearly needed, but it is interesting to note that clinicians working with adults have documented a similar phenomenon: After entering counseling, many adults with ADHD report positive treatment outcomes relative to symptoms and impairments, but curiously report lower self-esteem, perhaps as a result of coming to grips with limitations that were previously downplayed (Wiggins et al. 1999).

Taken together, these findings suggest that within our hypothetical group of 18 freshmen with ADHD, we can reasonably anticipate that many of the students would have a long history of social difficulties. Although it is difficult to predict the proportion of our group for whom this would be true, we can anticipate that social problems would be most likely for those with HI symptoms. We can also anticipate that the students themselves would have an overly positive assessment of their own social performance, even though peer relationships may have been clearly strained.

Academic Underachievement Children with ADHD are also likely to exhibit academic underachievement, which in some cases can include learning disabilities (LD).[7] Methods of defining LD vary widely and, as a result, varying rates of comorbid LD are found in the ADHD literature (Barkley 2006). Higher rates of comorbid LD are often found among school samples as compared to community or clinic samples for the simple reason that LD are most commonly diagnosed by school professionals (Staller 2006) who are likely to directly observe the poor study habits, disruptive classroom behavior, low test grades, and the troubled relationships with teachers (Robin 1998). Hence, studies conducted in differing settings are inconsistent on the question of comorbidity. Using a conservative definition of LD, Barkley (1990) found that 19 % of children with ADHD had comorbid reading disabilities, 24 % had comorbid spelling disabilities, and more than 26 % had comorbid math disabilities.[8] Based on such research, it appears that LD occurs much more frequently among children with ADHD than it does in the general population. So, in our hypothetical group of 18 adolescents, we could expect that roughly three to five will have a comorbid learning disability, based on Barkley's conservative definition, but this would not mean that the remaining 13–15 students would be academically successful. Rather, students with ADHD are likely to lag behind in their classwork, even when LD is not diagnosed (Kent et al. 2011). As such, academic impairment would still be a common concern for most of our hypothetical group, even if it did not warrant a separate diagnosis or special services.

In elementary schools, the academic problems stemming from ADHD often manifest as failure to complete assignments and less overall productivity relative to peers; but in secondary schools, ADHD is associated with lower grades, special service use, and higher rates of grade retention and drop-out as compared to undiagnosed peers (Anastopoulos and Shelton 2001). Obviously, the demands for student independence in secondary school are much greater than elementary school, particularly in regards to organization and assignment tracking. Adolescents with

[7] The temporal relationship between ADHD and specific LDs depends partly on how the latter condition is defined. If, for example, a traditional definition of LD is used (i.e., significant discrepancy between cognitive abilities (IQ) and measured academic achievement), ADHD can seemingly precede or even lead to LD because poor classroom performance over time can lead to cumulative deficits in academic performance that eventually reach the threshold for "significant discrepancy."

[8] In this study, LD was defined by a statistically significant discrepancy between IQ and achievement, as well as an academic lag 1.5 standard deviations below the norm-referenced mean. Modern definitions of LD have abandoned such discrepancy-based models, but many school districts still use them.

ADHD often struggle with these expectations and are likely to overestimate their academic performance in a manner that mirrors the PIB in social interactions. As a result, it is not unusual for secondary school students with ADHD to avoid special academic help (e.g., tutoring) when grade performance is well below parent and teacher expectations, or even below the child's own stated academic goals.

Research on the achievement goals of students with ADHD helps to clarify this troubling contradiction. For example, research suggests that children with ADHD tend to prioritize *performance-avoidance* goals over *performance-approach* goals, whereas children without the disorder tend to exhibit the opposite goal structure. In other words, children with ADHD are generally motivated to avoid appearing incompetent, whereas children without ADHD appear motivated to outperform their peers. Not surprisingly an orientation toward performance-avoidance goals is associated with ineffective learning strategies and an intolerance for academic challenge (Barron et al. 2006; Olivier and Steenkamp 2004).

So in our hypothetical group of freshmen, many would exhibit the performance-avoidance goal structure, such that successes seem unrewarding and failures are avoided or covered up with face-saving strategies. For example, an adolescent with ADHD who receives a good grade on a quiz might seem unaffected; attributing his success to luck or a temporary lapse in the teacher's demanding teaching style. Any student who views success in this way is unlikely to find the experience rewarding, thus missing the connection between the accomplishment and the behaviors that led to that accomplishment. Conversely, when placed in a potentially aversive situation such as playing a new sport, the same adolescent might mock or shun the activity. It is not unusual to see adolescents with ADHD "goof off" or easily give up in situations where failure or frustration is anticipated. For instance, an adolescent might passively participate in a basketball game, loosely following the action by walking the court, but avoid the ball or immediately pass the ball off whenever it comes into his possession. Children and adolescents with ADHD use such tactics to avoid the embarrassment of conspicuous incompetence by appearing disinterested, derisive, or oppositional. Similar self-protective behaviors can arise in any demanding activity with a perceived audience. Of course, adolescents of all stripes use these strategies at times, but the underlying goal structure that perpetuates these strategies appears to be unusually common among adolescents with ADHD.

Strained Relationships with Adults Children with ADHD often experience strained relationships with adults to a degree much greater than their peers. Of particular concern is the relationship between children and their parents or guardians, even at very early ages. For example, Stormshak and colleagues (2000) found that among a sample of 631 high-risk Kindergartners, hyperactivity was associated with elevated levels of punitive discipline by parents, which was defined as threatening with punishments, yelling, feeling angry when disciplining, and spanking or hitting the child. In general, it appears that parents of children with ADHD are more likely to resort to aggressive parenting tactics than parents of typically developing children (e.g., Edwards et al. 2001). Parents of children with ADHD often fail to reinforce appropriate behavior and instead focus on punishing unwanted behavior.

As a result, some children appear to exhibit behavior problems simply to gain adult attention. For some families, the preoccupation with inappropriate behavior leads to a pattern of harsh punishment that increases in severity over time. Among adolescents, ADHD is associated with more severe parent-adolescent conflict, especially in the case of oppositional behaviors. Thus, it is not surprising that parental measures of family cohesion and family interaction have been shown to negatively correlate with symptoms of ADHD, suggesting that as symptom severity increases, the quality of family functioning declines (Klassen et al. 2004).

ADHD is also associated with strained relationships with teachers. Teacher–student relationship difficulties may be partly attributable to a general lack of teacher understanding of ADHD that has been noted among preservice and early career teachers (Kos et al. 2004). Teachers report that students with ADHD create stress in the classroom, especially when there are social impairments and oppositional or aggressive behavior. Classroom observations confirm that students with ADHD command significantly more time from their teachers than their peers, and much of this time is spent in negative interaction (Greene et al. 2002). The inference is that students who demand lots of attention and have difficult interactions with teachers are likely to be perceived negatively, thus damaging the student–teacher relationship. However, this impact may not be limited to the student–teacher dyad, as it appears that such frustration can generalize to other students in the classroom, so that other classmates experience negative interactions with the teacher as well (Stormont 2001).

At the secondary school level, teacher relationships with students are further complicated by setting demands. Unlike elementary schools, where students generally interact with the same teacher throughout the entire day, student–teacher relationships in secondary schools are confined to the discrete and disconnected classroom arrangements typical in these settings. Rather than forming strong connections with one or two teachers, many secondary students—with or without ADHD—feel disconnected from their teachers (Gewertz 2004); but the lack of student–teacher connectedness is potentially more impactful for students with ADHD. We have found, for example, that teacher ratings of their relationships with ADHD students vary widely over time and between teachers (Evans et al. 2005), suggesting that teachers have differing capacities for building relationships with at-risk students.

So among our hypothetical sample of 18 freshmen, we would anticipate strained relationships with parents and teachers. We find that it is often difficult to identify teachers who have positive impressions of students with ADHD, even when they are unaware of the diagnosis. The inconsistency of ADHD stemming from performance deficits (as opposed to skill deficits) serve to frustrate attempts to informally intervene. When teachers try to help a student with poor study skills, for example, the effort often seems wasted because the student soon returns to their previous performance levels. Similarly, we find that many parents have a hands-off approach to school-related issues by the time their children reach secondary school, attributable to a long and seemingly unproductive history of trying to help. The "*three-steps-forward-and-two-steps-back*" phenomenon that marks chronic behavior problems can lead both parents and teachers to believe that they have "tried everything" only to find that nothing seems to work.

Causes of Attention Deficit Hyperactivity Disorder

We will leave our hypothetical sample of high school freshmen for a moment to discuss potential causes of the disorder. Although no definitive cause of ADHD has been found, current research has given rise to neurobiological explanations of the disorder. Neurobiological explanations of the disorder assume an internal, within-child cause of the behavioral symptoms and impairments of ADHD. At face value, this research would seem to suggest that psychosocial interventions—like those commonly used in counseling—would have limited effectiveness; however, environmental events change the individual's neurobiology. Therefore, it is wrong to assume that disorders with a biological basis are always best treated with medical interventions. Changes in the environment can have similar impacts.

Cognitive Deficits Theories of ADHD help to explain the associated deficits and impairments, and provide testable hypotheses regarding the nature and psychological mechanisms of the disorder. To date, there is no single, definitive theory of ADHD. Rather, several competing theories are found in the literature, and these theories have stimulated various avenues of research. Of all current theories of within-child causes, the most influential appear to involve two psychological phenomena: (1) dysregulation in the behavioral inhibition system (BIS); and (2) deficits in executive functioning. Of course, there are overlaps and inconsistencies in these theories, but the associated research has advanced enough to inform counseling strategies.

The BIS is a mental process posited to limit and control behavioral responses to environmental cues. Such processes are, in theory, a necessary prerequisite for self-control, as inhibition provides time for an individual to carefully consider situations, behavioral options, and the anticipated future consequences related to those options. There are several components to this system, which Barkley (2006) describes as the inhibition of prepotent (i.e., immediately reinforcing) responses, the ability to discontinue behavioral responses based on environmental feedback, and the ability to screen out interfering or distracting stimuli. For children and adolescents with ADHD, the BIS seems to be underdeveloped, particularly the ability to inhibit prepotent responses (Nigg 2006), and this hypothesized deficit seems to explain why children and adolescents with ADHD often have difficulties delaying gratification, or to forego short-term rewards for long-term gains. An immediate small reward is far more salient for children with ADHD than delayed large rewards, and theoretically this is because children with ADHD are less able than normally developing peers to inhibit their natural drive for immediate reward. Research examining risk-taking and gambling behaviors seems to confirm this hypothesis: Children with ADHD tend to make riskier and more impulsive decisions than their normal peers in pursuit of immediate, short-term gains (e.g., Garon et al. 2006).

When the BIS functions properly, it sets the stage for complex cognitive processes. The higher order cognitive processes afforded by the BIS are often referred to as the executive functions (EF). Several regions of the brain appear to play some role in EF, based on findings from neuroimaging studies, but the prefrontal cortex of the brain is believed to be the seat of executive processes. Interestingly, imaging studies suggest that these areas of the brain differ in physical size and activation levels between children with and without ADHD (Nigg 2006). Such findings seem to support an EF-deficit model of ADHD, but due to several competing theories (e.g., Barkley 2006; Brown 2006; Zelazo et al. 2003), it is difficult to answer this question definitively. Moreover, there is continuing debate as to the degree to which ADHD impairment is explained by EF deficits (Bunford et al. 2015). Still, commonalities among the competing definitions along with the emerging research on EF allows for some broad generalizations. According to Barkley (2006), EF is generally believed to include nonverbal working memory, verbal working memory (i.e., internalized speech), and planning and foresight for future events.[9] Educators often refer to these cognitive abilities as *metacognition* or *self-regulated learning;* but despite the differing terminology, the concepts are generally similar (Garner 2009).[10]

By almost any definition, research suggests an association between ADHD and deficits in EF across the lifespan, but this is not true for every individual with the disorder. Moreover, EF deficits are associated with other disorders, including ODD and CD, and are not unique to ADHD. Thus, current definitions of EF are not sensitive or specific enough to be used in diagnosis (Sergeant et al. 2002). Similar limitations have been noted for several neuropsychological tests that are purported to measure EF, including the Stroop (Homack and Riccio 2004) and Wisconsin Card Sorting Test (Romine et al. 2004). Such tests appear best suited for assessing strengths and weaknesses among children with ADHD and, in rare instances, to measure change over time (Seidman 2006), but diagnostic validity is highly questionable.

Despite such concerns, the continuous performance test (CPT) is a neuropsychological test that is widely used in the diagnosis of ADHD. Several version of the CPT are available, but generally all require examinees to discriminately respond to rapidly presented stimuli. Research on attention during CPT performance has been mixed, partly due to the lack of a standardized CPT format (Börger and van der Meere 2000), but it appears that children with ADHD make more omission (i.e., failing to respond to stimuli) and commission (i.e., "false alarm") errors than their typically developing peers (Vaughn et al. 2011). However, similar to other neuropsychological tests, the performance overlap between ADHD and non-ADHD

[9] For simplicity, a fourth component of executive functions proposed by Barkley (2006), namely *self-regulation of affect,* will be addressed in Chap. 5.

[10] Technically, executive functions and self-regulated learning may not be completely synonymous because the latter can vary even when executive functions are strongly developed. Thus, it appears that executive functions "support a broad range of self-learning constructs," but do not perfectly predict self-regulated learning (Garner 2009, p. 423). Given the potential for confusion among these closely related concepts, some researchers have proposed clarifying the language; but for our purposes here, we will consider the terms roughly interchangeable.

groups precludes reliable diagnosis on the basis of this one measure alone. So although there are aggregate group differences, no specific error pattern or response style on the CPT is pathognomic (Preston et al. 2005). Poor performance on the CPT only suggests general central nervous system dysfunction that may or may not be related to attention deficits or impulsivity (Homack and Reynolds 2005).[11]

More recently, researchers have examined the possibility of remediating the cognitive deficits associated with ADHD through "cognitive training" (CT) and neurofeedback. For example, working memory CT programs are intended to improve individuals' ability to temporarily store, rehearse, process, update, and manipulate verbal and nonverbal information (Rapport et al. 2013). Commercial purveyors have succeeded in selling CT products to school districts around the country on claims of improved cognitive and academic outcomes for individuals with LD, but recent meta-analyses challenge these claims. When researchers examine "near-transfer" outcomes, which are performance domains similar to what appears in the software (e.g., verbal and visuospatial working memory), CT programs appear to have moderate to large effects in the short term. However, when researchers examine "far-transfer" effects, which are performance domains with implications for the classroom (e.g., word decoding and math achievement), the effects are small and temporary (Melby-Lervåg and Hulme 2013). Taken together, there is little evidence to suggest benefits from CT for student achievement or behavior, even though there may be some immediate, near-transfer gains (Rapport et al. 2013).

Similarly, researchers have examined neurofeedback procedures that are intended to remediate the unusual hypoarousal in the prefrontal cortex associated with ADHD (Loo and Barkley 2005). Neurofeedback procedures provide instant feedback to subjects based on electroencephalogram, sometimes in the form of hands-free videogame interactivity (e.g., control of characters). Similar to CT, the immediate effects of neurofeedback are compelling (e.g., immediate reduction in parent ratings of ADHD symptoms), but the lack of research on long-term, far-transfer outcomes has been a limitation (see Hodgson et al. 2014; Sonuga-Barke et al. 2013). Researchers conclude that neurofeedback is *probably* (Lofthouse et al. 2012) or *probably* efficacious for ADHD (Evans et al. 2014), but long-term and far-transfer outcomes are still unsubstantiated.

Genetics In recent decades, research into potential biological causes of ADHD has increased, but to date no definitive cause has been discovered (Nigg 2013; Sergeant 2004). Still, there is some compelling evidence that ADHD is genetically inheritable, based on family studies, twin studies, and molecular genetic research. One of the most important implications of these findings is that biological parents of children with ADHD experience higher rates of ADHD-consistent impairments than do parents of children without ADHD. Interestingly, nonbiological parents also report unusually high levels of ADHD-consistent impairment, which may suggest

[11] Interestingly, some research suggests that behavioral observations during the CPT task correlate more strongly to parent and teacher ratings than did the actual test results. Thus, scores may be more ecologically valid when augmented with observation data than when used in isolation (e.g., Teicher et al. 2004).

that the expression of ADHD traits has a social learning component that affects family members in unidirectional or reciprocal ways. Or perhaps there is a "nonrandom selection bias," whereby adults with ADHD select partners and adoptive children with similar qualities (Epstein et al. 2000, p. 592). In any event, these findings suggest that interventionists are likely to discover a history of ADHD-consistent impairments among close relatives of the target child.

Twin studies suggest much higher concordance rates among identical twins ($rs > 0.80$) as compared to fraternal twins ($rs < 0.50$), suggesting some genetic basis for the disorder (Coolidge et al. 2000; Nigg 2006). In recent years, genome scans have improved the quality of this research, but have unfortunately led to equivocal findings. Inconsistencies are not necessarily surprising because genome scans are exploratory in nature and are not particularly powerful in detecting putative genes in complex traits such as ADHD. In contrast, candidate gene studies are more targeted and powerful than genome scans, but require specific hypotheses prior to analysis. Based on research of the neurotransmitters affected by stimulant medications and "knockout" gene studies[12] with mice, investigators have targeted specific genes associated with dopaminergic, adrenergic, and serotonergic systems in the brain. In general, there appears to be associations between ADHD and specific dopamine transporter and receptor genes (Nigg 2013; Waldman and Gizer 2006), but complications have plagued this research (see Box 2.1 for more details). When trying to interpret these findings for new practitioners, we point out that perhaps the most important message is that ADHD appears to "run in families." ADHD is not the fault of parents or how they have chosen to parent, although there are parenting strategies that are clearly more effective than others. Parents should not blame themselves, although at the same time there might be changes at home that can benefit their child.

Box 2.1

Complications in Genetic Studies of Attention Deficit Hyperactivity Disorder Although genetic research is promising, there are important limitations that deserve attention. First, the relationship between genes and ADHD is exceedingly complex, but the methodologies used to examine this relationship are oftentimes crude. On one hand, it seems clear that ADHD phenotype is consistent with a polygenetic model with multifaceted variations in genetic penetrance, not a simple Mendelian inheritance model. On the other hand, most candidate gene studies focus on single polymorphisms (i.e., single genetic variables), which is undoubtedly an oversimplified approach. It is likely that multiple markers within specific genes are involved in the etiology of the disorder. Second, there are concerns that the genetic expression of

[12] In "knockout" gene studies, researchers remove specific genes to assess their impact in laboratory animals.

ADHD is differentially affected by factors such as age, sex, and environmental influences. Thus, many variables need to be controlled before researchers can confidently identify specific genetic causes, but to date, most studies have not addressed these issues adequately. Third, genetic research has been complicated by the heterogeneous nature of ADHD. For example, some candidate gene studies have found associations and linkages for specific specifiers of ADHD, but not for others. As a result, some researchers have attempted to associate genetic variations to the specific deficits that are presumed to underpin the disorder—a concept referred to as *endophenotypes*—rather than the DSM-defined symptoms. Endophenotypes, such as EF deficits, do not seamlessly align with the current diagnostic criteria for the disorder, so such research may someday clarify the genetic contribution to ADHD, but currently the implications are unclear.

Neuroanatomy Attempts to determine physical differences in the brains of children with ADHD compared to their nonaffected peers using brain imaging techniques have also been wrought with methodological problems and inconsistent findings. Although this research has periodically uncovered neuroanatomical anomalies, researchers have historically used varying imaging techniques, varying measurement criteria, small sample sizes, and varying approaches for establishing diagnoses (Hendren et al. 2000). For example, magnetic resonance imaging (MRI) has been used in pathophysiology studies of ADHD and other mental disorders, but given the high costs associated with MRI and the lack of a standard technique for interpreting the results, the related literature continues to have serious limitations (Horga et al. 2014). Based on the best MRI research, it appears that children with ADHD have less total brain volume than their unaffected peers (Krain and Castellanos 2006). Specifically, it appears that an asymmetry in the prefrontal cortex seen in normal development is less pronounced for children with ADHD. Further, children with ADHD appear to have lower cerebellar volume and smaller corpora callosa than their normal peers (Durston 2003; Krain and Costellanos 2006). However, more research is needed to better understand the role of comorbid conditions and medication on neurophysiology, as these factors may help to explain some, but perhaps not all, of the neuroanatomical differences among children with ADHD (Seidman et al. 2005).

Other physical differences associated with ADHD are readily observable. On average, children with ADHD are smaller in height and weight than their normal peers. This difference is thought to be related to growth delays brought about by dysregulated neurotransmitter activity in the brain, which has a temporary growth-stunting effect mediated by the neuroendocrine system. Interestingly, physical disparities seem to disappear over time, as young adults with ADHD and their normal peers are comparable in height and weight (Spencer et al. 1998). Differences in stature between children with and without ADHD may also be attributable to the effects of psychostimulant medications, especially in young children, as psychostimulants appear to stunt growth in some children (Swanson et al. 2006). However, stimulant use does not explain all of the differences in stature between children with and without ADHD (Spencer et al. 1998).

Implications The causes of ADHD are still unclear, but the preponderance of evidence to date suggests the following:

1. ADHD is a neurobiological disorder.
2. Boys outnumber girls in terms of diagnoses, but these differences may partly explained by referral biases.
3. The cognitive deficits underlying ADHD appear to involve, but are not necessarily limited to, the following:
   a. Behavioral inhibition.
   b. Executive functioning.
4. ADHD is genetically determined in part, but the genetic root of the disorder is not fully understood.
5. ADHD is often shared by family members, including siblings, parents, and even unrelated caregivers.
6. ADHD is associated with anatomical abnormalities, both in terms of brain structures and physical stature.
7. To date, no neuropsychological, genetic, or medical tests can be reliably used to diagnose ADHD.

Our final point is drawn from the limitations associated with neuropsychological, genetic, and medical tests in ADHD diagnosis. Some clinicians may use one or more of these indicators as part of a comprehensive evaluation, but the diagnostic criteria currently in use require that the child's behaviors are assessed, through direct observation or the use of adult raters. So, although objective means of assessment offer a potentially interesting avenue for additional research, the current diagnosis still requires clinical judgment, based on behavior-based symptom expression and related impairment.

Given the state of affairs, it is not surprising that criticisms regarding the subjectivity of an ADHD diagnosis persist. Some critics have even likened the reliance on behavioral symptoms (rather than clear biological markers) to the antiquated medical diagnoses of the eighteenth and nineteenth centuries (e.g., Millar 1996). In medicine, many diagnoses have evolved from simple symptomatic descriptions to more refined definitions based on biological etiology. Obituaries from 200 years ago record "dropsy," "consumption," and "lockjaw" as causes of death, but these diagnoses have disappeared from the medical literature. What explains these changes? The case of dropsy is particularly informative because it simply described harmful collections of fluid in the body. Of course, we now know that several conditions can cause this symptom, including kidney damage and cardiovascular disease. As a medical diagnosis, dropsy was insufficient to inform accurate treatment because techniques that might work for one case would not necessarily work for another. In comparison, consumption and lockjaw—both descriptions of symptoms and not etiologies—were useful in identifying patients suffering from conditions that were later found to be caused by bacteria. So, although the early descriptions of these illnesses were incomplete, the symptom-based diagnosis proved useful in finding effective treatments and precautions. In the years leading up to the identification of antibiotics to treat tuberculosis (i.e., consumption), for example, epidemiological efforts to quarantine patients experiencing tertiary symptoms of the illness may have prevented wider contagion.[13] A similar pattern of discovery was true of tetanus. Initial diagnoses were made on the basis of "lockjaw," but then epidemiological insights led to effective precautions (e.g., cleaning open wounds). By the time that the tetanus bacterium was identified and a vaccine was developed, incidence rates had already declined due to effective prevention.

We wonder whether the current symptom-based diagnostic criteria of mental illnesses accurately inform treatment, similar to "lockjaw," or whether the current definitions are inadequate, similar to "dropsy." Are we feebly describing complex psychological phenomena that will be radically reconceptualized in the next 50–100 years? There is no way to know, but certainly the diagnosis of ADHD will continue to evolve, and our current conceptualization will someday seem quaint and naïve. Even so, it may also hold true that the psychosocial treatments developed in the past two decades will remain relevant and useful for generations, similar to epidemiological advances of the past. For now, we assume that the descriptive diagnosis of ADHD is accurate enough to advance palliative psychosocial treatments, recognizing that alternatives may someday supplant our efforts.

Developmental Trajectory

Like all forms of child psychopathology, ADHD follows a developmental course, with risk factors and symptoms changing over time. There are two aspects of development with clear implications for the practices described in this book: (1) the persistence of ADHD into adolescence; and (2) the potential for a developmental trajectory from ADHD to serious conduct problems.

Persistent ADHD

ADHD was once thought to be limited to early childhood, but studies show that many children continue to exhibit symptoms well into adolescence and adulthood (APA 2000; Barkley 2006; National Institute of Mental Health Consensus Forming Panel 2000; Tucker 1999). It is now estimated that approximately 70–87% of

[13] Given poor record keeping in the 1800s and early 1900s, it is difficult to know with certainty how effective quarantine conditions were for slowing the spread of tuberculosis. Still, some epidemiologists believe that public education and quarantine reduced the nationwide incidence rate, even though the resulting tuberculosis asylum system was the scene of terrible outbreaks and mass illness.

children with ADHD continue to exhibit symptoms and impairments in adolescence (Sibley et al. 2011). In contrast, self-reports of adolescents and young adults seemed to suggest significantly lower rates of ADHD persistence, perhaps due to inaccurate self-appraisals (i.e., PIB). Based on parent reports and diagnostic criteria adjusted for developmental norms, ADHD appears highly persistent. In other words, adolescents can outgrow the diagnostic criteria, but not necessarily the disorder because even when the symptoms attenuate over time, the impairments may not. Hyperactivity and impulsivity appear more likely than inattention to improve with time, but it may be that hyperactivity and impulsivity simply become less noticeable. It is far more likely for an adolescent or young adult to report subjective feelings of restlessness, rather than exhibiting physical overactivity (Barkley 2006). Hence, counselors working with this population are likely to notice mild fidgetiness, such as knee bouncing or finger drumming, or to hear complaints of racing thoughts, sleeplessness, or impatience.

Based on such findings, the DSM-5 requires only five symptoms of either inattention or hyperactivity-impulsivity for diagnosis of individuals 17 years or older, although it maintains a six symptom per factor threshold for younger children. The new criteria also allow for diagnosis on the basis of a "few" symptoms prior to age 12 and not necessarily evidence for impairment in childhood (APA 2013). These changes are meant to improve diagnostic accuracy among adults who may not recall these details. We believe the symptom threshold adjustments in DSM-5 may begin to address the developmental variability typical of the disorder, but additional considerations are still warranted. It is possible—perhaps even likely—that the age-adjusted symptom thresholds actually lead to new complications, including overdiagnosis among adolescents and adults (Gibbons 2013).

ODD and CD

As mentioned at the beginning of this chapter, children with ADHD are more likely than their undiagnosed peers to develop conduct problems, including ODD or CD (Sibley et al. 2011), with somewhere between 45 and 84% of adolescents with ADHD exhibiting these comorbidities (Barkley 2006). Such research suggests a developmental trajectory of behavior problems, beginning in early childhood with ADHD and, in some cases, progressing to include more serious conduct problems. Waschbusch (2002) conducted a meta-analysis of studies examining the comorbidity of ADHD and conduct problems and found that ADHD and ODD/CD co-occur more frequently than would be expected by chance; on average, the impairments associated with comorbid ADHD and ODD/CD are more severe than for the constituent diagnoses alone; and the comorbid ADHD and ODD/CD group experiences the earliest and most persistent behavior problems. The latter finding is particularly troubling, as conduct problems often precede antisocial personality disorder in adulthood—a chronic condition with serious social and legal implications (Sibley et al. 2011).

What do we mean when we say "conduct problems?" The diagnosis of ODD describes children who frequently exhibit negative, noncompliant, and disobedient behaviors, particularly in interactions with adults. Children diagnosed with ODD often rebel against the authority of parents and teachers by ignoring or actively defying adult commands. Thus, adults frequently describe these children as difficult or argumentative. Children with CD can also exhibit oppositional behaviors, but CD is often more severe because it is marked by violations of rules and social norms. For example, children with CD deceive, steal, and manipulate peers and adults for personal gain. In some cases, children with CD are outwardly aggressive and bully or otherwise physically coerce others. In the most severe cases, conduct disordered children and adolescents are callous and malicious toward others, either directly or indirectly. The research leading up to the DSM-IV(-TR) suggested that children with CD can be categorized as either early-onset or late-onset, depending on the child's age when the first symptom of CD appears. For children with early onset CD, which begins prior to age ten, the prognosis is grim; these children appear to have the most serious long-term behaviors and the highest likelihood of adult psychopathology, including antisocial personality disorder. Late onset CD is associated with social influences, including deviant peer affiliation, which makes this group more amenable to intervention than early-onset CD (McMahon and Kotler 2006). These distinctions have been maintained in the DSM-5, along with a specifier to identify cases lacking prosocial behaviors, which is predictive of the more severe outcomes.

We now return to our hypothetical group of 18 high school freshmen with ADHD. By definition, these adolescents will have impairments related to the disorder prior to age 12,[14] and as mentioned previously, the observed ratio of boys to girls among children who have a diagnosis of ADHD suggests that roughly six of these cases would be girls. How many children in this group will develop more serious conduct problems in later childhood or adolescence? By averaging estimates provided in the literature (cf. Barkley et al. 1990; Becker and McCloskey 2002; Lahey et al. 1994; McMahon and Kotler 2006; Vitelli 1998; White et al. 1994), we would predict that roughly five of these hypothetical adolescents would meet criteria for comorbid ODD, and another three would meet criteria for comorbid CD. Interestingly, there has been little research on girls with severe behavior problems, so predictions of gender ratios in the group of students with comorbid conduct problems are untenable. Based on the scant research available at this time, it appears that girls with CD may be underdiagnosed because their deviant behaviors are likely to be covert and their aggressive behaviors are likely to be nonphysical. Girls are much more likely to use social exclusion, rumors, and gossip as a means to harm their peers. Nonphysical forms of aggression, referred to as *indirect, social,* or *relational aggression,* are commonly overlooked by parents and teachers, which might explain why girls are not considered as aggressive as boys (Archer and Coyne 2005).

[14] The age-of-onset criterion (AOC) first appeared in the DSM-III and was set at age seven based on clinical judgment rather than research. The AOC remained in subsequent versions of the DSM "more out of tradition" than for any other reason (Barkley and Biederman 1997, p. 1207), up until the change to age 12 in the DSM-5.

Family Risk Factors Given the serious implications of antisocial behavior, it is not surprising that a growing literature has focused on the risk factors that help predict which children with ADHD are more likely to develop conduct problems. Much of this research has focused on family risk factors. For example, noncompliance with parental requests among boys with ADHD appears to play a key role in the development of later antisocial behavior (Lee and Hinshaw 2004). Also, inconsistent parenting practices (Wymbs et al. 2015), lack of parent monitoring (Walther et al. 2012), and exposure to family violence (Becker and McCloskey 2002) appear to predict higher rates of conduct problems among children and adolescents. For this reason, many established treatments for DBDs target parenting strategies (e.g., Kazdin 2005).

One of the most commonly cited models of familial influence on behavior disorders is Patterson's (1982) *coercive family process*. According to Patterson, caregivers inadvertently reinforce their child's noncompliant behavior by removing or reducing commands after the child defies the adult. When a parent makes a command, the child may initially refuse by saying "no," or by trying to diffuse responsibility onto siblings or others. Most children will be defiant at times, but there appears to be a group of children who have a predisposition toward noncompliant behaviors as a result of temperament. When confronted with such challenges, parents often amplify their demands, which can lead to even greater defiance by the child. The resulting back-and-forth between parent and child is essentially a power struggle, with both sides becoming increasingly insistent and aggressive. Parents of children with difficult temperaments will encounter such challenges and, when unable to manage their frustration effectively, give in to their child's disobedience on occasion. Such allowances have the effect of negatively reinforcing the problem behavior by removing the command, and the parent unwittingly rewards the child's defiance. Children are then more likely to escalate their defiant behaviors in the future whenever parents set limits or make demands that the child finds odious. The result is that parent–child interactions become increasingly confrontational over time.

Social Risk Factors In addition to familial influences, there are also peer influences that lead to the development of conduct problems. Although it is developmentally appropriate for adolescents to prioritize peer interactions over familial interactions, problems can arise when adolescents rely too heavily on their peer group for support and guidance (Taffel 2001). Given the social difficulties associated with ADHD, this developmentally appropriate turn toward peers can introduce new risks. Research suggests that children with ADHD commonly gravitate toward peer groups that welcome and reinforce antisocial behavior. For example, Marshal and colleagues (2003) found that children with ADHD reported that their friends were more accepting of deviant behaviors when compared to normally developing peers. These affiliations may help to explain a link between ADHD and an increased risk of alcohol and substance abuse (Lambert and Hartsough 1998; Molina and Pelham 2003; Smith et al. 2002). In cases of persistent ADHD and comorbid CD, the risk of substance abuse rises precipitously for cigarettes, tobacco, marijuana, and other illicit drugs (Molina and Pelham 2003).

Treatment Outcomes Research

Although much is known about prevalence rates, associated features, impairments, and comorbidities, the research on treatments for adolescents with ADHD and related disorders is less established. Several treatment options have been researched, but many have proven to be ineffective and, at times, even contraindicated. Some treatment options, such as dietary restrictions and relaxation training are generally unsupported in the professional literature (Barkley 2006), and others lack research with adequate scientific rigor to meet the requirements for strong empirical support (e.g., neurofeedback, as discussed above). In general, only three treatment domains are strongly supported for the treatment of ADHD: (1) stimulant medications; (2) behavior management; and (3) the combination of the two (Evans et al. 2014; Sibley et al. 2014). To support our later discussion of counseling techniques, we will now review the empirically supported behavior interventions.

Behavior Management

Given the limitations associated with stimulant medications and the trepidation on the part of many parents and children to opt for stimulants (see Box 2.2), behavior management can represent a more acceptable adjunct or alternative intervention. Oftentimes behavior management is advocated in the school setting, occasionally requiring teacher training on issues related to disruptive behaviors and the implications for the classroom (DuPaul et al. 2014). These efforts can include ongoing behavioral consultation with a school psychologist or other mental health professional (Evans et al. 2007; Schultz and Cobb 2005; Schultz et al. 2008; Wells et al. 2000). Behavior management is also commonly prescribed for parents, as exemplified by several parent training programs that appear to be effective for families of children with ADHD (Fabiano et al. 2009). Still, the relative ease and convenience of medications causes some to question whether these efforts are cost effective. If, for example, an inexpensive medication can safely deliver similar results, does it make sense to invest time and money in parent and teacher consultation? Researchers have examined this question many times, but perhaps the single most influential study has been the landmark Multimodal Treatment Study of Children with ADHD.

Box 2.2

Medication Therapy for ADHD Psychostimulant medications (e.g., methylphenidate and dextroamphetamine) are widely researched and generally supported in the professional literature. We acknowledge that in many cases, children and adolescents with ADHD are unlikely to fully benefit from their experiences in school without medication therapy. However, there are several critical limitations.

1. *Medications do not cure ADHD.* Medications provide temporary improvements in specific symptoms (The MTA Cooperative Group, 1999a), but some impairments, such as social skill deficits, are less responsive (Hoza et al. 2005). Even when medications reduce aggressive or noncompliant behavior, it does not replace problem behaviors with prosocial alternatives, nor do medications help children overcome the lasting effects of negative social reputations.
2. *Medications are controversial.* Prescriptions for ADHD medications have increased over time (e.g., Olfson et al. 2002; Robison et al. 2002; Zuvekas and Vitiello 2012) and vary considerably based on geography and family demographics (Cox et al. 2003). Based on such findings, some argue that medications are used out of convenience rather than legitimate medical necessity (e.g., Breggin 2001). However, it may be more accurate to conclude that medications are the option of choice when alternative treatments are unavailable, infeasible, or unacceptable.
3. *Long-term medication use in understudied.* There is a general lack of research on the long-term impact of medications, leading to concerns that stimulant use in childhood could potentially lead to illicit substance abuse in adulthood. In a meta-analysis of the relevant research, Wilens and colleagues (2003) concluded that stimulant medications actually *reduce* the risk of later substance abuse. In fact, stimulant use was associated with as high as a 1.9-fold risk reduction. However, the potential connection between stimulant medications and later drug use is still debated in the professional literature and in the lay press, causing many parents to shy away from medication as a treatment option for their children.
4. *Medication studies rarely include adolescents.* Although there is some indication that medications can benefit both children and adolescents (e.g., Sibley et al. 2014), the limited research specifically examining outcomes for adolescents has suggested that the benefits wane with age. It is unclear whether this is a function of physical maturity or adolescents who continue to warrant medication therapy represent the most severe (i.e., less responsive) cases, but in either event, pharmacotherapy for adolescents is generally less effective than it is for younger children.
5. *Medication compliance is poor.* Swanson (2003) found that parents discontinued stimulants in as much as 45 % of cases in as little as 10 months. Pharmaceutical companies have attempted to redress patient noncompliance issues by producing once-daily medications and providing families with information regarding the relative safety and effectiveness of stimulants. Still, many children express a desire to discontinue due to side effects, such as poor sleep and headaches (Doherty et al. 2000). By adolescence, an estimated 50–62 % of patients discontinue medications, sometimes without their parents' knowledge or consent (Molina et al. 2009; Pappadopulos et al. 2009).

The Multimodal Treatment Study (MTA) To answer questions regarding stimulant and behavioral treatment options, the National Institute of Mental Health (NIMH) and the US Department of Education funded a large, multisite study known as the Multimodal Treatment Study of Children with ADHD (MTA; MTA Cooperative Group 1999a, 1999b, 2004a, 2004b). The study, which included 579 children in first through fourth grades from seven sites across the USA and Canada, was the largest clinical trial conducted by the NIMH in child psychopathology up to that point. Participants in the MTA met the DSM-IV criteria for ADHD-C subtype, and were randomly assigned to one of four treatment conditions: medication only (MedMgt), behavior modification only (Beh), a combination of medications and behavior modification (Comb), and a community comparison condition (CC) (MTA Cooperative Group 1999a).

The treatment protocols offered to MTA participants who received medication or behavior modification were designed by experienced clinicians and physicians to adhere to rigorous, best practice standards. Children randomly assigned to the medication arm of the study (including both MedMgt and Comb groups) first went through a medication "wash out" period and then received a double blind, placebo controlled trial of Methylphenidate (in this case Ritalin®), which was randomly titrated with multiple dose repeats over 28 days to establish an optimal dose. Children who did not respond well to Methylphenidate or who appeared to benefit most from the placebo condition received additional medication trials with alternative stimulants, including dextroamphetamine and pemoline. Nonstimulant options were made available in cases where stimulants proved ineffective or the side effects were unacceptable. Once an optimal dose was found, participants began a 13-month open-label continuing treatment phase that was closely monitored by physicians in communication with families and teachers. Additional medication trials were initiated for those participants who exhibited problems (e.g., clinically significant symptoms) during the continuing treatment phase. To assess the initial medication trials and monitor progress over time, researchers collected behavior and side-effect ratings from parents and teachers, charted these data, and collaboratively problem-solved medication issues (Greenhill et al. 1996). In short, the medication titration strategy was more rigorous and data driven than is typically seen in community settings.

The behavior modification arm of the MTA was comprised of several components, including parent training, school consultation, and a summer treatment program. Parent training occurred primarily in small group sessions led by doctoral level clinicians for 1.5–2 hours at a time for up to 27 sessions. Sessions focused on evidence-based behavioral interventions, such as school–home daily report cards and token economies. To support these efforts, some session topics touched on issues not typically found in shorter parent training programs, including parental stress management, communication strategies with schools, and helping children improve their social functioning. To individualize and problem-solve the behavior plans that came out of the group meetings, clinicians met with parents individually on a monthly basis (Wells et al. 2000).

The summer treatment component of the MTA was an intensive 8-week behavioral program modeled on Pelham's Summer Treatment Program (STP; Pelham et al. 2000). Undergraduate paraprofessionals trained in the STP treatment protocol provided behavior modification, social skills training, sports skills training, and classroom strategies, during 8 hour sessions that met every weekday. In the fall following summer treatment, MTA paraprofessionals provided behavioral consultation for teachers that led to the creation of classroom interventions to address student academic and social needs during the school year (Wells et al. 2000). Given the investment in time and resources in both the medication and psychosocial treatment arms of the MTA, it is clear that the treatment protocols were far more intensive than what is typically delivered in school- or community-based practice.

After 14 total months of treatment, the MTA researchers administered outcome measures. Results suggest that all four groups (MedMgt, Beh, Comb, and CC) experienced improvement in ADHD symptoms post-treatment. When comparing group means, it appeared that the two groups receiving the intensive medication protocol (MedMgt and Comb) experienced significantly better outcomes than either the Beh or CC groups. Hence, the MTA researchers concluded that the medication protocol was the key intervention component that proved beneficial. To a much lesser extent, behavior therapy was also successful, but it did not appear to offer significant advantages over the community care condition, or to significantly improve outcomes for the Comb group over the MedMgt group. In other words, MedMgt and Comb groups were not significantly different from one another, and the Beh and CC groups were not significantly different from one another (The MTA Cooperative Group 1999a). The MTA results can be summarized as follows: Comb ≈ MedMgt > Beh ≈ CC. It should be noted that these results and conclusions were based primarily on analyses of symptoms and not functional impairments.

Reinterpreting the MTA Since the initial results of the MTA study were published, several researchers have provided alternative interpretations. It is important to note that the MTA employed an "intent-to-treat" (ITT) design, whereby participants were randomly assigned to treatments and their outcomes were assessed based on original assignments regardless of treatment adherence. All treatment protocol deviations that occurred after randomization were essentially ignored, allowing for varying compliance rates. The benefit of the ITT strategy is that it maintains as many participants as possible in the study (i.e., avoids attrition) and mimics clinical practice, but it makes interpretation of the results more difficult. For example, Smith and colleagues (2006) point out that two-thirds (67%) of the CC group actually received medications in the community. Hence, the nonsignificant differences between the Beh and the CC group suggest that behavior modification was indistinguishable from community-based care where the majority of children received some medication. Also of note, participants in the Beh condition actually received tapered services after the first 9 months, with some only meeting with researchers monthly by the 14-month endpoint. Given that medications were continued up to that point, it may seem like an unfair comparison between the behavioral treatments that had been tapered in the Comb and Beh conditions and the medication treatment that remained active in the Comb and MedMgt conditions. However, the initial rationale of the MTA held that psychosocial treatments would result in coping strategies that would last beyond the study timeframe. Since that time, many have come to believe that most behavioral treatments tend to be effective only as long as they are in place, so this rationale has been questioned. Interestingly, most of the Beh group participants who eventually started medications did so at or following the tapering of behavioral interventions, suggesting that many families attempted to supplement treatment at about the same time that investigators were transferring prime responsibility for behavior intervention to parents and teachers (Arnold et al. 2004).

In their review of the MTA, Conners and colleagues (2001) concluded that the Comb condition contributed to better outcomes in comparison to the MedMgt condition, similar to findings regarding the Summer Treatment Program (Pelham et al. 2000). Moreover, using measures of functional impairments, an advantage for behavioral interventions emerges. For example, behavioral interventions appeared to outperform medications on outcomes related to homework compliance (Langberg et al. 2010). Although the MTA Cooperative Group did not interpret the data to suggest significant benefits for behavior modification, the team noted that parents preferred treatment options that coupled behavior therapy with stimulant medications. Further, a group of participants (6%) who were randomly assigned to the MedMgt and Comb conditions discontinued the study to avoid the medications, suggesting dissatisfaction with a pharmacological approach to treatment for some of the participants (The MTA Cooperative Group 1999a).

Children in the MTA study were followed and reevaluated 10 months post treatment (24 months after starting the study). The results of these follow-up evaluations suggest that all participants continued to exhibit significant behavioral benefits over baseline, but the benefits deteriorated by roughly half for the MedMgt and Comb groups (MTA Cooperative Group 2004a). Further, it appeared that participants who had taken stimulant medications continuously throughout the study exhibited significant height and weight suppression, as compared to the participants who had not taken medications.

Implications of the MTA When presenting the MTA results to practitioners we try to emphasize practical implications, or "clinical significance." In other words, we focus on the proportion of participants in each condition who appeared to meaningfully benefit. Depending on the measures used, we can divide the participants into those who experienced a desirable and reliable change (RC) and those who did not (see Jacobsen and Truax 1991 for a discussion of these terms). Although the MTA investigators did not report percent of respondents meeting RC criteria in any of the manuscripts we could find, the percent achieving RC on parent ratings for participants in the three treatment groups (Beh, MedMgt, and Comb) can be calculated from data reported by Karpenko and colleagues (2009). Based on these data, 36% of participants met RC on a measure of broad functional impairments (the Columbia Impairment Scale); 48% on a measure of problem behaviors at home (Home Situation Questionnaire); 54% on a measure of homework compliance (Homework

Problems Checklist); and 60 % on a measure of social skills (Social Skills Rating Scale). We believe that these estimates offer a simple benchmark by which to compare intervention efforts, while recognizing that no efforts to date have been 100 % successful.

The other takeaway message from the MTA is that even though behavior interventions have limits, a multimodal treatment including behavioral interventions can address the functional impairment of the disorder and potentially reduce unwanted side effects. For example, investigators in the MTA noted that at the end of treatment (14 months), children in the Comb condition received less medication on average than the MedMgt group, suggesting that when behavior modification is combined with medication therapy, lower doses of medication are required to achieve satisfactory results. The medication offset afforded by behavioral interventions is a promising finding, as the side effects associated with stimulants (e.g., growth suppression) or other medications are more likely to occur at higher doses (MTA Cooperative Group 2004b). Thus, we advocate behavior management strategies for ADHD regardless of other treatments. The important caveat is that behavior treatments must be developmentally appropriate, and this was the principal concern that launched our research on the CHP.

Challenging Horizons Program

The CHP started in November of 1999 as a collaborative development project between administrators and educators at one middle school and the second author (SWE). The goal of the collaboration was to develop a set of middle school-based interventions to improve the social, behavioral, and academic impairment of students with ADHD. Prior to that time, little research had been conducted with secondary school-age adolescents. Anticipating frequent modifications during those formative years, the CHP launched as an after-school program independent of the activities of the school day. Specific techniques and interventions were included in the CHP based on the empirical literature with children, then modified, removed, or replaced based on experiences in the middle school setting. Some strategies widely used in schools were purposely omitted from the CHP due to a lack of evidentiary support. For example, the CHP dedicated little time for homework, even when parents and teachers complained about students being behind in their work, because simply completing work in the after-school program would not necessarily improve homework compliance in the future. Instead, we focused on helping parents establish time for homework (see Chap. 6) and then trained adolescents to improve their organization systems for managing school supplies, tracking assignments, and meeting deadlines. Similarly, staff in the CHP did not advocate for accommodations or other similar services at school because those strategies are unlikely to improve coping skills (see Harrison et al. 2013). The goals of the CHP interventions are to help adolescents independently meet age-appropriate expectations of their parents and teachers. To this end, we expanded beyond traditional behavior management to include *training interventions* (Evans et al. 2014). As we discussed earlier, behavior management interventions involve changing the adult-implemented contingencies in the setting in which change is desired and outcomes measured, as exemplified by the interventions tested in the Beh condition of the MTA study. In contrast, training interventions involve helping youth develop coping skills and rehearsing them to a point of competence. Counselors coach youth to exhibit transferable skills and may even provide reinforcement and punishment based on reports from raters in target settings, such as home and school. We added training interventions to the CHP package because there are many practical limitations to relying on behavior management with adolescents, including the fact that adolescents spend a large amount of time outside of direct adult supervision. A large portion of evidence-based treatments for adults is comprised of training interventions (e.g., Solanto 2011) and we find that many adolescents are at a point of transition to this approach.

After School Model The after school model of the CHP has operated two to three days per week for 2.5 hours per session over the course of an entire academic year. Interventions include academic interventions (see Chap. 4), an Interpersonal Skills Group (ISG; see Chap. 5), and parent training (see Chap. 6). In addition, we also target sports skills training in order to provide an opportunity to practice social skills (e.g., frustration tolerance in the face of disappointment) and to provide practice in sports that adolescents commonly play, while in a controlled environment. We also include brief mentoring meetings with CHP counselors to provide adolescents opportunities to share their concerns, initiate special interventions to augment program services and to receive coaching and encouragement on personal goals. Finally, there are parent meetings that include psychoeducation about ADHD and specific parenting practices that can be useful with adolescents.[15]

Mentoring Model The mentoring model of the CHP was designed to extend the interventions found effective in the after school program to the regular school day through consultation with teachers. The consultation process of the mentoring model is similar to traditional behavior consultation commonly provided in schools, but focuses specifically on the CHP interventions that have shown promise. We refer to it as the mentoring model because teacher consultees assume a "mentoring" role with students. The authors recently completed a large randomized trial of the mentoring model as compared to the after school version of the CHP. Although we are still evaluating those results, two early findings stand out. First, participants randomly assigned to the after-school model of the CHP dropped out of treatment at a rate much higher than those assigned to the mentoring model. Although approximately 80 % of those in the after-school program remained in treatment over the course of the entire academic year, almost 100 % of those in the mentoring model of the program persisted in treatment. Second, on almost all measures of outcomes, participants in the after school program improved more than those in the mentor-

[15] We address counseling strategies in the next chapter and then discuss some parent training issues in Chap. 6; however, we do not discuss the recreational component of the CHP specifically in this volume.

ing version (Schultz et al. 2014). Our interpretation of these findings is that under optimal conditions, the CHP is delivered in a manner to guarantee feasibility and student engagement, while allowing for the maximum dosage possible.

Integrated Model Given our previous findings, we have recently started work on another delivery strategy that we refer to as the integrated model. In the integrated version of the CHP, interventions occur during study halls (or similar times during the day), thereby providing a dosage comparable to the after-school program. We have found that many secondary students receive small, supervised study halls each day where time is provided for them to complete their assignments, but specific skill development is not targeted. For this reason, we have started work on the integrated version of the CHP as an alternative to the traditional study hall. We modified the CHP curriculum so that teachers and SMH professionals could implement the interventions during these periods. Substantive modifications were required along with new training and support procedures to ensure that the academic and ISG interventions were prioritized. We are in the midst of late stage refinements to the procedures and gathering additional pilot data, but early findings with a small number of adolescents are encouraging from a feasibility and efficacy perspective.

Efficacy of the CHP To date, there have been nine empirical articles published in peer-reviewed journals focusing on the efficacy of the CHP. These articles report the results of three randomized trials, one large trial using a quasi-experimental design, and other small studies from the treatment development process. Three studies have included random assignment to the CHP or to a control group (Evans et al. 2011; Evans et al. 2014; Molina et al. 2008) and one included random assignment of schools, but not participants (Evans et al. 2007). Sample sizes in these four studies ranged from 20 to 79, and three were conducted at the middle school level and one in high schools. A large trial with over 300 middle school students with ADHD who were randomly assigned to either the after-school model, the mentoring condition, or community care for an academic year was just completed and initial results have been presented (Schultz et al. 2014), but not yet published.

Some of our findings have surprised us. For example, we have found that contrary to our early hypotheses, the CHP interventions do not necessarily improve academic performance, but there appears to be a benefit from the standpoint of prevention—students who receive the CHP are less like to experience a performance "crash" at some point during the school year (Schultz et al. 2009). We have also found relationships between organization and report card grades, suggesting that organization is necessary but not necessarily sufficient to ensure strong academic performance (Evans et al. 2009; Sadler et al. 2011). We have also found that parents have been actively involved in parenting training groups offered at the schools, but there has been little uptake when we have offered individual parent or family sessions (Evans et al. 2011; Evans et al. 2014). Perhaps our most important discovery has been the broad receptivity to implementing the CHP interventions in schools, even during the regular school day. We return to these findings in later chapters and discuss the implications for broader school-based practices.

Conclusion

ADHD is a neurodevelopmental disorder with complex biological bases that researchers are only starting to understand. Still, it is clear that ADHD is not simply a social construction or a product of faulty parenting or underperforming schools. Individuals with ADHD appear to have biologically based deficits in attentional capacity and activity regulation. Although we can demonstrate these differences in aggregated group research, the differences are too inconsistent to inform diagnosis at this time. Nevertheless, counselors can confidently inform adolescents and their parents that the disorder is not anyone's fault, nor is it a moral or personal failing. ADHD describes a pattern of cognitive deficits that cause some individuals to lag behind same-age peers in areas of attention and activity regulation. In some cases, the related behavior problems seem to progress to more serious conduct problems (and other mental health concerns), so treatments designed to address the chronic nature of the disorder are warranted.

Among the treatments tested for ADHD and conduct problems, most of the research evidence to date supports stimulant medications and behavior management. These treatments do not cure the underlying biological causes, but are effective at reducing the related symptoms and functional impairments. Researchers have debated the relative contributions of these options, but it is clear that behavior management can contribute meaningfully to any treatment package, whether or not medications are included. We point out that, to be effective, behavioral treatments must be adapted to match a child's developmental level, and it was this concern that spurred the research on the CHP. After a series of pilot studies and clinical trials, the benefits of the CHP are becoming clear. We will explore our procedures in the CHP in the following chapters.

References

Amador-Campos, J. A., Forns-Santacana, M., Guàrdia-Olmos, J., & Peró-Cebollero, M. (2006). DSM-IV Attention deficit hyperactivity disorder symptoms: Agreement between informants in prevalence and factor structures at different ages. *Journal of Psychopathology and Behavioral Assessment, 28,* 23–32.

American Psychiatric Association. (2000). *Diagnostic and statistical manual of mental disorders* (4th ed., text revision). Washington DC: Author.

American Psychiatric Association. (2013). *Diagnostic and statistical manual of mental disorders* (5th edn.). Washington DC: Author.

Anastopoulos, A. D., & Shelton, T. L. (2001). *Assessing attention-deficit/hyperactivity disorder.* New York: Kluwer Academic/Plenum Publishers.

Archer, J., & Coyne, S. M. (2005). An integrated review of indirect, relational, and social aggression. *Personality and Social Psychology Review, 9,* 212–230.

Arnold, L. E., Chuang, S., Davies, M., Abikoff, H. B., Conners, C. K., Elliott, G. R., … Wigal, T. (2004). Nine months of multicomponent behavioral treatment for ADHD and effectiveness of MTA fading procedures. *Journal of Abnormal Child Psychology, 32,* 39–51.

Bagwell, C., Molina, B. S. G., Pelham, W. E., & Hoza, B. (2001). Attention-Deficit Hyperactivity Disorder and problems in peer relations: Predictions from childhood to adolescence. *Journal of the American Academy of Child and Adolescent Psychiatry, 40,* 1285–1292.

Barkley, R. A. (2006). *Attention-Deficit Hyperactivity Disorder: A handbook for diagnosis and treatment* (3rd edn.). New York: Guilford.

Barkley, R. A., Anastopoulos, A. D., Guevremont, D. C., & Fletcher, K. E. (1991). Adolescents with ADHD: Patterns of behavioral adjustment, academic functioning, and treatment utilization. *Journal of the American Academy of Child and Adolescent Psychiatry, 30,* 752–761.

Barkley, R. A., & Biederman, J. (1997). Toward a broader definition of the age-of-onset criterion for attention-deficit hyperactivity disorder. *Journal of the American Academy of Child and Adolescent Psychiatry, 36,* 1204–1210.

Barkley, R. A., Fischer, M., & Edelbrock, C. S. (1990). The adolescent outcome of hyperactive children diagnosed by research criteria: An 8-year prospective follow-up study. *Journal of the American Academy of Child and Adolescent Psychiatry, 29,* 546–557.

Barron, K. E., Evans, S. W., Baranick, L. E., Serpell, Z. N., & Buvinger, E. (2006). Achievement goals of students with ADHD. *Learning Disability Quarterly, 29,* 137–158.

Becker, K. B., & McCloskey, L. A. (2002). Attention and conduct problems in children exposed to family violence. *American Journal of Orthopsychiatry, 72,* 83–91.

Börger, N., & van der Meere, J. (2000). Visual behaviour of ADHD children during an attention test: An almost forgotten variable. *Journal of Child Psychology and Psychiatry, 41,* 525–532.

Breggin, P. R. (2001). *Talking back to Ritalin: What doctors aren't telling you about stimulants and ADHD* (Rev. Ed.). Massachusetts: Perseus Publishing.

Brown, T. E. (2006). Executive functions and attention deficit hyperactivity disorder: Implications of two conflicting views. *International Journal of Disability, Development and Education, 53,* 35–46.

Bunford, N., Brandt, N. E., Golden, C., Dykstra, J. B., Suhr, J. A., & Owens, J. S. (2015). Attention/deficit hyperactivity disorder symptoms mediate the association between deficits in executive functioning and social impairment in children. *Journal of Abnormal Child Psychology, 43,* 133–147.

Burns, G. L., Boe, B., Walsh, J. A., Sommers-Flanagan, R., & Teegarden, L. A. (2001). A confirmatory factor analysis on the DSM-IV ADHD and ODD symptoms: What is the best model for the organization of these symptoms? *Journal of Abnormal Child Psychology, 29,* 339–349.

Conners, C. K., Epstein, J. N., March, J. S., Angold, A., Wells, K. C., Klaric, J., Wigal, , T (2001). Multimodal treatment of ADHD in the MTA: An alternative outcome analysis. *Journal of the American Academy of Child and Adolescent Psychiatry, 40,* 159–167.

Coolidge, F. L., Thede, L. L., & Young, S. E. (2000). Heritability and the comorbidity of attention deficit hyperactivity disorder with behavioral disorders and executive function deficits: A preliminary investigation. *Developmental Neuropsychology, 17,* 273–287.

Cox, E. R., Motheral, B. R., Henderson, R. R., & Mager, D. (2003). Geographic variation in the prevalence of stimulant medication use among children 5 to 14 years old: Results from a commercially insured US sample. *Pediatrics, 111,* 237–243.

Diener, M. B., & Milich, R. (1997). Effects of positive feedback on the social interactions of boys with attention deficit hyperactivity disorder: A test of the self-protective hypothesis. *Journal of Clinical Child Psychology, 26,* 256–265.

Doherty, S. L., Frankenberger, W., Fuhrer, R., & Snider, V. (2000). Children's self reported effects of stimulant medications. *International Journal of Disability, Development & Education, 47,* 39–54.

DuPaul, G. J., Gormley, M. J., & Laracy, S. D. (2014). School-based interventions for elementary school students with attention-deficit/hyperactivity disorder. *Child and Adolescent Psychiatric Clinics of North America, 23,* 687–697.

DuPaul, G. J., Power, T. J., Anastopoulos, A. C., Reid, R., McGoey, K. A., & Ikeda, M. J. (1997). Teacher ratings of attention-deficit hyperactivity disorder symptoms: Factor structure and normative data. *Psychological Assessment, 9*(4), 436–444.

Durston, S. (2003). A review of the biological bases of ADHD: What have we learned from imaging studies? *Mental Retardation and Developmental Disabilities Research Reviews, 9,* 184–195.
Edwards, G., Barkley, R. A., Laneri, M., Fletcher, K., & Metevia, L. (2001). Parent-adolescent conflict in teenagers with ADHD and ODD. *Journal of Abnormal Child Psychology, 29,* 557–572.
Epstein, J. N., Conners, C. K., Erhardt, D., Arnold, L. E., Hechtman, L., Hinshaw, S. P., … Vitiello, B. (2000). Family aggregation of ADHD characteristics. *Journal of Abnormal Child Psychology, 28,* 585–594.
Erhardt, D., & Hinshaw, S. P. (1994). Initial sociometric impressions of attention-deficit hyperactivity disorder and comparison boys: Predictions from social behaviors and from nonbehavioral variables. *Journal of Consulting and Clinical Psychology, 62,* 833–842.
Evans, S. W., Allen, J., Moore, S., & Strauss, V. (2005). Measuring symptoms and functioning of youth with ADHD in middle schools. *Journal of Abnormal Child Psychology, 33,* 695–706.
Evans, S. W., Brady, C. E., Harrison, J. R., Bunford, N., Kern, L., State, T. & Andrews, C. (2013). Measuring ADHD and ODD symptoms and impairment using high school teachers' ratings. *Journal of Clinical Child and Adolescent Psychology, 42*(2), 197–207.
Evans, S. W., Owens, J. S., & Bunford, N. (2014). Evidence-based psychosocial treatments for children and adolescents with attention-deficit/hyperactivity disorder. *Journal of Clinical Child and Adolescent Psychology, 43*(4), 527–551.
Evans, S. W., Schultz, B. K., DeMars, C. E., & Davis, H. (2011). Effectiveness of the challenging horizons after-school program for young adolescents with ADHD. *Behavior Therapy, 42,* 462–474.
Evans, S. W., Schultz, B. K., White, L. C., Brady, C., Sibley, M. H., & Van Eck, K. (2009). A school-based organization intervention for young adolescents with attention-deficit hyperactivity disorder. *School Mental Health, 1,* 78–88.
Evans, S. W., Serpell, Z. N., Schultz, B., & Pastor, D. (2007). Cumulative benefits of secondary school-based treatment of students with ADHD. *School Psychology Review, 36,* 256–273.
Fabiano, G. A., Chacko, A., Pelham, W. E., Robb, J., Walker, K. S., Wymbs, F., Pirvics, L., et al. (2008). A comparison of behavioral parent training programs for fathers of children with attention-deficit/hyperactivity disorder. *Behavior Therapy, 40,* 190–204.
Fabiano, G. A., Pelham, W. E., Coles, E. K., Gnagy, E. M., Chronis-Tuscano, A., & O'Connor, B. C. (2009). A meta-analysis of behavioral treatments for attention-deficit/hyperactivity disorder. *Clinical Psychology Review, 29,* 129–140.
Gaub, M., & Carlson, C. L. (1997). Gender differences in ADHD: A meta-analysis and critical review. *Journal of the American Academy of Child and Adolescent Psychiatry, 36,* 1036–1045.
Gadow, K. D., Drabick, D. A., Loney, J., Sprafkin, J., Salisbury, H., Azizian, A., et al. (2004). Comparison of ADHD symptom subtypes as source-specific syndromes. *Journal of Child Psychology and Psychiatry, 45,* 135–1149.
Garner, J. K. (2009). Conceptualizing the relations between executive functions and self-regulated learning. *The Journal of Psychology, 143,* 405–426.
Garon, N., Moore, C., & Waschbusch, D. A. (2006). Decision making in children with ADHD only, ADHD-anxious/depressed, and control children using a child version of the Iowa gambling task. *Journal of Attention Disorders, 9,* 607–619.
Gewertz, C. (2004). Student-designed poll shows teenagers feel lack of adult interest. *Education Week, 24,* 6–7.
Gibbons, E. (2013). Changes to DSM-5 ADHD diagnosis. *Communique, 42*(3), 1–31.
Greene, R. W., Beszterczey, S. K., Katzenstein, T., Park, K., & Goring, J. (2002). Are students with ADHD more stressful to teach? *Journal of Emotional and Behavioral Disorders, 10,* 79–90.
Greenhill, L. L., Abikoff, H. B., Arnold, L. E., Cantwell, D. P., Conners, C. K., Elliott, G., Hechtman, L., Wells, K., et al. (1996). Medication treatment strategies in the MTA study: Relevance to clinicians and researchers. *Journal of the American Academy of Child and Adolescent Psychiatry, 34,* 1304–1313.
Hartman, C. A., Willcutt, E. G., Rhee, S. H., & Pennington, B. F. (2004). The relation between sluggish cognitive tempo and DSM-IV ADHD. *Journal of Abnormal Child Psychology, 32,* 491–503.

Hartung, C. M., Willcutt, E. G., Lahey, B. B., Pelham, W. E., Loney, J., Stein, M. A., et al. (2002). Sex differences in young children who meet criteria for attention deficit hyperactivity disorder. *Journal of Clinical Child and Adolescent Psychology, 31,* 453–464.

Harris, M. J., Milich, R., Johnston, E. M., & Hoover, D. W. (1990). Effects of expectancies on children's social interactions. *Journal of Experimental Social Psychology, 26,* 1–12.

Harrison, J. R., Bunford, N., Evans, S. W., & Owens, J. S. (2013). Educational accommodations for students with behavioral challenges: A systematic review of the literature. *Review of Educational Research, 83,* 551–597.

Hendren, R. L., De Backer, I., & Pandina, G. J. (2000). Review of neuroimaging studies of children and adolescent psychiatric disorders from the past 10 years. *Journal of the American Academy of Child and Adolescent Psychiatry, 39,* 815–827.

Hinshaw, S. P., Zupan, B. A., Simmel, C., Nigg. J. T., & Melnick, S. (1997). Peer status in boys with and without attention-deficit hyperactivity disorder: Predictions from overt and covert antisocial behavior, social isolation, and authoritative parenting beliefs. *Child Development, 68,* 880–896.

Hodgens, J. B., Cole, J., & Boldizar, J. (2000). Peer-based differences among boys with ADHD. *Journal of Clinical Child Psychology, 29,* 443–452.

Hodgson, K., Hutchinson, A. D., & Denson, L. (2014). Nonpharmacological treatments for ADHD: A meta-analytic review. *Journal of Attention Disorders, 18,* 275–282.

Homack, S. R., & Reynolds, C. R. (2005). Continuous performance testing in the differential diagnosis of ADHD. *The ADHD Report, 13*(5), 5–9.

Homack, S., & Riccio, C. A. (2004). A meta-analysis of the specificity and sensitivity of the Stroop Color and Word Test for children. *Archives of Clinical Neuropsychology, 19,* 725–743.

Horga, G., Kaur, T., & Peterson, B. S. (2014). Annual Research Review: Current limitations and future directions in MRI studies of child- and adult-onset developmental psychopathologies. *Journal of Child Psychology and Psychiatry, 55,* 659–680.

Hoza, B., Gerdes, A. C., Mrug, S., Hinshaw, S. P., Bukowski, W. M., Gold, J. A., … Wigal, T. (2005). Peer-assessed outcomes in the multimodal treatment study of children with Attention Deficit Hyperactivity Disorder. *Journal of Clinical Child and Adolescent Psychiatry, 34,* 74–86.

Jacobson, N. S., & Truax, P. (1991). Clinical significance: A statistical approach to defining meaningful change in psychotherapy research. *Journal of Consulting and Clinical Psychology, 59,* 12–19.

Karpenko, V., Owens, J. S., Evangelista, N. M., & Dodds, C. (2009). Clinically significant symptom change in children with attention-deficit/hyperactivity disorder: Does it correspond with reliable improvement in functioning? *Journal of Clinical Psychology, 65,* 76–93.

Kazdin, A. E. (2005). *Parent management training: Treatment for oppositional, aggressive, and antisocial behavior in children and adolescents*. New York: Oxford University.

Kent, K. M., Pelham, W. E., Molina, B. S. G., Sibley, M. H., Waschbusch, D. A., Yu, J., … Karch, K. M. (2011). The academic experience of male high school students with ADHD. *Journal of Abnormal Child Psychology, 39,* 451–462.

King, S., & Waschbusch, D. A. (2010). Aggression in children with attention-deficit/hyperactivity disorder. *Expert Review of Neurotherapeutics, 10,* 1581–1594.

Klassen, A. F., Miller, A., & Fine, S. (2004). Health-related quality of life in children and adolescents who have a diagnosis of attention-deficit/hyperactivity disorder. *Pediatrics, 114,* 541–547.

Kos, J. M., Richdale, A. L., & Jackson, M. S. (2004). Knowledge about attention-deficit/hyperactivity disorder: A comparison of in-service and preservice teachers. *Psychology in the Schools, 41,* 517–526.

Krain, A. L., & Costellanos, F. X. (2006). Brain development and ADHD. *Clinical Psychology Review, 26,* 433–444.

Lahey, B. B., Applegate, B., McBurnett, K., Biederman, J., Greenhill, L., Hynd, G. W., … Shaffer, D. (1994). DSM-IV field trials for attention deficit hyperactivity disorder in children and adolescents. *American Journal of Psychiatry, 151,* 1673–1685.

Lambert, N. M., & Hartsough, C. S. (1998). Prospective study of tobacco smoking and substance dependencies among samples of ADHD and non-ADHD participants. *Journal of Learning Disabilities, 31,* 533–544.

Landau, S., & Moore, L. A. (1991). Social skill deficits in children with attention-deficit hyperactivity disorder. *School Psychology Review, 20,* 235–251.

Langberg, J. M., Arnold, L. E., Flowers, A. M., Epstein, J. N., Altaye, M., Hechtman, L., et al. (2010). Parent-reported homework problems in the MTA study: Evidence for sustained improvement with behavioral treatment. *Journal of Clinical Child and Adolescent Psychology, 39,* 220–233.

Lee, S. S., & Hinshaw, S. P. (2004). Severity of adolescent delinquency among boys with and without attention deficit hyperactivity disorder: Predictions from early antisocial behavior and peer status. *Journal of Clinical Child and Adolescent Psychology, 33,* 705–716.

Lofthouse, N., Arnold, L. E., Hersch, S., Hurt, E., & DeBeus, R. (2012). A review of neurofeedback treatment for pediatric ADHD. *Journal of Attention Disorders, 16,* 351–372.

Loo, S. K., & Barkley, R. A. (2005). Clinical utility of EEG in attention deficit hyperactivity disorder. *Applied Neuropsychology, 12,* 64–76.

Marshal, M. P., Molina, B. S., & Pelham, W. E. (2003). Childhood ADHD and adolescent substance use: An examination of deviant peer group affiliation as a risk factor. *Psychology of Addictive Behaviors, 17,* 293–302.

McMahon, R. J., & Kotler, J. S. (2006). Conduct problems. In D. A. Wolfe & E. J. Mash (Eds.), *Behavioral and emotional disorders in adolescents: Nature, assessment, and treatment* (pp. 153–225). New York: Guilford.

Melby-Lervåg, M., & Hulme, C. (2013). Is working memory training effective? A meta-analytic review. *Developmental Psychology, 49,* 270–291.

Millar, T. (1996). *The myth of attention deficit disorder. New westminster*. British Columbia: Palmer Press.

Molina, B. S. G., Hinshaw, S. P., Swanson, J. M., Arnold, L. E., Vitiello, B., Jensen, P. S., Houck, P. R., et al. (2009). The MTA at 8 years: Prospective follow-up of children treated for combined-type ADHD in a multisite study. *Journal of the American Academy of Child and Adolescent Psychiatry, 48,* 484–500.

Molina, B. S. G., & Pelham, W. E. (2003). Childhood predictors of adolescent substance use in a longitudinal study of children with ADHD. *Journal of Abnormal Psychology, 112,* 497–507.

National Institute of Mental Health Consensus Forming Panel. (2000). National institutes of health consensus development conference statement: Diagnosis and treatment of attention-deficit/hyperactivity disorder (ADHD). *Journal of the American Academy of Child and Adolescent Psychiatry, 39,* 182–193.

Nigg, J. T. (2006). *What causes ADHD? Understanding what goes wrong and why*. New York: Guilford.

Nigg, J. T. (2013). Attention deficits and hyperactivity-impulsivity: What have we learned, what next? *Development and Psychopathology, 25,* 1489–1503.

Ohan, J. L., & Johnson, C. (2002). Are the performance overestimates given by boys with ADHD self-protective? *Journal of Clinical Child Psychology, 31,* 230–241.

Olivier, M. A., & Steenkamp, D. S. (2004). Attention-deficit/hyperactivity disorder: Underlying deficits in achievement motivation. *International Journal for the Advancement of Counseling, 26,* 47–63.

Olfson, M., Marcus, S. C., Weissman, M. M., & Jenson, P. S. (2002). National trends in the use of psychotropic medications by children. *Journal of the American Academy of Child & Adolescent Psychiatry, 41,* 514–521.

Owens, J. S., Goldfine, M. E., Evangelista, N. M., Hoza, B., & Kaiser, N. M. (2007). A critical review of self-perceptions and the positive illusory bias in children with ADHD. *Clinical Child and Family Psychology Review, 10,* 335–351.

Pappadopulos, E., Jensen, P. S., Chait, A. R., Arnold, L. E., Swanson, J. M., Greenhill, L. L., Newcorn, J. H., et al. (2009). Medication adherence in the MTA: Saliva methylphenidate samples

versus parent report and mediating effect of concomitant behavioral treatment. *Child and Adolescent Psychiatry, 48,* 501–510.
Patterson, G. R. (1982). *Coercive family process*. Eugene, OR: Castalia.
Pelham, W. E., Fabiano, G. A., & Massetti, G. M. (2005). Evidence-based assessment of attention deficit hyperactivity disorder in children and adolescents. *Journal of Clinical Child and Adolescent Psychology, 34,* 449–476.
Pelham, W. E., Gnagy, E., Breiner, A. R., Hoza, B., Hinshaw, S. P., Swanson, J. M., ... McBurnett, K. (2000). Behavioral versus behavioral and pharmacological treatment in ADHD children attending a summer treatment program. *Journal of Abnormal Child Psychology, 28,* 507–525.
Pelham, W. E. Jr., & Hoza, B. (1996). Intensive treatment: A summer treatment program for children with ADHD. In E. D. Hibbs & P. S. Jensen (Eds.), *Psychosocial treatments for child and adolescent disorders: Empirically based strategies for clinical practice* (pp. 311–340). Washington: American Psychological Association.
Preston, A. S., Fennell, E. B., & Bussing, R. (2005). Utility of a CPT in diagnosing ADHD among a representative sample of high risk children: A cautionary study. *Child Neuropsychology, 11,* 459–469.
Rapport, M. D., Orban, S. A., Kofler, M. J., & Friedman, L. M. (2013). Do programs designed to train working memory, other executive functions, and attention benefit children with ADHD? A meta-analytic review of cognitive, academic, and behavioral outcomes. *Clinical Psychology Review, 33,* 1237–1252.
Robin, A. L. (1998). *ADHD in adolescents: Diagnosis and treatment*. New York: Guilford.
Robison, L. M., Skaer, T. L., Sclar, D. A., & Galin, R. S. (2002). Is attention deficit hyperactivity disorder increasing among girls in the US? *CNS Drugs, 16,* 129–137.
Romine, C. B., Lee, D., Wolfe, M. E., Homack, S., George, C., & Riccio, C. A. (2004). Wisconsin card sorting test with children: A meta-analytic study of sensitivity and specificity. *Archives of Clinical Neuropsychology, 19,* 1027–1041.
Sadler, J. M., Evans. S. W., Schultz, B. K., & Zoromski, A. K. (2011). Potential mechanisms of action in the treatment of social impairment and disorganization in adolescents with ADHD. *School Mental Health, 3,* 156–168.
Schultz, B. K., & Cobb, H. (2005). Behavioral consultation for adolescents with ADHD: Lessons learned in the challenging horizons program. *Report on Emotional & Behavioral Disorders in Youth, 5,* 91–99.
Schultz, B. K., Evans, S. W., & Langberg, J. (2014). *Interventions for adolescents with ADHD: Results of a clinical trial.* Paper presented at the annual meeting of the National Association of School Psychologists, Washington, DC.
Schultz, B. K., Evans, S. W., & Serpell, Z. N. (2009). Preventing academic failure among middle school students with ADHD: A survival analysis. *School Psychology Review, 38,* 14–27.
Schultz, B. K., Reisweber, J., & Cobb, H. (2008). Mental health consultation in secondary schools. In S. Evans, M. Weist & Z. Serpell (Eds.), *Advances in school-based mental health interventions* (Vol. 2). New York: Civic Research Institute.
Sciutto, M. J., Nolfi, C. J., & Bluhm, C. (2004). Effects of child gender and symptom type on referrals for ADHD by elementary school teachers. *Journal of Emotional and Behavioral Disorders, 12,* 247–253.
Seidman, L. J. (2006). Neuropsychological functioning in people with ADHD across the lifespan. *Clinical Psychology Review, 26,* 466–485.
Seidman, L. J., Valera, E. M., & Makris, N. (2005). Structural brain imaging of attention-deficit/hyperactivity disorder. *Biological Psychiatry, 57,* 1263–1272.
Sergeant, J. (2004). EUNETHYDIS—searching for valid aetiological candidates of attention-deficit hyperactivity disorder or hyperkinetic disorder. *European Child & Adolescent Psychiatry, 13,* i43–i49.
Sergeant, J. A., Geurts, H., & Oosterlaan, J. (2002). How specific is a deficit of executive functioning for Attention-Deficit/Hyperactivity Disorder? *Behavioural Brain Research, 130,* 3–28.

Sibley, M. H., Kuriyan, A. B., Evans, S. W., Waxmonsky, J., & Smith, B. H. (2014). Pharmacological and psychosocial treatments for adolescents with ADHD: An updated systematic review of the literature. *Clinical Psychology Review, 34,* 218–232.
Sibley, M. H., Pelham, W. E., Molina, B. S. G., Gnagy, E. M., Waschbusch, D. A., Biswas, A., Karch, K. M., et al. (2011). The delinquency outcomes of boys with ADHD with and without comorbidity. *Journal of Abnormal Child Psychology, 39,* 21–32.
Skinner, B. F. (1974). *About behaviorism.* New York: Alfred A. Knopf.
Smith, B. H., Barkley, R. A., & Shapiro, C. J. (2006). Attention-deficit/hyperactivity disorder. In E. J. Mash & R. A. Barkley (Eds.), *Treatment of childhood disorders* (3rd edn.). New York: The Guilford Press.
Smith, B. H., Molina, B. S., & Pelham, W. E. (2002). The clinically meaningful link between alcohol use and attention deficit hyperactivity disorder. *Alcohol Research and Health, 26,* 122–129.
Sonuga-Barke, E. J. S., Döpfner, M., Dittmann, R. W., Simonoff, E., Zuddas, A., Banaschewski, T., European ADHD Guidelines Group, et al. (2013). Nonpharmacological interventions for ADHD: Systematic review and meta-analyses of randomized controlled trials of dietary and psychological treatments. *The American Journal of Psychiatry, 170*(3), 275–289.
Spencer, T., Biederman, J., & Wilens, T. (1998). Growth deficits in children with attention deficit hyperactivity disorder. *Pediatrics, 102,* 501–506.
Staller, J. A. (2006). Diagnostic profiles in outpatient child psychiatry. *American Journal of Orthopsychiatry, 76,* 98–102.
Stormont, M. (2001). Social outcomes of children with AD/HD: Contributing factors and implications for practice. *Psychology in the Schools, 38,* 521–531.
Stormshak, E. A., Bierman, K. L., McMahon, R. J., Lengua, L. J., & Conduct Problems Prevention Research Group. (2000). Parenting practices and child disruptive behavior problems in early elementary school. *Journal of Clinical Child Psychology, 29,* 17–29.
Swanson, J. (2003). Compliance with stimulants for attention deficit/hyperactivity disorder: Issues and approaches for improvement. *CNS drugs, 17,* 117–131.
Swanson, J., Greenhill, L., Wigal, T., Kollins, S., Stehli, A., Davies, M., Wigal, S., et al. (2006). Stimulant-related reductions of growth rates in the PATS. *Journal of the American Academy of Child and Adolescent Psychiatry, 45,* 1304–1313.
Taffel, R. (2001). *The second family: How adolescent power is challenging the american family.* New York: St. Martin's Press.
Teicher, M. H., Ito, Y., Glod, C., & Barber, N. I. (1996). Objective measurement of hyperactivity and attentional problems in ADHD. *Journal of the American Academy of Child and Adolescent Psychiatry, 35,* 334–343.
The MTA Cooperative Group. (1999a). A 14-month randomized clinical trial of treatment strategies for attention-deficit/hyperactivity disorder. *Archives of General Psychiatry, 56,* 1073–1086.
The MTA Cooperative Group. (1999b). Moderators and mediators of treatment response for children with attention-deficit/hyperactivity disorder. *Archives of General Psychiatry, 56,* 1088–1096.
The MTA Cooperative Group. (2004a). National Institute of Mental Health Multimodal Treatment Study of ADHD follow-up: 24-month outcomes of treatment strategies for attention-deficit/hyperactivity disorder. *Pediatrics, 113,* 754–761.
The MTA Cooperative Group. (2004b). National Institute of Mental Health Multimodal Treatment Study of ADHD follow-up: Changes in effectiveness and growth after the end of treatment. *Pediatrics, 113,* 762–769.
Tucker, P. (1999). Attention-deficit/hyperactivity disorder in the drug and alcohol clinic. *Drug and Alcohol Review, 18,* 337–344.
Vaughn, A. J., Epstein, J. N., Rausch, J., Altaye, M., Langberg, J., Newcorn, J. H., Wigal, T., et al. (2011). Relation between outcomes on a continuous performance test and ADHD symptoms over time. *Journal of Abnormal Child Psychology, 39,* 853–864.
Vitelli, R. (1998). Childhood disruptive behavior disorders and adult psychopathy. *American Journal of Forensic Psychology, 16,* 29–37.

Waldman, I. D., & Gizer, I. R. (2006). The genetics of attention deficit hyperactivity disorder. *Clinical Psychology Review, 26,* 396–432.

Walther, C. A. P., Cheong, J., Molina, B. S. G., Pelham, W. E., Wymbs, B. T., Belendiuk, K. A., et al. (2012). Substance use and delinquency among adolescents with childhood ADHD: The protective role of parenting. *Psychology of Addictive Behaviors, 26,* 585–598.

Waschbusch, D. A. (2002). A meta-analytic examination of comorbid hyperactive-impulsive-attention problems and conduct problems. *Psychological Bulletin, 128,* 118–150.

Waschbusch, D. A., & King, S. (2006). Should sex-specific norms be used to assess attention-deficit/hyperactivity disorder or oppositional defiant disorder? *Journal of Consulting and Clinical Psychology, 74,* 179–185.

Webb, J. T., Amend, E. R., Webb, N., Goerss, J., Beljan, P., & Olenchak, F. R. (2005). *Misdiagnosis and dual diagnosis of gifted children and adults: ADHD, bipolar, OCD, Asperger's, depression, and other disorders.* Scottsdale, AZ: Great Potential Press.

Weis, R., & Totten, S. J. (2004). Ecological validity of the Conners' continuous performance test II in a school-based sample. *Journal of Psychoeducational Assessment, 22,* 47–61.

Wells, K. C., Pelham, W. E., Kotkin, R. A., Hoza, B., Abikoff, H. B., Abramowitz, A., Schiller, E., et al. (2000). Psychosocial treatment strategies in the MTA study: Rationale, methods, and critical issues in design and implementation. *Journal of Abnormal Child Psychology, 28,* 483–505.

Wheeler, J., & Carlson, C. (1994). The social functioning of children with ADD with hyperactivity and ADD without hyperactivity: A comparison of their peer relations and social deficits. *Journal of Emotional and Behavioral Disorders, 2,* 2–13.

White, J. L., Moffitt, T. E., Caspi, A., Bartusch, D. J., Needles, D. J., & Stouthamer-Loeber, M. (1994). Measuring impulsivity and examining its relationship to delinquency. *Journal of Abnormal Psychology, 103,* 192–205.

Wiggins, D., Singh, K., Getz, H. G., & Hutchins, D. E. (1999). Effects of brief group interventions for adults with attention deficit/hyperactivity disorder. *Journal of Mental Health Counseling, 21,* 82–92.

Wilens, T. E., Faraone, S. V., Biederman, J., & Gunawardene, S. (2003). Does stimulant therapy of attention-deficit/hyperactivity disorder beget later substance abuse? A meta-analytic review of the literature. *Pediatrics, 111,* 179–186.

Wolraich, M. L., Lambert, E. W., Baumgaertel, A., Garcia-Tornel, S., Feurer, I. D., Bickman, L., et al. (2003). Teachers' screening for attention deficit/hyperactivity disorder: Comparing multinational samples on teacher ratings of ADHD. *Journal of Abnormal Child Psychology, 31,* 445–455.

Wymbs, B. T., Wymbs, F., & Dawson, A. E. (2015). Child ADHD and ODD behavior interacts with parent ADHD symptoms to worsen parenting and interparental communication. *Journal of Abnormal Child Psychology, 43,* 107–119.

Zelazo, P. D., Muller, U., Frye, D., & Marcovitch, S. (2003). The development of executive function: Cognitive complexity and control-revised. *Monographs of the Society for Research in Child Development, 68,* 93–119.

Zuvekas, S. H., & Vitiello, B. (2012). Stimulant medication use in children: A 12-year perspective. *American Journal of Psychiatry, 169,* 160–166.

Part II
The Challenging Horizons Program

Chapter 3
Counseling Adolescents with ADHD

The necessity for bringing the child into a good relationship to his mentor is of prime importance. The worker cannot leave this to chance; he must deliberately achieve it and he must face the fact that no effective work is possible without it.
August Aichhorn, from *Wayward Youth* (1925)

In the previous chapter, we discussed behavior disorders—specifically attention deficit hyperactivity disorder (ADHD), oppositional defiant disorder (ODD), and conduct disorder (CD)—as well as the associated social and academic impairments seen among adolescents with these disorders. Clearly, adolescents with disruptive behaviors are an underserved, at-risk group. But despite the overwhelming challenges this population faces, research suggests that psychosocial interventions can have a positive impact (Sibley et al. 2014). The primary task for counselors is to establish effective alliances with adolescents—a goal that often eludes adults—while motivating meaningful behavior changes in several settings. Our aim in this chapter is to describe our strategy for establishing the therapeutic relationship with adolescents as a foundation for intervention. In contrast to some other sources on this topic, we go beyond relationship building to include how counselors can introduce contingencies for behavioral performance that fit with (and even expand) the therapeutic alliance.

Even though we approach disruptive behaviors as chronic conditions, much of the theoretical basis of our approach comes from the literature on brief therapies. As we will make clear, our approach to counseling is not brief in terms of the length of time we engage with adolescent clients, their families, and their teachers; but rather in the time and scope of each individual session. In particular, we draw extensively from solution-focused therapy, which has gained increasing attention in the child and adolescent mental health literature. Solution work is the guiding "tone" or leitmotif within our counseling interactions. We also draw from motivational interviewing (Miller and Rollnick 2013, 2002) and traditional cognitive-behavioral

B. K. Schultz, S. W. Evans, *A Practical Guide to Implementing School-Based Interventions for Adolescents with ADHD,* DOI 10.1007/978-1-4939-2677-0_3

therapies (CBT) to guide some interactions with clients, but as we will show, we primarily focus on behavior management and solution work throughout. In this chapter, we provide an overview of the current state of research on solution-focused counseling and then introduce our approach to building solution-focused relationships with adolescents.

A Brief History of Brief Therapy

Early pioneers of brief psychotherapies (e.g., de Shazer 1985, 1988; Watzlawick et al. 1974) were disappointed with traditional therapies that, in their view, tediously examined client complaints session after session. Despite the extended time and effort, traditional psychotherapies still resulted in ambivalent outcomes for many clients. The problem, according to brief therapists, is the faulty theoretical bases of traditional therapies. Early models, such as Sigmund Freud's Psychoanalysis or Alfred Adler's Individual Psychology, are based on logically circular theories that cannot be invalidated. If, for example, a client's presenting complaint is believed to be caused by unconscious intrapsychic conflicts, then even the client herself is unable to explain the causal forces. In therapy, the client slowly searches for these unconscious forces through tangential means (e.g., dream analysis, hypnosis); all the while, her continuing symptoms point to the need for *more* therapy.[1] From the standpoint of clinical practice, this virtually ensures that therapy will be a protracted endeavor because the murky, almost metaphysical goals are unattainable for most clients, and success is defined by the therapist rather than the client. Watzlawick and colleagues (1974) explain that:

> …if a "neurotic" symptom is merely seen as that tip of the iceberg, and if in spite of many months of uncovering therapy it has not improved, this "proves" the correctness of the assumption that emotional problems may have their roots in the deepest layers of the unconscious, which in turn explains why the patient needs further and even deeper analysis. Open-ended, self-sealing doctrines win either way, as in the bitter joke about the patient who after years of treatment still wets his bed, "but now I understand why I do it." (p. 56)

In contrast, brief therapists set their sights on limited and clearly defined goals, rather than all-encompassing, idealistic pursuits that are almost certain to disappoint.

[1] The philosopher Karl Popper criticized Freud's Psychoanalysis and Adler's Individual Psychology because the underlying theories cannot be falsified; thus, according to Popper, these therapies cannot be considered scientific, although still potentially useful. Popper came to this conclusion even though he personally admired Alfred Adler. In a famous lecture, Popper told the following story: "Once, in 1919, I reported to [Adler] a case which to me did not seem particularly Adlerian, but which he found no difficulty in analyzing in terms of his theory of inferiority feelings, although he had not even seen the child. Slightly shocked, I asked him how he could be so sure. 'Because of my thousand-fold experience,' he replied; whereupon I could not help saying: 'And with this new case, I suppose, your experience has become thousand-and-one-fold'" (Popper 1963). Popper's point was that Adler simply looked for cases to validate his theory and found evidence everywhere, rather than testing whether predictions based on his theory held. The former strategy is pseudo-scientific and dogmatic, where the latter is scientific and flexible.

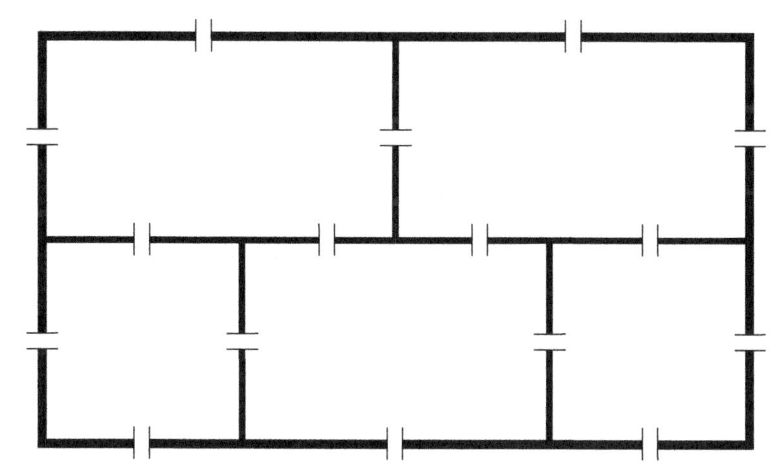

Fig. 3.1 The five-room house puzzle. *Instructions*: Draw a single, continuous line that passes through all doors only once, without breaking through walls or lifting the pencil from the paper. The line can start anywhere inside or outside the house and end anywhere inside or outside the house

The term "brief" refers primarily to a limited time period, but this limit is made possible by a deliberate decision to focus on specific, attainable goals set by the client. Rather than digging for an unresolved psychological crisis, the brief therapist helps clients solve observable problems in the here-and-now.

As an analogy, consider the five-room house puzzle (see Fig. 3.1).[2] In this puzzle, a single continuous line must be drawn through all the doors (indicated as gaps), without breaking through walls, and only passing through each door once. The line can start anywhere inside or outside the house and end anywhere inside or outside the house, but the pencil cannot be lifted from the paper. I (BKS) first encountered this puzzle in elementary school and attempted a solution countless times. I drew the five-room house figure on my notebooks, on scrap paper, and even inside of workbooks and textbooks, determined to solve it. In my best efforts, I could draw a line through all but one door, but ultimately I would get trapped by previous moves and could not reach the final door. (We encourage readers who are not familiar with the puzzle to try it now before reading further).

The five-room house puzzle (and others like it) demonstrates that many difficulties do not yield to straightforward "commonsense" approaches to solution, no matter much time and energy is expended. Consider families of adolescents with ADHD and other behavior problems. As we discussed in the previous chapter, these families often experience extreme patterns of parent-child conflict and often express the feeling that they have "tried everything and nothing works." In our clinic, we met a frustrated single father whose 13-year-old son had frequent behavior problems at school. The father valued a strong work ethic and had received awards for years

[2] Murphy (2008) and Watzlawick et al. (1974) use the nine-dot puzzle to make the same point.

of dedicated service at his job, without a single missed workday. His son had been previously diagnosed with ADHD but was found ineligible for any special services at his school. Still, school staff called the father at work on an almost weekly basis to describe another instance in which his son either got into verbal confrontations or out-of-control horseplay with other students. In most instances, these behaviors simply disrupted classroom activities and the son received in-school disciplinary actions (e.g., lunch detention), but occasionally the problems escalated into physical confrontations and out-of-school suspensions. The out-of-school suspensions placed a significant burden on the father because it meant that he had to rely on extended family members to "babysit" his son during the day. In desperation, the father resorted to ever-increasing forms of punishment. At first the son lost access to his videogame console for 1 week, but when the son was suspended from school again, this restriction stretched into 3 weeks. When this proved ineffective, the father also took away television, phone, and Internet privileges for several weeks at a time. When this strategy failed, the father began stripping all enjoyable items from the son's room, including hand-held games, board games, music CDs, radio, and even posters the son had tacked to his walls. Eventually the son's room was barren, with only a bed and a dresser, and yet his behaviors did not improve—in fact, his behavior *worsened.*

Similar situations are discussed widely in the relevant literature, and this example is far from unique. From the father's perspective, the removal of privileges was a perfectly rational way to punish the son's behaviors, and indeed, punishments are a vital component of behavior modification efforts. However, the father over-relied on these strategies, to the point of trapping himself and his son in an endless cycle of *infraction-punishment-infraction*. The father's response was to do more of the same, even though the evidence was clear that what he was doing was not working. His unquestioned assumption was that his son would change his behavior once the consequences became adequately punishing; thus, if the behavior did not improve, the solution was *more punishment*.

Now think about the five-room puzzle again. What many readers probably already know is that the puzzle is mathematically impossible as long as one "rule" is presumed: two-dimensionality. No matter how many times the puzzle is attempted under this assumption, success cannot be realized. After several years of struggling with this puzzle as a child, a friend finally demonstrated the way out of the trap. He approached the puzzle the same way I did, up until the point where he had one door left and no obvious way of getting to it. Then he folded over the corner of the paper and, without lifting his pencil, used the back of the paper as a bridge to the remaining door (see Fig. 3.2). In other words, my friend literally *bent* the rule I had imposed on myself. Nowhere in the instructions was it specified that the paper could not be folded, and once this clever (albeit anticlimactic) solution was demonstrated, I not only solved the five-room puzzle, but also learned to question the rules of other puzzles I encountered from that point forward.

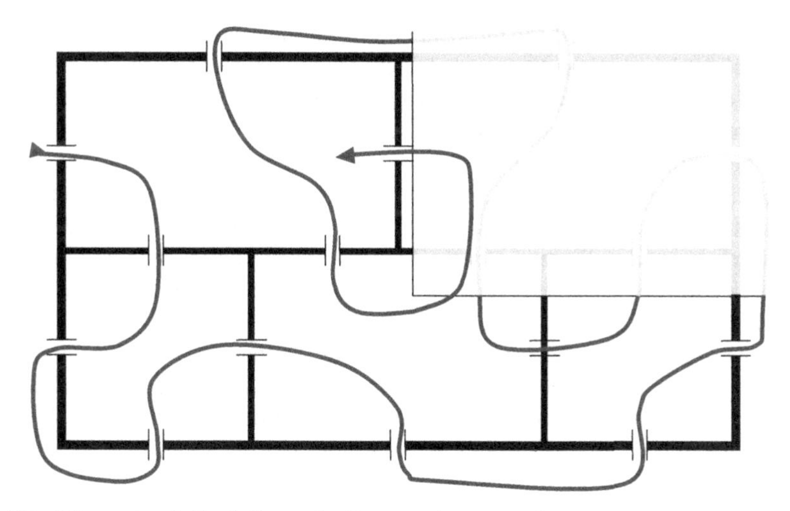

Fig. 3.2 A "second-order" solution to the five-room house puzzle

Watzlawick and colleagues (1974) argue that counseling is a process of helping clients change the way they approach their problems. Such change can occur on two levels. On the first level, called *first-order change*, problems are solved through straightforward means. If a room is too dark, for example, the solution is to turn on a light. If a faucet is leaking, the solution is to tighten or replace the appropriate plumbing. Most everyday problems are solved through first-order change, and very rarely do first-order problems necessitate counseling. But occasionally we run into problems that cannot be remedied by first-order change alone. In the five-room house puzzle, for example, the solution is not straightforward; a two-dimensional approach is doomed to failure no matter how many times it is tried. What is required is a *second-order change*, which is an approach to problem-solving that questions both the explicit and implicit rules of the task. Conceptually, second-order change occurs at a higher, "meta" level, where rules, assumptions, and experiences are analyzed as well as the actual task itself. For readers who were unfamiliar with the five-room house puzzle and could not immediately see the mathematical impasse, the solution in Fig. 3.2 probably had the "*oh, I get it*" effect that is characteristic of second-order change.

When applying the puzzle analogy to counseling, there is one important caveat: *Clients are most likely to use solutions they create for themselves*. In other words, people prefer to credit personal change to their own volition. Psychologists have long studied change in therapy and it is clear that many people are unlikely to take "advice" or be persuaded by anyone they do not trust, respect, feel closely affiliated with (Cialdini 2008), or when they feel angry (Gino and Schweitzer 2008). An adolescent client with disruptive behaviors often represents the worst-case scenario: She is angry because she was referred against her will, she sees little need for change, and she suspects the counselor is a proxy for her parents and teachers. We argue that the basic principles of brief therapy, as described by Watzlawick and others, are well suited for these situations because the brief counselor aligns with the client in an attempt to expand strengths the adolescent already possesses. The brief counselor is a *coinvestigator* who assists the client in a search for simple and acceptable solutions that are likely to advance the client's short- and long-term goals. The counselor does not impose her goals on the client, as is the case in some therapies. If unwelcomed guidance worked to change adolescents' problem behaviors, most counseling would be unnecessary because parents and teachers would have struck upon an effective sermon long before the complaints culminated in referral. In contrast, the brief counselor encourages the client to set their own goals and then collaborates with the client to find acceptable solutions.

In view of the caveat regarding the ownership of change, all counselors working with children and adolescents have to avoid falling exclusively into the role of advice-giver, but this may be particularly challenging for counselors who have limited time with adolescents. Carefully consider the following forms of everyday advice-giving:

"You need to _____."
"You should | ought to _____."
"I want | need you to _____."
"Why did | don't you ____?"

In each instance, a solution is prescribed rather than elicited. The last example is particularly noteworthy because it is an example of a "*Why*" question. "Why" questions deserve special attention because inexperienced counselors often over-rely on this line of questioning: *Why didn't you bring your materials to class today? Why did you shove that kid?* Such questions almost began "I don't know" response, and this is precisely the reaction from many adolescents. "Why" questions can make clients defensive, and yet for every "Why" question a counselor might ask, there is a much better "What" or "How" question: "*What made you leave your things in your locker?*" "*How did things between you and Darnell get so scary?*" Such questions sound less judgmental than "Why" questions and are generally perceived as nonconfrontational. Of course, the conversational inflection of the counselor's question ultimately shades how the client interprets a question, so a neutral or even "confused" approach is advisable. We find that whenever the counselor is feeling "stuck," it is better to ask clarifying questions or to even admit feeling stuck than it is to offer uninvited advice or value judgments.

Although clients generally do not respond well to advice-giving, there is an interesting trade-off: When clients feel ownership over positive changes—even small changes—the benefits can spill over into many areas of their lives. As de Shazer (1985) explains, "…no matter how awful or how complex the situation, a small change in one person's behavior can make profound and far reaching differences in the behaviors of all persons involved" (p. 16). This belief sets brief therapists apart from therapists operating from traditional theories because the latter have maintained that even if some client complaints were alleviated, the underlying psychopathology would cause new symptoms to crop up in other areas. In other words, the deeper root cause of the disorder has to be treated or else apparent victories in one area would be lost to *symptom substitution*. Of course, research in recent decades has shown that actually the opposite is true: When clients make gains in psychotherapy, those gains often lead to additional gains outside of psychotherapy (see Tyron 2007 for an excellent review of this literature).

Insights such as the difference between first- and second-order change, the futility of advice-giving, and the power of small changes form the philosophical basis of brief therapies. In short, the aim in brief therapy is to help clients discover effective second-order solutions through a cooperative client-counselor relationship. Contrary to the claims of early critics, brief therapies are not simply less-of-the-same-old-therapies, but rather a pragmatic and future-oriented approach to achieving specific client goals (Budman 1981). In this way, brief therapies represent a fundamental break with many traditional schools of psychotherapy.

Solution-Focused Brief Therapy

A specific approach to brief therapy, called solution-focused brief therapy (SFBT), was first outlined by Steve de Shazer, Insoo Kim Berg, and their colleagues at the Brief Family Therapy Center in Milwaukee. The clinical team at the Brief Family Therapy Center carefully observed and documented interactions in counseling sessions that led to client success. Typically, one therapist would work with a client while the rest of the clinical team observed from behind a one-way mirror. Near the end of each session, the therapist would leave the therapy room and consult with the team to develop a case conceptualization. The team worked from multiple theoretical angles to conceptualize the client's complaints, with each questioning the client's self-imposed rules and presuppositions that had led to the impasse. Afterwards, the therapist would return to the room and offer the client feedback and a homework assignment designed to help the client find a possible solution.

The assignments in SFBT often seem strange or counterintuitive. For example, de Shazer (1985) relays the story of a mother and her young child's uncontrollable temper tantrums. After reflection, the team encouraged the mother to dance around her child during his next emotional outburst to change the normal sequence of events to see if this change would uncover some possible solutions the mother had not considered. In the follow-up session, the mother reported that the dancing worked to break the chain of events that had previously escalated into more serious behavior problems, helping the mom rethink the problem (p. 126). In another example, de Shazer (1988) describes a case where the therapist encouraged the parent to squirt her daughter with a squirt gun during her next uncontrollable temper tantrum as a means of approaching the problem in a new way. Although the parent did not actually use the squirt gun, the thought caused her to laugh at the child's behavior, which changed the outcome (p. 91). In yet another case, de Shazer (1988) describes a 10-year-old boy who wet his bed most nights. The assignment for the family was to break with their tradition of having the mother wake the son in the morning and instead have the father fulfill this role. In a later session, the parents reported that this change stopped the bed wetting incidents, so the counselor assigned that each night the parents flipped a coin to see who would initiate the morning routine without the boy knowing what to expect. In the end, this assignment completely ended the bed wetting incidents (pp. 54–56).

Due to the seemingly bizarre nature of the therapeutic assignments, SFBT quickly gained a reputation as an odd therapy. As de Shazer explains (1988), SFBT is unusual in that it focuses almost exclusively on solutions, whereas traditional therapies focus mostly on client problems. In most schools of psychotherapy, there is an assumption that to solve client problems, two conditions are necessary: (1) a complete understanding of the cause of the problem, and (2) custom-designed solutions for each problem. Brief therapies, such as SFBT, challenge these assumptions. Brief therapists believe that solutions can be created on the basis of problem descriptions alone, as long as the client's interpretations and ascribed meanings to the problems are understood. In the five-room house puzzle analogy, for example, it is not necessary to grasp the mathematical proof for why the puzzle is impossible to immediately see the usefulness of the solution. Likewise, the switch from problems to solutions drastically reduces the amount of time clients spend in therapy (hence, *brief therapy*), yet still has the potential for achieving meaningful change.

Solution-focused therapists also generally believe that specific therapeutic techniques can illuminate solutions for a wide range of problems. Although the assignments that the SFBT therapists recommended in the above examples seem tailor-made for specific situations (i.e., idiosyncratic), formulaic tasks can be used to arrive at such solutions, and these techniques are transferable across many client complaints. In de Shazer's early work (1985), these transferable techniques mostly comprise specific questions and activities that were found to lead to positive client change in early case studies. Based on these observations and client satisfaction with SFBT, de Shazer and his team discovered that meaningful improvements in the initial complaint area could be achieved in as few as five to six sessions.

Consequently, solution-focused counselors spend little, if any time, trying to uncover the *causes* of the presenting problems. Solution-focused counselors do not routinely delve into experiences of the distant past, nor do they attempt to root out unconscious motivations, internal psychic conflicts, ulterior motives, irrational thinking, or roadblocks to self-actualization.[3] Rather, the emphasis is on encouraging clients to (1) do *more* of what moves clients toward their goals and (2) do *less* of what moves clients away from their goals. The principal aim, of course, is to help clients identify instances of success and then amplify those behaviors. Note the inherent presumption of past success in the problem area: Previous successes often serve as the jumping-off point for change. The techniques in SFBT are designed

[3] In our work with adolescents with ADHD, we rarely discuss the disorder or attempt to understand all of the potential cognitive deficits at play. Instead, we focus almost entirely on functional outcomes.

to uncover and reorient the client to the coping skills he or she already possesses, which might require clients to approach the problem in new ways in order to reexamine their strategy.

Key Ingredients of Solution-Focused Counseling

Although there is some inconsistency in the literature regarding the necessary core elements of SFBT, Franklin and colleagues (2001) suggest that three specific techniques are vital: the miracle question, scaling questions, and compliments.[4] We will describe each of these techniques to give readers a sense of the process of solution-focused therapy, and then later explain how this style of counseling (not necessarily the techniques themselves) has been integrated into our work with secondary students with disruptive behaviors.

The Miracle Question Perhaps the most well-known technique in SFBT, the miracle question is a strategy for helping clients describe what will be different when the presenting complaint is resolved. Ideally, the miracle question challenges clients to think specifically about how their actions and behaviors will be different in the future. Generally, the question is posed as such:

> Suppose that tonight, while you're asleep, a miracle happens and this problem is completely solved. What will be different tomorrow? What will be your first clue that things have changed for the better? (Adapted from de Shazer 1997, pp. 375–377)

At first blush, the miracle question may seem overly simplistic, but actually can be difficult to use in practice (de Shazer 1997). When asked the miracle question, many children and adolescents will focus on how *others* should change, such as how their parents or teachers should change. Children are dependent on adults to varying degrees, so it is understandable why initial attempts at goal setting often lead to "they" statements: "*They* [my parents] *will stop fighting.*" "*They* [my teachers] *will get off my back!*" Child therapy is unlike adult therapy in that young clients have limited power over their environments, so change often comes in the form of coping strategies rather than life-altering resolutions. But the purpose of the miracle question is to get clients to describe how their behavior will be different. So, after offering adequate time for clients to think about the question and respond, counselors might follow up with questions such as:

> So, after all those changes, what will you do differently?
> When things change for the better, how will you respond?
> If we could watch a video called "After the Miracle," what would we see you doing?

Note how the miracle question changes focus from problems to solutions—from a frustrating past to a desirable future. Once the client describes this desirable future, the counselor is provided with a clearer picture of the client's goal, and the client

---

[4] According to Franklin et al. (2001), these defining elements of SFBT were reviewed and approved by both Steve de Shazer and Insoo Kim Berg in 1997 in personal communication.

can start to imagine what behaviors might be helpful to achieve that goal. Also notice that the counselor uses "presuppositional" language (Selekman 1997, p. 60). Rather than talking about change as simply a possibility (e.g., "*If* things change for the better…"), the language suggests that the desired change is inevitable (e.g., "*When* things change for the better…"). Presuppositional language is used to convey the counselor's confidence in positive change and hopefully instill the same sense of inevitability in clients.[5]

Scaling Questions Scaling questions are another technique commonly used within SFBT. Early pioneers of SFBT found that some concepts were difficult for clients to explain. For example, de Shazer (1997) points out that the discussion of degrees of depression or anxiety can be overly abstract (p. 377). In early clinical experiences, SFBT therapists found that by having clients describe concerns relative to an imaginary "scale," these impressions were easy to track. Thus, SFBT therapists often ask clients to rate their concerns along "scales." For example, a therapist might ask:

> On a scale from "one" to "ten," with "ten" meaning that everything was going great and there was no problem, and "one" meaning that nothing was going right and everything is bad, where would you rate your concern right now? (Adapted from de Shazer 1997).

The point of the scaling question is to provide a metric by which therapists can get clients to clearly imagine small improvements. For example, if a client responds that his complaint is currently overwhelming and he rates the experience as a "two" on the scale, the therapist can then have the client imagine what the client would be doing differently when he or she improves a little:

> Okay, so right now things are a "two." What would it take for things to feel like a "three" or a "four"?
> How would things be different at "four"?
> What would have to change for things to be a "four"?

Or alternatively, this technique can be used to explore client strengths that keep them from sliding further down the scale. In this way, resiliency factors can be discovered and perhaps expanded upon. For example, the therapist might ask:

> So you're at a "two," which means you're not completely bottoming out. What good things are keeping you from feeling like a "one"?

When confronted with this question, many adolescents point to the support they get from family and friends, or possibly point to upcoming events that they are looking forward to. In each of these cases, the counselor is given ideas for how to expand on the adolescent's preexisting strengths. With some further exploration, for example, the counselor might help the adolescent identify behaviors that make it possible for

[5] In a classic social psychology experiment, researchers found that children who received teacher encouragement that presupposed success outperformed children who were lectured and persuaded (e.g., "*You should…*") on outcomes related to classroom rule compliance and academic performance (Miller et al. 1975). In our view, the presuppositional language of SFBT is a fantastic example of how to apply these lessons to counseling.

family and friends to be even more supportive, or increase the likelihood of having more things to look forward to in the future.

Alternatively, it is not unusual to find that the scaling question yields the extreme low response. No matter the numbers or the size of the scale, many teens seem to be perpetually at the outer limits. When this occurs, it may help to rescale, using excessive anchors that assure a response somewhere in the middle of the scale. The counselor might say, "*So things are a 'one' right now? Hmmm... Well, maybe we think of 'one' and 'ten' differently, so let's try this again.*" Then the counselor might explain that a "one" is tantamount to "*aliens from the Centaurus galaxy attacking the earth, enslaving all mankind, and making us watch C-SPAN all day, every day.*" Conversely, clients who overstate how well things are going can be told that a "ten" means; "*the sun is shining, the birds are singing, and there are rainbows in the sky.*" We find that dramatic humor often works well in these situations, assuming the situation allows for humor. But in any event, it seems that for some adolescents, the more extreme the anchor, the better. Obviously, calamitous situations that could actually occur (e.g., "Your boyfriend breaks up with you") should never be used as anchors because the counselor could inadvertently exaggerate how "catastrophic" and unmanageable such events would be. For this reason, we recommend preternatural descriptions of the undesirable anchor, such as unprecedented cosmic events or impossibly bad weather events.

Over time, the use of scaling questions offers the therapist a practical way to informally measure progress. When, for example, a client returns and reports that they feel two or three degrees better than before, the counselor can then explore the behaviors and situations that led to improvement: "*What are you doing differently now that you're higher up the scale?*" "*How did you turn things around?*" In this way, the counselor can more easily help clients identify those strengths and coping mechanisms that can be expanded upon in the future (Murphy 1997, 2008; Selekman 1997). In some cases, counselors can even track outcomes using the scaling questions to know whether and when counseling has been successful.

Compliments Another key element of SFBT is the use of compliments and occasional between-session tasks. These two elements traditionally are introduced together, typically at the end of each session. As mentioned previously, SFBT counselors traditionally use a break in the session to formulate feedback and then return to offer the client final thoughts and observations. During this feedback, SFBT counselors often use praise to reinforce positive client behaviors and coping mechanisms. The counselor might start out by saying:

I'm impressed with how you have dealt with this concern so far!
I'm impressed with how you value _____.
There are some kids who may have given up, but you're really hanging in there!
It says a lot about you that you _____.
You've clearly tried lots of things to make things better.

In all these statements, the client's strengths and resiliencies are highlighted in the hope that this recognition will increase and amplify the successful behavior.

When providing compliments, however, there are two general concerns. First, compliments must be genuine. Adolescents are very adept at detecting disingenuous praise, and adults who offer bogus cheerleading are often ignored and discredited (Taffel 2005). Of course, for adolescents whose behaviors are particularly challenging, it can be difficult to find specific traits to genuinely compliment. In these cases, reframes are often useful. For example, combative behavior can be reframed as a need for independence: "*I'm impressed with how important it is to you to be independent.*" Or, "*I'm impressed with how important it is to you to come up with your own solutions.*" Similarly, procrastination might be complimented as, "*Some kids may have blown off the assignment altogether, but it really says a lot about you that you ultimately saw it through.*"

Second, adults often misuse compliments and this can have the same chilling effect as disingenuous compliments. For example, when at-risk adolescents start to experience success, well-intentioned adults might heap on praise in the hopes that somehow the adolescent has turned a corner. Parents and teachers often say, "*I knew you could do it!*" Or, "*I'm so proud of you!*" Of course, these are wonderful sentiments and, from a behavioral standpoint, one would expect such praise to be highly rewarding; but praise is unrewarding for adolescents who do not value the adult's opinions. To illustrate this problem, consider the following true case example: An adolescent who was struggling in school worked with a paraprofessional to develop some basic study strategies and to organize his bookbags, binders, and assignment tracking system. After some time, teachers started to comment that the student turned in more assignments than before and that his grades were improving. At midterm, a positive report went home and, in an attempt to praise his son, the father said, "I knew you could do it!" Almost immediately thereafter, the adolescent resorted to his old habits and his grades again plummeted. He lost his assignment notebook and missing schoolwork started to pile up. When the paraprofessional asked about the setback, the adolescent admitted that he purposely sabotaged his own academic performance because he did not want his father to take credit for the improvements. The father's praise had backfired.

The important lesson here is that counselors have to be mindful of how adolescents are likely to receive compliments and not assume that all praise is welcomed. In general, we encourage counselors to withhold value-based appraisals—either positive or negative—until it is clear that the adolescent will value the feedback. As an alternative, counselors can ask clients for their appraisal of events. For example, if an adolescent earns higher grades in school than at previous times (e.g., a *B* in a class that he previously failed), the counselor might ask, "*What do* you *think? Were you shooting for a B?*" Although we might assume that this is a breakthrough moment, the adolescent might actually have worked harder than ever before and quietly expected an *A*, and now harbors doubts that he can ever be an *A* student. A compliment in this situation (e.g., "*Way to go! It's awesome that you earned a B!*") could easily backfire. In other situations, counselors can ask if the adolescent wants feedback: "*Do you want to know what I think?*" But when asking such questions, counselors should be prepared to be told "No!"

At the same time that compliments are offered, SFBT counselors often encourage clients to try a homework assignment. As mentioned previously, these homework assignments can seem bizarre, but the purpose is to help clients reexamine the problem in order to uncover strengths or exceptions that the client might broaden. In the case of de Shazer's bed wetting problem described above, for example, the decision to have the father wake the boy rather than the mother was based on the fact that the father encountered fewer bed wetting incidents than the mother. Because this represented an exception to the problem, the counselor explored the exceptions by having the father wake the boy every morning between sessions. When this task proved successful, the counselor then made the morning routine random by having the parents secretly flip a coin each night to determine who initiated the morning routine. In this way, the boy could not anticipate who would wake him. Note that the underlying cause of the bed wetting is inconsequential. Neither the family nor the counselor needed to know *why* the bed wetting events occurred in order to find an effective solution (de Shazer 1988, pp. 54–56).

Of course, exceptions to problems are not always immediately obvious. In these cases, formulaic tasks are sometimes assigned to uncover possible solutions. One classic task is the "first session formula task" (de Shazer 1985, p. 187). Here, counselors encourage clients to take time between sessions to observe the things that they would *not* want to change, and then report these things back to the counselor. The point of this exercise is to focus the client on potential strengths and coping mechanisms already available that could potentially be strengthened. Such assignments are a common element of SFBT and, when implemented correctly, move clients closer to their goals. Of course, it is common for clients to ignore the task, and this may be especially true among reluctant adolescents. For this reason, counselors should choose straightforward homework tasks and explain how they might benefit the adolescent. Alternatively, the counselor can offer two or three homework options and let the adolescent choose which one is most doable (Hay and Kinnier 2001).

Summary of the Keys to SFBT We have briefly summarized some of the key elements of SFBT, but readers should be aware that neither our list nor our descriptions are exhaustive. Rather, we offer this overview to simply illustrate the solution-focused approach, and how the techniques in SFBT build on a common theme. In practice, the techniques flow from one to another, so a counselor's structuring of a single SFBT session might go as follows: (1) listening carefully to the client's complaint and making use of therapeutic microskills (e.g., active listening, reflection, reframing); (2) using the miracle question to clarify goals; (3) using scaling questions to identify helpful behaviors and client strengths; and then (4) offering compliments and a homework assignment designed to uncover and amplify coping strategies. The common theme, of course, is the cooperative search for solutions. The counselor does not force a solution through begging, pleading, lecturing, advice-giving, or persuading; rather, the client and counselor work together to uncover or rediscover strategies already within the client's repertoire that have been helpful in the past to solve the problem in question or others like it.

Research on Solution-Focused Counseling

Clinical trials examining solution-focused counseling outcomes have been rare, and most published studies to date have suffered from methodological flaws. In their thoughtful review of all controlled trials conducted prior to 2000, Gingerich and Eisengart (2000) state, "...we cannot conclude that SFBT has been shown to be efficacious. We do, however, believe that [studies] provide initial support..." (p. 493). The authors came to this conclusion after noting that only 5 of the 15 controlled studies in their review adhered to 80% or more of the recommended guidelines for clinical research outlined by the American Psychological Association (Task Force on Promotion and Dissemination of Psychological Procedures 1995). In these "well-controlled" studies, solution-focused counseling appeared to lead to statistically significant—yet generally modest—client improvements across several referral problems (e.g., depression, prison recidivism, substance abuse). Most of the remaining studies appeared to be "poorly controlled," meeting less than half of the recommended research standards. Results in these latter studies were mixed and difficult to interpret. Thus, by the start of the past decade, research support for solution-focused counseling appeared somewhat promising, but clearly SFBT could not be considered an empirically validated option.

Since that time, more studies have been published focusing specifically on the application of solution-focused approaches with children and adolescents, and much of this research has been conducted in schools. For example, Newsome (2004) conducted a secondary school-based study of an eight-week small group application of SFBT for students with learning disabilities and a history of classroom behavior problems. The author examined whether group participation improved student grades and school attendance relative to a comparison group who did not receive the intervention. Group activities in the treatment condition focused mostly on academic goal setting (using the miracle question), self-ratings (using scaling questions), identifying exceptions to problems, and an activity called "A letter from the future" that was designed to help students identify effective coping skills (p. 339). Results suggest that the group participants experienced a statistically significant improvement in grades relative to the control group, but the effect size was modest. No differences were noted in terms of school attendance. Although somewhat encouraging, the results are difficult to interpret because participants were not randomly assigned to the experimental conditions; rather, students were admitted into the SFBT group based on class schedule and availability. Thus, the results might be attributable to a selection bias. In a follow-up article, Newsome (2005) reports that teacher ratings of the students who participated in the eight-week SFBT improved significantly from pre- to post-treatment in social skills and classroom behaviors. However, without comparisons to the control condition, it is unclear if these changes are attributable to the intervention or some other factor.

Franklin and colleagues (2008) examined the impact of one-to-one SFBT sessions for middle school students identified by teachers with disruptive classroom behaviors. Five to seven sessions were provided for 30 children at one school, and 29 students at another school were recruited as no-treatment control participants.

Fig. 3.3 Even effective techniques can be misused

When the groups were compared over three time points (pretest, posttest, and 1-month follow-up), it appeared that the treatment group experienced significant reductions in externalizing and internalizing symptoms relative to control as rated by teachers, and significant reductions in externalizing behaviors relative to control according to participant self-reports. However, like the Newsome study, the participants were not randomly assigned to experimental condition, so the results might be attributable to preexisting differences between the treatment and control groups.

Overall, it appears that the research on SFBT continues to suffer the same methodological limitations discussed in Gingerich and Eisengart's (2000) review. In our review of recent studies, we did not find any instances that meet all of the conditions necessary to be considered a true experimental design. Most research designs are quasi-experimental due to a lack of sufficient comparison groups.[6] Recommendations offered by Gingerich and Eisenhart are still unheeded, even after more than a decade of additional research. For example, researchers have not focused on specific populations (e.g., specific diagnoses) in order to improve external validity. The studies we reviewed make attempts at defining the target population, but labels such as "at-risk" and "bullying victims" are poorly defined. Also, Gingerich and Eisenhart recommend that researchers carefully define SFBT, yet in the studies we reviewed, procedures were inconsistently identified and, in some cases, researchers used as few as three specific techniques to define SFBT. For example, Franklin and colleagues required that all sessions conducted as part of their study include the miracle question. In our view, this is a rather narrow definition of SFBT (even though it was supported by de Shazer and Berg) that reminds us of the humanistic critique of manual-based research as inflexible. Moreover, it seems odd to require specific techniques in every session when the literature recommends their selective use (e.g., de Shazer 1988). How could a counselor use the miracle question in every session and still maintain novelty and genuineness? Although we doubt that SFBT has ever been interpreted as rigidly as the illustration in Fig. 3.3, this intentionally

[6] When conducting research in schools, it is often difficult to conduct randomization to condition because of the difficulties this can create for the school schedule, so the limitations in the studies above are not necessarily surprising.

absurd depiction underscores why we believe it is important to define therapies based on their objectives as well as techniques (see Chap. 1).

Solution-Focused Behavior Interventions

Early in our research, we found that counselors-in-training had difficulties helping adolescents with disruptive behaviors because the counselors' goals for treatment (e.g., reduced impulsivity, fewer disruptive behaviors) were often not shared by the client. As a result, the path to change was not always clear and the impasse of first-order change attempts was realized almost immediately. Counselors could effectively manage behavior problems within the setting (i.e., during our after-school program, within one-to-one counseling sessions), but problem behaviors often persisted outside of those settings. Even when sessions were marked by compliance and harmony, parents or teachers rarely reported change at home or school. This is not surprising, as straightforward behavior management strategies rarely generalize beyond the treatment setting (see Chap. 2). As a result, new counselors in the CHP were frequently frustrated by what seemed like an impossible task, and the therapeutic alliance suffered when sessions were experienced as autopsies of new problems (i.e., weekly crises) that occurred in school or in the community.

For these reasons, we started to modify our predominately behavioral approach to include strategies that, in our judgment, seemed promising for generalizing gains across multiple settings. One of our first modifications was to emphasize a cooperative focus on solutions, thereby offering the counselor a strategy for guiding the adolescent toward attainable and effective coping strategies while maintaining the client-counselor relationship. Even client complaints that seemed intractable or overwhelming could be addressed from the standpoint of coping skills. For example, older adolescents with disruptive behaviors often have difficulties with their employers, but this does not mean that they are incapable of new behaviors that might reduce or avoid vocational difficulties. Similarly, adolescents have difficulties with their peers that can be approached from a solution-focused standpoint. Consider the following scenarios. In both, high school students bring concerns to the attention of a school-based paraprofessional that we refer to as a *skills coach.*[7]

Scenario A A high school senior meets with the skills coach between classes and describes a confrontation with his immediate supervisor at his job in a local café. The coach encourages the adolescent to explain his side of the events and based on his description it becomes clear that the adolescent became very agitated after his supervisor caught him taking an unauthorized break.

[7] In these scenarios, we use verbatim transcripts from actual counseling sessions recorded during our studies. The only changes made to these transcripts were the removal of excessive verbal markers (e.g., "um, um…") and information that could identify the clients. In all cases, informed consent was acquired from parents and the adolescents prior to taping, and our consent procedures were approved by the Institutional Review Board at James Madison University and Ohio University.

Coach: What did you actually say?
Adolescent: Uh…
C: …don't sugarcoat it…
A: I said, "This is bullshit!"
C: And what did he say?
A: He said, "You got to do what you got to do." So I called my mom, and I said, "How bad do you think it would be if I quit?" I told her the scenario and stuff, and she could hear him [the supervisor] over the phone, saying stuff. And she said, "You got to do what you got to do." And so—but she was like, "You can call a meeting [with the café manager]," so I called in today and we're going to have a meeting Monday with the big, head bosses.
C: So you haven't quit—or did you tell him that you were going to quit?
A: I told him I was, like, this close (*holds fingers close together*), but I don't…I don't know. I don't think I quit because I could go in today, if I wanted, I guess.
C: Okay.
A: But, we're going to have this big meeting or something… But yeah, a real crappy day yesterday.
C: Yeah. So what do you hope to accomplish with the meeting?
A: Um, the thing is, if I go back there, it's going to be all awkward and stuff. I just hope to leave on good terms.
C: Okay.
A: Because, like, I don't want to get a new job, but I have to because in four weeks [the season ends] anyways.
C: That's right, we talked about that before.

The coach and adolescent discuss several related concerns that had been the topic of previous sessions, which all seem to point to the fact that the adolescent has been having a difficult time coping in several areas of his life, including his family, his friends, and his supervisor at work. After a few minutes reflecting on these events, the coach brings the discussion back to the incident at work the previous night.

C: Is he [the supervisor] going to be at the meeting next week?
A: Yeah.
C: What do you think you can do [in the meeting] to advocate for yourself?
A: I guess I just have to stand my ground. Because I, like, made a good point and I definitely want to stand by [it]. Like, the work is definitely unfair—it seems like I put in a hundred percent all day, and I get, like, no time to mess around. And everyone else puts in, like, twenty percent—two hours of work—and get paid the same amount as I do. So, I don't find that fair.

The adolescent then describes an earlier event at work when he and a coworker were told they could not have a break. When the adolescent protested, the supervisor reportedly said that breaks and other "freedoms" were being abused.

C: I'm stuck on the comment that he thought that if you and [a coworker] were given any freedom that you would abuse it. Why do you think he thinks that?[8]

A: Huh. (pauses for a moment) I can speak for [the coworker]. Like, he has a really bad habit of just, like, walking off. Sometimes when he has a line [of customers waiting]… Like, it's not like…like he walks off and leaves me hanging—sometimes it ends up being that, but he doesn't intend it to be like that. And like, me and him are close, we're like best friends at work. He's cool… He's like, getting in trouble a lot lately for walking off and leaving me to do the job. I don't really have a problem with it because if I, like, ask him, "Hey, I got to go use the bathroom," or something, "Can you cover me real quick?" and he has no problem with it at all.

Scenario B In this second scenario, another high school senior describes a recent social misunderstanding with a fellow athlete on the track team.

Adolescent: He [the peer] got his worst time and he was, like, his best time would have gotten him into the finals, but he got his worst time of the season. As did I.
Coach: So what do you say to a kid in that situation?
A: I would've said…I was going to say, "Oh, there's always next year. No, wait, [the school is] going to cut funding, so they're going to cut indoor track."
C: Did you say that to him?
A: Yeah.
C: How did he react to it?
A: He was like, uh, he was still trying to be mopey.
C: So it was like a joke, right?
A: No. What's funny is, is like I said it, "oh, next year—no wait, they're going to cut funding," and he was like, "Yeah! So, it's going to be the last year," or something like that.
C: So what do you say to someone in that situation?
A: (Speaking as if he's talking to his teammate) "So what? You sucked. You know you can do better—use that, get better."

The adolescent then digresses from the topic and describes unrelated events that occurred the same day. Eventually, the coach is able to redirect the adolescent back to this incident.

C: So after you talked to that guy, do you think he felt better?
A: (laughing) No!
C: Did it make him feel worse?
A: I don't know. I'm just a bad comforter, 'cause, you know, I'll sit there and go, "You had it rough? I had it tougher," or something like that—trying to make them feel better by it, you know. Like, things could be worse.

After a few minutes exploring the incident, the coach asks the adolescent to rate himself along a scale from −3, meaning that he was completely ineffectual in his at-

[8] This question may have been better phrased as, "*What gives your supervisor that impression?*"

tempt to console his peer, to +3, meaning that he was completely effectual.[9] Prior to this meeting, the adolescent had chosen "appearing competent" as a personal goal, and the scale was designed to reflect moving toward (positive numbers) or moving away (negative numbers) from this goal.

C: How would you rate yourself on your competence level [during this incident]?
A: I thought it was kinda' like a 2 (the second-highest rating). I wrote that down… Sometimes I tried to be funny and it wouldn't work…but I wasn't worried too much about doing good 'cause this was my last indoor meet.

These scenarios, which both involve 17-year old boys, highlight several interesting facets of counseling adolescents with ADHD. First, the dialogue is dysfluent. The adolescents' speech patterns seem to reflect a disorganized approach to thinking about interpersonal experiences. In the first scenario, the boy was unsure whether he had actually quit his job, and his retelling of the events jumps around in time so that the beginning, middle, and end of the story are jumbled. Similarly, the boy in the second scenario seems to confuse what he *thought* about saying with what was actually said. This makes the counselor's job difficult, as she has to ask several clarifying questions in order to understand what happened. Second, there is often a pattern of unsuccessful behavior cycles that go largely unexamined. For example, the adolescent in Scenario A seems convinced that when confronted by an adult, he must "stand his ground," even though it leads to more conflict; but interestingly, he is reluctant to confront coworkers who are possibly taking advantage of his friendship. The adolescent in Scenario B seems to believe that he is naturally "not a good comforter," so therefore any efforts to change his behaviors are doomed to failure. Third, and perhaps most important, the dysfluent speech patterns and limited insight makes it unclear what the boys would target for change in the future, if anything. In fact, both boys seem to conclude that no real changes are necessary, even though they were clearly troubled by the events. When potential goals are implied (e.g., planning for the meeting at work, trying different social skills), both boys seem to retreat. So, what goals are these boys truly working toward? Even in the second scenario where a previous attempt at defining a goal had been made ("appearing competent"), was the adolescent accurate in his self-appraisal? Such complications are the norm when counseling adolescents with ADHD and conduct problems.

In our experience, solution-focused counseling appears to be useful because the concrete nature of goal setting, feedback, and self-evaluation (i.e., "*How can I keep moving toward my goal?*") lends itself particularly well to the cognitive deficit areas of this population (e.g., poor memory, lack of foresight, disorganized thoughts). As we discussed in Chap. 2, adolescents with disruptive behaviors appear to experience a disconnection between behavior and its consequences, so that a pairing between a behavior and a punishment is less salient than is typically seen among normally developing adolescents. Solution-focused strategies seem to work by "externalizing" (using Barkley's (2006) idiom, pp. 327–330) and concretizing the *behavior → consequence* connection. In contrast, overly abstract approaches to problem solu-

[9] As we discuss in Chap. 5, we use this scale frequently when helping adolescents to set and then assess their performance on their social goals.

tion are likely to be ineffective due to the dysfluent and disorganized thought patterns, which might partially explain the disappointing results of research on cognitive therapies for children and adolescents with ADHD. As readers might anticipate from the scenarios above, a discussion of the irrationality of these boys' interpretations of these events is unlikely to succeed.

Yet, it should be pointed out that the classic SFBT model is not likely to be effective, either. We have found that three basic changes to the traditional SFBT approach (e.g., de Shazer 1985, 1988) are warranted:

1. We target a specific population with an identifiable psychiatric diagnosis.
2. Our approach is "brief" in terms of therapeutic focus and session length, but not in terms of total sessions conducted.
3. When clients are "stuck," we carefully introduce behavioral interventions.

On the first point, it should be noted that solution-focused counseling was originally intended to be applicable to a wide range of client concerns. In early writings on SFBT, for example, de Shazer and his colleagues describe the application of the therapy to parent training, addictions, eating disorders, and even delusional thinking. By targeting our efforts to adolescents with a specific diagnosis, which is premised on client *problems*, it may seem incongruous to begin with a focus on client strengths and solutions. After all, we start the intervention anticipating specific problems (e.g., disorganization, poor homework compliance). However, our goal as practitioners and researchers has been to construct an effective intervention program for a specific at-risk population; so in our view, anything that safely improves client outcomes should be considered. Utility trumps theoretical purity: We implement techniques that have been shown to be effective (or at least promising), even if the underlying theories are incompatible.

On the second point, traditional applications of solution-focused therapy are typically less than 10–12 sessions. When applied to ADHD and conduct problems, which can be chronic and pervasive, 12 or fewer sessions is usually inadequate. We know that when psychosocial interventions are removed, for example, disruptive behaviors can return to levels that would be expected if no specialized treatments had been attempted (The MTA Cooperative Group 2004). Thus, our application of solution-focused counseling typically occurs over several months, an entire school year, or even several years. Some may argue that by extending solution-focused counseling over such long periods, we are no longer providing "brief" or "solution-focused therapy," but we argue that our interventions are still "brief" in the sense that we deliberately limit our focus to observable goals in the here-and-now. In fact, we find that the elements of solution-focused counseling lend themselves quite well to long-term intervention because the techniques can be applied across several client concerns, affecting multiple environments. Similar modifications have been made by researchers examining the long-term application of solution-focused strategies to whole institutions, such as alternative schools (e.g., Franklin and Streeter 2005). Adolescents with disruptive behaviors need extended practice generating solutions for a wide range of problems before we can expect the learned skills to generalize to other settings.

The third point is actually our motivation for writing this book. As we explained in Chap. 1, there has historically been a gap between research and practice, due in part to disagreements about what constitutes "evidence" for best practices in psychotherapy. On the one hand, proponents of the evidence-based practice movement advocate an empirical approach, and, on the other hand, proponents of what we have termed the humanistic perspective advocate varied and flexible research methods that reflect the idiosyncratic nature of the therapeutic process. Our strategy for bridging this gap is to think of therapy as consisting of external factors (e.g., family stressors), nonspecific elements (i.e., common factors), and specific elements (e.g., therapeutic techniques) (see Fig. 1.2). Proponents of the humanistic perspective tend to emphasize the common elements of therapy, and evidence-based movement enthusiasts seem to emphasize the specific elements. But clearly, all elements are transactional, and each is vital for understanding how psychotherapy improves client outcomes. When training psychologists for clinical practice, we describe the therapeutic relationship as a conduit through which interventions—ideally evidence-based interventions—are introduced and implemented. This is similar to the frequently espoused notion of "flexibility within fidelity" proposed by Kendall and colleagues (2008), in that we adapt our procedures to the needs of the situation and adjust our sessions accordingly.

In our research, we have trained counselors to utilize solution-focused skills as a means of establishing this relationship because it appears that SFBT has some benefits for adolescents with disruptive behaviors as a standalone approach, as we discussed above. The difficulty is how and when to introduce behavioral interventions within this relationship, as some interventions have objectives that are ostensibly incompatible with SFBT. For example, SFBT emphasizes a cooperative client-counselor relationship that is largely directed by the client's goals, yet the counselor might suspect that a specific intervention matches a need the client does not readily recognize. How does the counselor proceed? Is it possible to implement the intervention and still maintain a solution-focused relationship with the client? We believe that it is possible, but we acknowledge that some of our practices are inconsistent with SFBT. In the remainder of this chapter and the ones that follow, we will describe how we synthesize these approaches.

Solution-Focused Relationships

As August Aichhorn's quote at the top of this chapter points out, it is imperative that counselors establish an effective relationship with troubled youths before progress can be made on any objective. Interestingly, Aichhorn's quote is over 80 years old and is still undeniably true; in the intervening years, no substitute has been found for the client-counselor relationship. The important question that remains is how best to establish this relationship and what to do with it after it is achieved. As we have pointed out, we believe that solution-focused counseling is a very promising means of building the therapeutic alliance, particularly for clients with ADHD and conduct problems, because clients drive the goal-setting process. We have no doubt that other approaches to counseling can be as effective or even more effective in some cases, but of the therapies that have been researched, solution-focused approaches seem to offer the best hope.

In our own research on psychosocial interventions, we have trained undergraduate counselors and paraprofessionals to use a solution-focused approach to relationship building. Although we have not detailed these efforts in our published research articles (mostly due to space constraints), we have increasingly relied on solution-focused strategies. To begin, we encourage counselors to use "non-problem" language in their first meeting with new clients. Non-problem language is a strategy where counselors purposely postpone discussions of the client's problems until after some initial connections are made between client and counselor.

Early Sessions

In early sessions, we encourage counselors to focus on neutral issues—things that are unrelated to the reason why the client was referred. We have used a semi-structured interview protocol we call the "Initial Appraisal Form" to help open a dialogue with adolescents (see Appendix A for the form; specific examples of questions are provided in Chap. 5). We encourage counselors to have adolescents respond to all of the items, but counselors are free to ask questions in a manner that matches the adolescent's comfort level and at the pace that feels appropriate, even if it means breaking the interview up over multiple sessions. In general, we find that the non-problem approach disarms reluctant adolescents. Most youths with disruptive behaviors are referred to counseling by their parents or teachers, so unlike traditional counseling with adult clients, client motivations and expectations for change are often less than ideal (Prout 2007). Murphy (1997) explains that clients have varying degrees of "customership" when it comes to counseling. Clients who are self-referred and motivated to solve problems can be considered "customers." Clients who see counseling as simply an opportunity to ruminate over their problems without making changes can be considered "complainants." And clients who do not wish to discuss problems or work toward solutions can be considered "visitors" (pp. 50–53). By and large, counselors can expect adolescent clients with disruptive behaviors to fluctuate between complainant and visitor. In Scenarios A and B above, these qualities are clearly visible. Thus, it is often important for counselors to rely on non-problem talk early in the relationship-building process. This is not just true of SFBT—many counselors recognize the need to set the referral question aside and discuss trouble-free topics at first. Taffel (2005), for example, explains that discussing pop culture, fashion, and television often helps to make the counseling scenario less stressful than the adolescent might have anticipated.

Impulsive Clients

Interestingly, hyperactive or impulsive adolescents may provide more information than anticipated in the first session. Counselors working with this population for the first time are often shocked to find that seemingly simple, non-problem questions can spark discussions that lead to the adolescent divulging personal information that most adults would keep secret. New counselors often express a sense of accomplishment following the first session because their client seems to have had a catharsis of self-disclosure. But of course, this is the nature of impulsivity, and it is important for counselors to be ready for a potential avalanche of client self-disclosure in the first meeting or two. In terms of customership, this behavior is consistent with the complainant, and the fact that the adolescent shares a lot of information does not necessarily mean that he is willing to make any meaningful change.

Three rules-of-thumb are worth noting here: (1) counselors should not overreact to client confessions; (2) counselors should not trust that all information provided by the client is accurate;[10] and (3) counselors should avoid disclosing information about their own lives. In other words, it is important for counselors to not be visibly shaken or horrified, even when adolescents divulge intense personal information. It is also important to verify the adolescent's perceptions of her relationships with parents and teachers for later challenges, but early in the process it is best to take all claims at face value. Finally, we strongly discourage counselors from providing too much personal information, outside of briefly pointing out mutual interest areas, because adolescents form opinions of adults in unpredictable ways. Unfavorable opinions of a counselor can undermine subsequent sessions.

Angry and "Resistant" Clients

Of course, the opposite is also possible; clients enter the first session and are reluctant to talk to the counselor at all. In these cases, adolescents are usually angry and frustrated that they have been referred for counseling and believe that they "do not belong" with the counselor. If, for example, the client is in counseling because he was referred by his parents and he angrily disagrees with this decision, the initial relationship may be difficult to establish. In some instances, even non-problem questions can be shut down with silence or painfully short answers. In such cases, we encourage counselors to try to find ways to actually *agree* with the client. The counselor may use scaling questions, such as:

> Sometimes kids are referred to me who don't need to be here. It happens quite a bit, actually. So how about we save ourselves a little time. On a scale from "one" to "ten," with

[10] Claims of abuse or suicidal thinking (or any other potentially dangerous situations) should be handled appropriately—always ensuring clients are safe—but we assume that readers have the appropriate background in these precautions.

"one" being "absolutely no need" and "ten" being "definitely a need," where would you rank your need to be here?

In almost every case, complainants and visitors will rank themselves a "one" (or below). When this occurs, the counselor can respond with investigative questions to determine the adolescent's impressions for why the referral was made. Depending on the situation, the counselor might ask:

Who was concerned enough about you that they thought you should be here? Or
What led to you getting sent here?

The point of these questions is not to stoke the adolescent's resentment at the referral source; rather, such questions have potential for outlining early goals. After listening to and reflecting the adolescent's dispute with the referral, the counselor might ask:

What would it take to prove to your parents/teachers that you do not belong here?
What would they need to see to convince them that counseling isn't necessary?
How might you "graduate" out of this program?
How will they know when you are better?

Based on the adolescent's responses to these types of questions, the counselor can start giving voice to the client's implicit or explicit goals. For example, a goal to convince the client's parents that counseling is unnecessary is a goal that many reluctant clients find acceptable. Of course, the methods by which such goals are met are typically synonymous with the purpose of the original referral. A parent might refer an adolescent because of arguments in the home and a goal to "prove" to the parents that counseling is unnecessary would essentially require improvement in that area.

Of course, these strategies are not always successful and adolescents often leave counseling before any real work can be done. Counselors should be ready for this possibility by preparing alternative strategies for continuing to work with the family or the school. Conversely, counselors should not assume that encouraging recalcitrant clients to attempt counseling is a guarantee that client outcomes will improve. Indeed, individual counseling is often just one component of a larger intervention, and it is this larger intervention that we describe in later chapters.

Conclusion

In this chapter, we have examined the basic objectives and techniques of solution-focused counseling and started to apply these concepts to individual work with adolescent clients with disruptive behaviors. We have used these techniques as part of our overall strategy to build an alliance with adolescents and to motivate them to engage in the interventions we introduce later. Our approach is admittedly unorthodox because we mix approaches to counseling that are based on seemingly incompatible theories; on the one hand, we use solution-focused strategies premised on the adolescent's strengths, and on the other hand we have a set of specific, manualized interventions in mind that target client weaknesses. Despite the surface contradiction, we find that using solution-focused strategies early in the relationship is effective in reducing the potential hesitancies many adolescents feel when starting work with a counselor. As we discussed, most adolescents with behavior problems enter the relationship against their will, often following a referral from a parent or teacher. Adolescents are also unlikely to recognize a need for counseling, unlike clients who self-refer. Thus, our initial work is devoted to helping adolescents set their own goals, even if that goal is to prove to their parents or teachers that they do not need counseling! We find that a solution-focused approach works well in these cases because it is largely nonconfrontational and it requires that the counselor pay close attention to how the adolescent client describes their goals.

Of course, adolescents with ADHD and conduct problems can also benefit from specific interventions targeting other goals that they may not initially endorse. At this point, we deviate from traditional solution-focused counseling to introduce manualized interventions, but continue to use the concepts of client-driven goal setting and scaling questions throughout the entire process. In the following chapters, we describe this process and provide some specific techniques outlined in our treatment manuals.

References

Barkley, R. A. (Ed.). (2006). *Attention-deficit hyperactivity disorder: A handbook for diagnosis and treatment* (3rd ed.). New York: Guilford Press.

Budman, S. H. (1981). Looking toward the future. In S. H. Budman (Ed.), *Forms of brief therapy* (pp. 461–467). New York: Guilford Press.

Cialdini, R. B. (2008). *Influence: Science and practice* (5th ed.). Needham Heights. MA: Allyn & Bacon.

de Shazer, S. (1985). *Keys to solution in brief therapy*. New York: W. W. Norton & Company.

de Shazer, S. (1988). *Clues: Investigating solutions in brief therapy*. New York: W. W. Norton & Company.

de Shazer, S. (1997). Radical acceptance. *Family, Systems, and Health, 15,* 375–378.

Franklin, C., & Streeter, C. L. (2005). *Solution-focused alternatives for education: An evaluation of Gonzalo Garza Independent High School*. Austin: University of Texas, Hogg Foundation for Mental Health.

Franklin, C., Biever, J., Moore, K., Clemons, D., & Scamardo, M. (2001). The effectiveness of solution-focused therapy with children in a school setting. *Research on Social Work Practice, 11,* 411–434.

Franklin, C., Moore, K., & Hopson, L. (2008). Effectiveness of solution-focused brief therapy in a school setting. *Children and Schools, 30,* 15–26.

Gingerich, W. J., & Eisengart, S. (2000). Solution-focused brief therapy: A review of the outcome research. *Family Process, 39,* 477–498.

Gino, F., & Schweitzer, M. E. (2008). Blinded by anger or feeling the love: How emotions influence advice taking. *Journal of Applied Psychology, 93,* 1165–1173.

Hay, C. E., & Kinnier, R. T. (2001). Homework in counseling. In H. G. Rosenthal (Ed.), *Favorite counseling and therapy homework assignments* (pp. 223–234). Philadelphia: Brunner-Routledge.

Kendall, P. C., Gosch, E., Furr, J. M., & Sood, E. (2008). Flexibility within fidelity. *Journal of the American Academy of Child and Adolescent Psychiatry, 47,* 987–993.

Miller, W. R., & Rollnick, S. (2002). *Motivational interviewing: Preparing people for change* (2nd edn.). New York: Guilford.

Miller, W. R., & Rollnick, S. (2013). *Motivational interviewing: Helping people change* (3rd ed.). New York: Guilford.

Miller, R. L., Brickman, P., & Bolen, D. (1975). Attribution versus persuasion as a means of modifying behavior. *The Journal of Personality and Social Psychology, 31*(3), 430–441.

MTA Cooperative Group. (2004). National institute of mental health multimodal treatment study of ADHD follow-up: Changes in effectiveness and growth after the end of treatment. *Pediatrics, 113,* 762–769.

Murphy, J. J. (1997). *Solution-focused counseling in middle and high schools*. Alexandria: American Counseling Association.

Murphy, J. J. (2008). *Solution-focused counseling in schools* (2nd ed.). Alexandria: American Counseling Association.

Newsome, S. (2004). Solution-focused brief therapy groupwork with at-risk junior high school students: Enhancing the bottom line. *Research on Social Work Practice, 14,* 336–343.

Newsome, S. (2005). The impact of solution-focused brief therapy with at-risk junior high school students. *Children & Schools, 27,* 83–90.

Popper, K. (1963). *Conjectures and refutations: The growth of scientific knowledge.* London: Routledge.

Prout, H. T. (2007). Counseling and psychotherapy with children and adolescents: Historical developmental, integrative, and effectiveness perspectives. In H. T. Prout & D. T. Brown (Eds.), *Counseling and psychotherapy with children and adolescents: Theory and practice for school and clinical settings* (3rd ed., pp. 1–31). Hoboken: Wiley.

Selekman, M. D. (1997). *Solution focused therapy with children: Harnessing family strengths for systemic change*. New York: Guilford Press.

Sibley, M. H., Kuriyan, A. B., Evans, S. W., Waxmonsky, J., & Smith, B. H. (2014). Pharmacological and psychosocial treatments for adolescents with ADHD: An updated systematic review of the literature. *Clinical Psychology Review, 34,* 218–232.

Taffel, R. (2005). *Breaking through to teens: A new psychotherapy for the new adolescence*. New York: Guilford.

Task Force on Promotion and Dissemination of Psychological Procedures. (1995). Training in and dissemination of empirically-validated psychological treatments: Report and recommendations. *Clinical Psychologist, 48,* 3–23.

Tyron, W. W. (2007). What ever happened to symptom substitution? *Clinical Psychology Review, 28,* 963–968..

Watzlawick, P., Weakland, J., & Fisch, R. (1974). *Change: Principles of problem formation and problem resolution.* New York: Norton & Company.

Chapter 4
Academic Interventions

I have little sympathy with the rather prevalent concept that man is basically irrational, and this his impulses, if not controlled, will lead to destruction of others and self. Man's behavior is exquisitely rational, moving with subtle and ordered complexity toward the goals his organism is endeavoring to achieve.
Carl Rogers, from *On Becoming a Person* (1961)

In the previous chapter, we explored a basic approach to counseling for engaging adolescents with attention deficit hyperactivity disorder (ADHD) and conduct problems. In this chapter, we move beyond the relational aspects of counseling and begin exploring specific interventions supported by research. Readers should recall that our overall approach to counseling is a combination of strategies that have shown promise in the research literature, even when those strategies are based on seemingly incompatible ideas. The integrative nature of this approach will become clearer in the following sections, but we anticipate that some readers may question how these elements fit together. For example, in our previous discussion of solution-focused counseling, we point to the importance of building on clients' existing strengths; however, in this chapter, we describe several interventions that are meant to mitigate clients' functional impairments. How can both aims be seamlessly integrated? Can a counselor align with an adolescent and encourage him to expand on a skill he occasionally uses with success, and in the next moment introduce a preplanned, step-by-step procedure for addressing specific impairments? Based on our research and clinical experiences, the answer is *Yes*. The key to combining various strategies in counseling is what we refer to as *shifting*, and this chapter describes the ways that counselors can shift between solution-focused counseling and preplanned behavior training.

Before we begin, however, we should explain that this chapter does not explore classroom management techniques or instructional consultation, which has been examined at length in other works (e.g., Erchul and Martens 2010). Instead, our goal

B. K. Schultz, S. W. Evans, *A Practical Guide to Implementing School-Based Interventions for Adolescents with ADHD*, DOI 10.1007/978-1-4939-2677-0_4

here is to describe specific interventions in one-to-one sessions with adolescents, with a focus on how the strategies are introduced, progress is monitored, and how adolescents can increasingly take up and independently monitor these strategies over time. In our experience, secondary students often rely on underdeveloped academic skills that become increasingly problematic as expectations and curriculum advance in the later grades. As such, these interventions have a diagnostic as well as a treatment function, as difficulties with these interventions might suggest that a more elaborate and intensive intervention is needed, consistent with a "response-to-intervention" model.

It is also important to mention that counselors should secure accurate and up-to-date information regarding academics prior to starting academic interventions. In our research, we have studied the work of counselors and paraprofessionals based in schools, with direct access to teachers, report cards, disciplinary reports, and in some instances electronic grade books. The ability to communicate with school professionals about academic interventions is absolutely paramount, and professionals working outside of the school setting will be more effective when they are able to maintain such collaboration. Counselors should also have access to their client's school materials, such as bookbags and binders, because discussion of academic skills without application is unlikely to be effective.

There is, of course, one additional assumption that should be clear from the previous chapters: A therapeutic relationship has been established between the counselor and the adolescent. As always, we begin with this relationship, and introduce specific interventions only after the adolescent trusts and respects the counselor.

Identifying Academic Goals

Just as adolescents enter counseling with varying levels of motivation for change, there are clear differences between adolescents in terms of motivation to achieve academically. As we discussed in Chap. 2, some adolescents intentionally do just enough classwork to pass classes, but avoid accomplishing more for a variety of reasons (e.g., failure is experienced as unbearably punishing). In other words, they purposely underachieve, pursuing only the most easily attainable goals possible (e.g., to avoid being the lowest performer in the class). Sometimes adolescents downplay academics altogether by dismissing classwork as "stupid" or "worthless." In this way, the sting is removed from failure because the adolescent has staked a claim to indifference. Parents and teachers often describe adolescents who use this strategy as "lazy" or "unmotivated," but the phenomenon is more complex than these labels might suggest. Adolescents generally adopt a dismissive attitude toward school largely in response to a long history of failure, not because of a disgust of learning. Still others avoid the appearance of failure by blaming their lack of success on their disorder. We have worked with adolescents who have stated, rather clearly, that they "can't do better because of ADHD." In our experience, this latter tactic is rare, but it is yet another way in which adolescents avoid conspicuous failures by not risking effort.

As Carl Rogers' quote at the top of this chapter suggests, human behavior *is* rational when considered in the context of goals; so, if a middle or high school student wants to avoid the appearance of incompetence, the strategies we just described are entirely (and exquisitely) rational. This is an important insight when counselors prepare to help adolescents change because direct challenges to the underlying motivations can easily miss the mark. If, for example, a counselor attributes purposeful underachievement to faulty logic, the experiential evidence actually favors the adolescent, who is keenly aware of their past failures and the fast benefit of lowered expectations. Similarly, counselors who attempt to cajole the adolescent by dramatizing the risks associated with school dropout can inadvertently reinforce the adolescent's dismissive attitude toward school. Miller and Rollnick (2002) describe such attempts as "advocacy," which they define as promoting a position or point of view, and argue that these efforts can actually increase client resistance (p. 49). In our view, such mistakes can have broader repercussions for at-risk adolescents because of the escapist motivations described above. When push comes to shove on the issue of academic achievement, school rejection offers the at-risk student an easy way out. Counselors are wise to keep this in mind.

Given these problems, counselors hoping to address academic impairments can begin by having adolescents set their own goals. For readers familiar with the counseling literature, this is not a momentous insight; however, the process of goal setting with adolescents can be quite challenging. Assuming that counseling was initiated at least in part on the basis of academic concerns, we often start with an open-ended question such as:

> I'm asking you—not your parents or your teachers—what kind of grades are *you* comfortable with?

In our experience, most adolescents will at least imply that they want to pass their current grade and eventually graduate high school. Of course, this is not always the case, but the majority of struggling students, when given the opportunity to voice their own goals, will admit that some academic success is important. Often the adolescent's goal is motivated by a desire to escape the domain of their parents or other adults rather than for intrinsic reasons, but such admissions can still be considered positive from a goal-setting standpoint. The counselor can support the fledgling goal through normalization (e.g., "Lots of teens I know have come to the same conclusion") or reflection (e.g., "So getting all the way through school is important to you"). In some cases, however, the adolescent's early goal statements will clearly be disingenuous, and the counselor might suspect that the adolescent is simply parroting the well-intentioned messages of their parents or teachers. In these instances, the counselor might argue *against* change as a method for making the adolescent consider their borrowed goals more carefully. For example, the counselor might ask, "What about the people who drop out of high school and go on to be successful athletes or musicians? Is that a possibility?" The intent of such statements is essentially paradoxical, and the point is to encourage the adolescent to argue the opposite position without the counselor having to advocate or defend an external value system (Miller and Rollnick 2002, pp. 89–91). For adolescents with ADHD and conduct problems, self-defined goals are often modest, and it is common for this discussion to end with simple goals, such as passing core classes (i.e., earning "D"s or better). Although this may be disappointing for many parents and teachers, such targets offer a wonderful starting point for academic interventions. Rather than push for overly ambitious goals, it is important for counselors to allow adolescents to drive this process, even if the initial goals seem timid.

Note here that we have focused on grades as the target of goals. Grades offer some advantage as components of counseling goals, including the frequency with which midterm grades and report cards are provided, and the ecological validity of these outcomes. But what about clients who claim to have no academic aspirations at all? To be sure, some adolescents will deny any desire to pass tests or quizzes, to earn passing grades, or to graduate from high school. The obvious mistake is for counselors to advocate for the school by repeating lectures about the importance of education that adolescents have certainly heard before. Instead, the counselor has essentially two choices: (1) to alter the counseling strategy by expanding services to the family and larger support systems as a whole; or (2) to maintain an alliance with the adolescent and ostensibly agree to help him prepare for dropout. The latter option should be reserved for situations where access to the family and larger support systems are impossible; and obviously, this strategy is paradoxical in nature—the hope is that the experience of preparing for dropout will give the adolescent pause. But in truth, many students opt to drop out of school each year, particularly students with disruptive behaviors, so these discussions might actually be the only time that adolescents honestly consider their plans for life after dropping out.

For the remainder of our discussion, we will assume that the adolescent client states a desire to graduate from school and that there are continued expectations for independent work outside of the classroom. As mentioned above, our experiences suggest that most adolescents express a desire to complete high school or an equivalent, but their short-term goals are often uninspired and pessimistic. Unfortunately, some parents and educators might share this pessimism and remove most expectations by overusing accommodations to the point that all schoolwork is completed and managed in the classroom; but again, we will assume in this chapter that some expectations for independent schoolwork are shared by adolescents, parents, and educators. Even meager goals offer an opportunity for counselors to support change.

The Executive Functions

As discussed in Chap. 2, contemporary theories of ADHD attribute inattention and hyperactivity/impulsivity to deficits in executive functions (EF). Although many questions surround the role and definition of EF in ADHD or other related disorders, the research suggests that it is important for counselors to be mindful of the deficits that clients with disruptive behaviors are most likely to experience, particularly in terms of how these deficits might moderate our interventions. To this end, we use a simplified definition based on EF as a means to anticipate and recognize these deficits in sessions. For ease, we summarize these elements with the acronym M.O.P., which stands for:

- *M*emory
- *O*rganization
- *P*lanning

To illustrate these elements, consider the common experience of daydreaming while reading. As you read, your eyes pass over each line on the page, but your mind wanders. You might think to yourself, "*A turkey sandwich would be really good right now. Do we have any turkey in the refrigerator? I bet there's still a little—enough to make a sandwich, anyway. And if I'm going to eat, I should probably do it soon because it's getting late and I don't want to eat too close to bedtime.*" Just then, your eyes reach the bottom of the page and you catch yourself: "*Wait, I missed everything on this page! I have no idea what's going on in the story. Maybe this is a sign that I should stop reading! No, I want to finish this chapter, so I'll reread this section, beginning with the last sentence I recognize.*"

Now think about all the individual mental processes in this scenario. To start, the mind wanders during reading. Of course, this is not unusual—such momentary lapses seem to be part of human cognition and are partly explained by internal states such as exhaustion, or external conditions such as distractions. Theoretically, these lapses occur more often for people with ADHD than for those without, but this difference is quantitative, not qualitative.[1] The subsequent mental events in our scenario, however, appear to underscore a true difference between people with and without ADHD, beginning at the point at which we "catch" ourselves off-task. In the scenario, the bottom of the page serves as a cue that our hunger has distracted us. For others, however, the bottom of the page may not have served as a cue at all, and the reader may have turned the page and continued to think about turkey sandwiches. Or, as alluded to in our example, the cue may have drawn attention to mounting frustration with the task and led to avoidance, rather than redoubling of effort. In any event, the scenario exemplifies the cognitive experience of inhibition ("*Wait, I missed everything on this page.*") and EF, which are the subsequent mental processes. In our example, the internalized dialogue demonstrates planning ("*I want to finish this chapter tonight...*"), organization ("*...so I'll reread this section...*"), and memory ("*...beginning with the last sentence I recognize.*"). As a result of this internal dialogue, we redirect our behavior and work backward through the book, scanning for the last sentence we recognize and then begin reading again.

Of course, any single example is insufficient to convey the depth and richness of the various theories of EF, but the image of the distracted reader is a useful analogy of the deficits supposedly underlying academic impairment. When listening to the school-related complaints made by clients with ADHD and conduct problems,

[1] Researchers often describe ADHD as representing the low end of a continuum of attention and behavior regulation skills, rather than a distinct cognitive trait (e.g., Nigg 2006).

counselors will hear clues that point to deficits in working memory, organization, and planning. Here, we will describe specific interventions designed to address each of these deficit areas as related to academic impairment, highlighting how counselors can integrate these strategies within sessions.

Memory

One of the most consistent neuropsychological findings regarding ADHD is that working memory is often below that of same-age peers, perhaps especially so in regards to nonverbal working memory (Willcutt et al. 2005). Based on such findings, we predict that adolescents with ADHD would manage their time poorly and have difficulties recalling procedures when imitating tasks that have been previously modeled for them (Barkley 2006). How might these deficits impact academic achievement? In our experience working with middle and high school students, these deficits often manifest as poor study skills. Adolescents with ADHD and other disorders seem to have difficulties applying study strategies to novel classroom material, and select procedures that are likely to be the most time consuming. In one study of our after-school program, we informally assessed study skills by asking participants to examine a list of nine items and then telling us how they would remember the list if a quiz were pending (see Table 4.1). Of the nine young adolescents present that day, six indicated that they would rehearse each word individually, either by writing each word repeatedly or by saying the words repeatedly in their head. Two participants realized that the words fell into categories (clothes, food, body parts) and indicated that they would memorize the categories, and the last participant suggested that she would use the first letter from each word to make a silly sentence.

Which strategy is most likely to lead to success? Based on the research, the last two strategies would fair best; however, given the limited details provided by the participants who recognized the categories, their attempts might still be lacking. The most promising strategy—building an acrostic—was given by the last participant, who perhaps not coincidentally exhibited the least amount of academic impairment of the group. Simple rehearsal strategies, like those endorsed by six of the nine participants, are the most protracted strategy of the three options provided, and are the least likely to result in long-term retention of the material (Forness et al. 1997; Mastropieri and Scruggs 1998). Although anecdotal, our experience with the middle school students prompted us to reconsider study skill strategies, because we

Table 4.1 List of nine everyday objects. (This list was adapted from Rafoth's (1999) Metacognitive Interview p. 111)

Scarf	Coat	Sock
Brownies	Hand	Foot
Apple	Hot dog	Ear

anticipate that boring and protracted study strategies will be quickly abandoned by adolescents with ADHD. Students at the middle school level have been exposed to basic study strategies several times in their classrooms, particularly if they have ever received special education, yet in our informal survey, most vastly underestimated the time-consuming nature of rehearsal strategies and failed to apply efficient and effective mnemonic strategies to the task at hand. Further, when asked how many words each expected to remember on the quiz, all but the last predicted 100 % accuracy.

Now imagine a secondary school student with poor study skills that have caused problems in history class, as evidenced by low grades on tests and quizzes. His poor performance so far has caused stress between the adolescent and his parents and teachers. When asked, the student responds that he wants to pass the class so he does not have to retake it again next year, so in effect he sets a goal to do just enough to pass (e.g., earn a "D" overall). The counselor is aware that high school curricula require students to commit concepts and definitions to memory and then recall these concepts on short-answer, multiple-choice, or matching-style test items, and this appears to create a mismatch with this student's deficits in working memory because of his difficulties following the steps necessary for successful study. How might a counselor be helpful in this scenario? In our view, these types of academic concerns are highly productive targets for counseling because it affords the opportunity to examine the strategies that adolescents use and how they talk themselves through challenges. In our example, the counselor might ask, "When you have a test or quiz coming up, how do you prepare for it?" Responses to such questions can be revealing. Some adolescents will openly admit that they do not prepare at all, and others will point to inefficient strategies that are unlikely to be successful, even if they are actually used.

Heretofore, our discussion has been consistent with the literature on solution-focused counseling, which centers on the client's strengths and past successes. But when we start to discuss specific study strategies, it becomes increasingly difficult in many cases to identify success as a foundation for moving forward. The adolescent might have had success in early elementary school, for example, but the strategies she employed at that time are unlikely to be helpful now. In fact, the tendency for struggling students to resort to simple rehearsal strategies may be an artifact of the "*write-your-spelling-words-five-times-each*" experiences of first and second grade. Similarly, adolescents with ADHD and other disorders often struggle to imagine what potential solutions might work for them, partly due to the cognitive deficits associated with this class of disorders. As a result, strategies such as the miracle question (see Chap. 3) can sometimes fall flat because the adolescent repeatedly responds "I don't know," or the adolescent's imagined miracle provides few clues for realistic solutions. When counselors encounter such impasses, we encourage them to flexibly shift between a solution- and problem-focused orientation. A problem-focused orientation is generally more directive and procedure-driven than the solution-focused orientation, so this shift is significant and deserves some discussion. Below, we describe a specific strategy for teaching a flashcard study strategy to adolescents. Although such study strategies are not unique to the Challenging Horizons Program (CHP), we use this example to highlight the shift from solutions to problems, and ultimately back to solutions again.

The goal of this intervention is to teach an effective approach for constructing flashcards prior to tests and quizzes. To shift into the intervention, counselor might offer the following segue:

> It sounds like social studies has given you the most trouble this year, and so far your strategy for studying for tests and quizzes has not worked because your grades are lower than you'd like.

Several components of the shift statement are important. First, a problem is identified, but it is presented in tentative and time-limited terms (e.g., "…it seems like…" "…so far your strategy…"). Second, the problems are depersonalized and discussed as if they are completely outside of the client. So, instead of saying that a client is "failing social studies," the counselor flips the statement and points out how the class has been problematic for them. So far, both of these strategies are entirely consistent with solution-focused counseling. However, the third component in the shift statement begins the transition toward problem solving, and that is the deduction that what the adolescent has done so far "has not worked" relative to her stated goals. Once the adolescent has had a moment to reflect on this, the counselor might then continue:

> I've worked with students in the past who found themselves in similar situations and we came up with some things that worked. Can I show you one of the tricks we came up with?

Here, the intervention is framed as a "trick" that has worked for similar clients in the past. Alternatively, if the counselor anticipates that the adolescent will resist any attempt to intervene, the shift might be framed as:

> If you spend more than an hour studying each night, then something might be wrong. There are much quicker ways to beat these kinds of tests so that you could at least pass. Can I show you what I mean?

This shift strategy is an appeal to the "work smarter not harder" principle, and the counselor purposely uses phrases like "beat the test" to align herself with the adolescent by making the test the "bad guy."[2]

Another shift strategy is as follows:

> We could try a strategy other people have used to pass tests. I can't make any promises that it will work, but we could try it between now and your next test to see if it's worth anything. What do you think?

Here, the intervention is purposely given a time limit and framed as a completely experimental endeavor. Again, as with all of the shifts demonstrated here, the intervention is presented in tentative terms, and the adolescent is given the option to refuse the technique. In instances where the adolescent refuses the intervention, the counselor can shift back to solution-focused strategies. For example, the counselor might say, "Okay, it's up to you how we proceed. What change do *you* want to try?" In instances where the adolescent is unable to come up with a promising solution,

---

[2] We caution practitioners to be careful to not suggest that the teacher is somehow the "bad guy." The tests, quizzes, and curriculum can be framed as such, but not other adults.

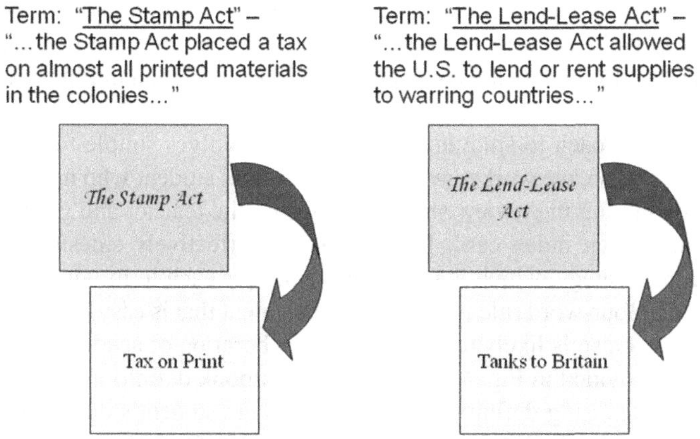

Term: "The Stamp Act" –
"...the Stamp Act placed a tax on almost all printed materials in the colonies..."

The Stamp Act

Tax on Print

Term: "The Lend-Lease Act" –
"...the Lend-Lease Act allowed the U.S. to lend or rent supplies to warring countries..."

The Lend-Lease Act

Tanks to Britain

Fig. 4.1 Examples of student-generated flashcards

the counselor can offer the problem-focused intervention as a backup plan: "Let's try your plan and, if it doesn't work on your next test, I'll show you the idea I have." In this way, we are encouraging adolescents to try their own solutions, but the counselor sets a limit for how many failed or unused strategies are attempted before the formal shift to directive problem solving. Without such limit setting, many disruptive adolescents will endlessly postpone change by offering insincere and unrealistic solutions. If this has already occurred, the counselor can flip the proposition and say, "Let's try this idea for a week and see what you think."

Once the adolescent agrees to see the intervention, or once the limits to her solutions are met, the intervention is introduced. If working with a middle school student, for example, the counselor might ask to see a list of vocabulary words that she is to learn. Assuming that the material lends itself to the intervention (i.e., one-to-one relationships between concepts and definitions), the counselor then describes a "new" approach to using flashcards. Because we anticipate that students with ADHD and related disorders will struggle with the procedural aspects of various interventions, two rules are introduced:

1. Each term is given its own physical flashcard.
2. The definitions associated with each term must be written in the student's own words, using no more than four words.

The key element here is the definition, which is purposely shortened by the second rule to provide a simple prompt for the student to recall the gist of the larger definition. In Fig. 4.1, we offer two examples from a middle school student who struggled in his American History class. Two of the terms he needed to remember were the "Stamp Act" and the "Lend-Lease Act."[3] Consistent with many textbooks, these terms were provided in bold print and then defined with paragraph-length expla-

[3] Obviously, these examples are taken from two separate lessons, the first in the fall and the second in early spring.

nations, so this provided a cue for the student when deciding which words were flashcard-worthy. The rule to limit the definition to just a few words is intended to force the student to process the concepts at a deeper level than might have occurred otherwise. As mentioned above, students with ADHD and related disorders often use a passive approach to studying that typically involves simple rehearsal strategies. In another case, we worked with a middle school student who made flashcards by physically cutting the review sheet provided by the teacher and gluing the parts on either side of an index card. In doing so, he effectively sidestepped the key element of the strategy, which is to actually consider each term when building the flashcards. The four-word rule is a procedural element that is easy for adolescents to remember, but it also is likely to force mental elaboration of academic concepts. In the examples provided in Fig. 4.1, the lengthy textbook definitions were shortened into somewhat amusing definitions. Even though the student's definition varied in style from the textbook, the process of building the flashcards under the four-word rule increased the student's retention of the larger concepts. The four-word rule is frustrating for many adolescents who think of studying as a passive exercise, but this temporary nuisance is often necessary for learning to occur. Therefore, making the cards and using the four-word rule is a critically important step in the learning process that should not be skipped by cutting and pasting definitions or having others create the cards for them.

After the student has created flashcards, the counselor encourages the student to go through the flashcards, reading the term and verbalizing the definition, and then flipping the card over to check for accuracy. If the student is incorrect, the flashcard is shuffled back into the pile, and the process is repeated until all cards are called correctly and set aside. Ultimately, students should try to get to a point where they can accurately call all of their flashcards without taking more than a few seconds for each card. So, for a set of 20 flashcards, the student should take no more than 60 s. To reward this accomplishment, we encourage counselors to tell students that when this goal is reached, study time is over. For improved test performance, the counselor can encourage students to review flashcards at their desk immediately prior to the test, but in general, the fluency goal acts as a trigger to end study sessions. In other words, once fluency with flashcards is achieved, the student can safely end their studies.

During initial counseling sessions when the intervention is introduced, the counselor will assist the student in constructing several flashcards, but the goal is to have students construct their own flashcards between sessions as a homework assignment. If clients return to follow-up sessions without flashcards, the counselor uses time in the session to create more. Once a set of flashcards is created, the counselor should randomly pick the word or definition side of the card to show to the student, requiring that the student learns the material both ways. As with other interventions, these strategies generally continue over an extended period, requiring some portion of time in each counseling session, until it is clear that the student is able to use flashcards independently. In our studies, we have required students to earn grades of 80 % or better on three consecutive tests or quizzes before officially withdrawing counselor support for the intervention. With this intervention and all others discussed in this volume, we encourage counselors to consider activity, privilege, and even tangible rewards if verbal praise alone is not enough to motivate the adolescent to improve their performance. We also encourage counselors to look for ways to generalize the skills outside of the counseling sessions. For example, the student might be required to produce an increasing number of flashcards outside of sessions as homework; but to ensure accuracy, counselors will need to monitor all efforts against feedback from teachers and parents.

Using these same general principles, we have also introduced note-taking strategies to address working memory deficits.[4] Students with ADHD and related disorders often struggle with note-taking or overestimate their ability to remember materials discussed in class, so note-taking is typically poor or nonexistent. When a specific intervention is introduced to address this problem it not only helps a student academically, it actually improves classroom behavior because it occupies the student during instruction—a time that might otherwise be spent daydreaming or disrupting others (Evans et al. 1995). We provide a checklist of these procedures in Module 4.1. In essence, counselors begin by reviewing how students currently take notes in class and then assess the quality of the notes by having students verbally explain what the relevant classroom topic was about. We find that this proves very difficult for many students, so we then shift into the note-taking intervention by asking if students want to see a "trick" to make their notes easier to understand. In most cases, we use a simple outline-style note-taking strategy, but this might vary based on class demands. In outline-style notes, students left-justify main ideas and indent supporting details. To demonstrate how this works, we use previous materials and ask questions such as, "What were the main ideas?" Through this process, we reconstruct the notes to see if the material makes more sense to the student afterward. In our after-school group sessions, we carried this concept one step further and provided "lectures" on fun topics (e.g., history of football, monster trucks) and compared the students' notes to our master copy at the end to generate an accuracy score. Through collaboration with teachers, counselors can arrange for similar activities, but using actual classroom materials. In Module 4.1, we assume that the counselor has access to such materials, but this may not always be realistic. As an alternative, this intervention can be introduced as a component of teacher consultation, with the teacher fulfilling the role of interventionist. More information about teacher consultation is provided in Chap. 7.

[4] Many teachers are moving toward alternative note-taking strategies, such as "guided notes," that are generated from classroom presentations. In the guided note strategy, the key terms are typically replaced with blanks, so students are still expected to take notes, but the writing burden is reduced. We encourage counselors to ask teachers about these expectations and to modify the procedures to fit each situation.

Organization

As discussed in Chap. 2, one of the most impairing aspects of ADHD is disorganization. Adolescents with ADHD are often highly disorganized with their personal belongings, mental processes, and even verbal behavior. The problem of disorganization is so profound in some instances that parents and teachers struggle to identify exceptions. Bookbags are often stuffed with unnecessary clothing; school binders overflow with loose and irrelevant papers; and an excavation of the adolescent's locker (if he uses one) is akin to an archeological dig back in time to long-lost grading periods. Even objects that the adolescent cherishes, such as computer games, movies, or magazines, are similarly jumbled. As a result, the adolescent often misplaces things. Parents of adolescents with ADHD tell stories of how their child lost or forgot critically important matters. In our clinical work, one mother admitted to driving to her son's high school one to two times each week to drop off something the son had misplaced or otherwise forgot to take with him in the morning. She saw the frequent trips back and forth to the school as frustrating, but less so than the reminder notices and phone calls about missing library books, unsigned permission slips, and lost equipment for extracurricular activities.

How can a counselor intervene in this scenario? Interestingly, some counselors see organizational concerns as being external to the counseling process. As Kapalka (2009) observes, organization interventions are often relegated to academic "coaching" services, perhaps because counselors see such concerns as trivial and unimportant (p. 144). In our experience in schools, classroom teachers typically address academic organization rather than school counselors, and in most cases this is only done for brief periods early in the school year. Moreover, not all teachers set clear expectations for how notebooks or other materials need to be organized, and fewer still collect those materials and provide feedback. Presumably, this lack of consistent support in this area is because most secondary teachers believe that their students are capable of staying independently organized. Among special education teachers, there is more focus on supporting student organization, but unfortunately many intervention plans (e.g., IEPs) reduce or even remove the expectation for independent organization altogether.

In our work with adolescents, we have developed an organizational skills intervention that appears very promising for alleviating some academic impairment. In fact, given our early clinical experience with these youth it was the first intervention we developed (Evans et al. 2004). Perhaps most importantly, the intervention is simple to implement and flexible enough to apply to virtually any academic setting. Typically, counselors need only 5–10 minutes of a single session to carry out all of the required steps. In secondary schools, where it is difficult to schedule meeting times, this aspect of the intervention makes it a feasible option for students who require help with organization. Thus, we have successfully taught these strategies to general and special education teachers and supported them while they integrated the intervention into the normal school day (see Evans et al. 2007, as well as Chap. 7 in this volume). Moreover, the basic strategies can be modified for use at home, and we have supported parents who have included similar strategies within parent–child behavior contracts (see Chap. 6).

For our purposes here, we will describe the organization intervention as used within the individual counseling setting and targeting school binders and bookbags. We start here with two assumptions. First, we assume that the adolescent is expected to independently keep their school materials organized. If, for example, a behavior plan has been written by the school that effectively eliminates all expectations for organization (e.g., homework is never assigned, all school materials are stored in the classroom), then organization interventions can seem pointless. Why would an adolescent work on improving a skill that is not needed? (We believe the removal of such expectations over the long-term is a disservice to the adolescent.) Second, we assume that the adolescent is using a multiple-subject binder, along with some independent means of transporting these materials between classes, and potentially between home and school. We will use the word "bookbag" to describe this latter object, but we have seen students use imaginative ways to use other objects for this same purpose. Students might use an electronic method to send needed documents back and forth between home and school, and we would consider the software system a type of bookbag.

The organization skills intervention establishes a set of criteria to facilitate the student's ability to sort and store paperwork, to identify assigned homework, and locate completed assignments when they are due. This intervention also targets general organization of books, clothing, and personal items. The counselor assists the adolescent by monitoring these behaviors, helping the adolescent to chart progress over time, and providing an organization chart and frequent feedback.

Consider the following true-case scenario of a seventh-grade student we will refer to as Tiffany. Tiffany had trouble organizing her classroom materials and constantly misplaced assignments and notes for her parents. She could not find her clothing for gym class, and often carried the wrong books home for homework. Tiffany's counselor discovered that her binder and bookbag were disorganized. At the start of the intervention, the counselor encouraged Tiffany to empty all of her belongings out of her binder and bookbag and then rebuild her organization system "from scratch." To help with this process, the counselor used the Organization Intervention Monitoring Record (see Appendix C), which was individualized in collaboration with Tiffany and listed several criteria that operationally define organization. During the beginning of subsequent individual sessions, Tiffany and her counselor checked her binder and bookbag organization against the organization checklist and recorded how many criteria were met. Together, Tiffany and her counselor would examine each criterion and mark a *yes* or *no* for each. At the bottom of the page, the number of successful criteria were summed and divided by the total number of checklist criteria, providing a percentage. Each column on the checklist represents one session, and the date was recorded at the top of each column so that graphs of performance over time could be easily interpreted.

In Tiffany's case, success in organization was primarily rewarded with verbal praise (e.g., "It looks like you met all of the criteria we targeted. Good for you!"). Alternatively, when Tiffany failed to meet any of the criteria, Tiffany's counselor assisted her as she corrected the problems. In cases where Tiffany met less than 50 % of the criteria, her counselor used an *over-correction* procedure by encouraging her to remove all disorganized items from that area and start over, piece-by-piece, building up the organization system again "from scratch." Tiffany met 100 % of the organization criteria over three consecutive sessions and her counselor started to fade the procedure by checking her bookbag and binder during every other session. Over time, Tiffany's organization habits improved, and her teachers reported fewer missing assignments.

Based on this scenario, it should be clear that the organization intervention involves several straightforward steps. First, an organization checklist is constructed with the student's active participation. Given that classrooms vary considerably, it is impossible to design a global form that would accurately apply to the organization expectations in all situations. As a result, the checklist provided in Appendix C is intended as a general guide and readers are encouraged to modify as needed. Once the checklist is created, however, the items stay as consistent as possible. The counselor uses the checklist to monitor the student's ability to maintain organization through regularly scheduled checks (two to three times per week at the beginning). We provide a guide for this intervention in Module 4.2.

In Tiffany's case, the counselor was able to adequately reinforce progress through praise, correction, and graphing of outcomes. However, some students might require more tangible rewards, even at the high school level. We have successfully used point systems for students who needed additional reinforcement, where the points were ultimately turned in for small gift cards or "prizes." In one instance, a high school student had a CD stolen from his car, so the counselor bought a replacement CD, displayed it in her office, and set a long-term goal of 50 organization points (one point per criterion met) for the student to earn the CD. Even though the point system was reminiscent of strategies used for younger students, the counselor successfully used humor to encourage the student to accept the challenge. On days that his organization fell short, the counselor would pick up the CD, hold it to her ear, and joke that she could hear the musician "crying" (e.g., "Wait, is that a tear in Kenny Chesney's eye?"). Within the context of their relationship, this type of gentle teasing always caused the student to laugh, without minimizing the need for the student to continue to improve his organization.

The example of Tiffany points out a general strategy for tapering the intervention once the student shows consistent success. For example, once 100 % of the organization criteria are met in four consecutive sessions, students can be given their own organization checklist and encouraged to self-monitor from that point forward. Ultimately, the hope is that counselors can turn this intervention over to the student for independent self-monitoring. We use several tapering strategies to achieve this goal across most interventions in the CHP (e.g., flipping a coin during sessions and only checking when it comes up heads, rolling a dice and only checking when the number is five or six), but generally rely on continued monitoring of some form to determine whether a return to regular checks are needed. Recall from Chap. 2 that students with ADHD and related disorders experience extreme performance fluctuations over the course of a school year, so success can unfortunately be fleeting.

It is not uncommon for students to require more than one session to set up an organization intervention depending on baseline performance. During this time, the student might label the different folders according to class, which typically include Science, Math, Social Studies, English, and Reading or Language Arts. To conveniently store handouts and assignments, the student might also label the pockets within each folder according to agreed upon guidelines. For example, the organizational checklist example in Appendix C indicates that the two pockets in each folder hold completed and uncompleted assignments, respectively.

During subsequent meetings, the counselor checks the targeted area(s) using the same checklist. When the student does not fully meet the criteria in any area, the counselor records that the criteria is unmet and then assists while the student corrects the problem. In other words, the score is based on how the organization system appears when the counselor first assesses it, not after the student corrects. Counselors can expect students to provide excuses for disorganization (e.g., "The bell rang, so I just threw it in my binder to get to my next class on time!" or "Another kid dropped my binder on the floor"), but regardless of the excuse, "No" is recorded in the checklist if the target is not completely met. To keep the checks interactive, counselor generally reads the items aloud and asks the student if the criterion is met. For example, the counselor might ask, "Are all the papers that are in the binder school related? What do you think? Is this magazine school related?"

The organization intervention typically requires close, consistent monitoring and frequent reinforcement for an extended period. In our research, students take 16 or more session of checking and prompting before demonstrating consistent improvement because there are three patterns of responding that often emerge. The first is what we call the "Immediate Responder" profile, where the student quickly adapts to the intervention and is successful over time. Such cases are rare, unfortunately, but our impression is that this is often the case for students who want to please the counselor. In the second pattern, the student responds quickly, but then struggles for a while and then slowly regains earlier levels of success. We refer to this pattern as the "Honeymoon Response" pattern because the early excitement seems to wear off and then the remainder of the time is a slow process toward long-term success. In the third pattern, the student seems to be inconsistent over time, but the trend is toward improvement. We refer to this pattern as the "Slow but Steady" response pattern. Based on our work with organization interventions, this last pattern is actually the most common (Evans et al. 2009). To some degree, the Slow but Steady response can be attributed to adjustments to contingencies or holiday breaks; but in any event, counselors should remain patient and persistent in implementing this intervention over extended periods. Disorganization is an integral deficit in ADHD and related disorders, and the chronic nature of the problem is unlikely to respond to short-term interventions.

Planning

The final aspect of our shortened definition of EF is planning, which is generally considered to be the cognitive ability of anticipating and preparing for contingencies in the future, based on experiences in the past. In Barkley's (2006) model of EF, he refers to this concept as *reconstitution,* which he defines as the ability to deconstruct past and future behaviors into hierarchical sequences. In other words, planning is the ability to visualize several behavioral sequences into the future and adjust current behavior accordingly. Neuropsychologists often measure planning abilities using puzzles that require multiple step solutions that have to occur in a specific sequence, and children with ADHD generally perform poorly on these tasks when compared to typically developing peers (Nigg 2006). In academics, deficits in planning often result in procrastination, last-minute scrambles to finish long-term projects, and a general difficulty in prioritizing activities in order of most to least urgent. Not surprisingly, teachers of students with ADHD frequently report problems with late and missing assignments, and students may find that they completed the wrong portion of an assignment or left a major project at home on the due date. Failure to effectively track daily homework assignments results in missing assignments, forgotten projects, and poor grades. Moreover, poor academic achievement may lead to conflict with parents or teachers and increase the risk for dropping out.

The assignment notebook intervention establishes a routine that helps students accurately record assignments, thereby providing accurate information when planning and prioritizing study time. Counselors will find that some students already use an assignment notebook occasionally, but many others will not have used it at all. The intervention typically requires communication with teachers to verify that the information in the assignment tracking system is correct, oftentimes by having teachers verify (e.g., write their initials next to) the records during class or after school. The counselor then briefly checks the assignment notebook during each session to see if assignments are recorded, and whether an identified teacher has verified the information. We have provided a brief checklist for practitioners in Module 4.3, along with a case example below.

One student, who we will call Sam, had significant trouble tracking his daily homework assignments. He frequently forgot to complete assignments or to turn them in. Sometimes he forgot which set of problems were due in his math class and, as a result, turned in the wrong assignments. Sam's science teacher reported that a major project was submitted a week late, resulting in a substantial point deduction. In fact, three of his core class teachers reported that his grades were negatively impacted by missing assignment scores. In one of our early sessions, Sam's counselor learned that he rarely used his assignment notebook, even though he kept it at the front of his binder. The counselor began by ensuring that Sam understood how the tracking system could work and briefly demonstrated her own system for tracking work assignments. She then provided specific instructions for the assignment tracking system we use in the CHP. She encouraged Sam to record all assignments before leaving his classes, making sure to write enough information to understand the assignment. For example, simply writing "math problems" is insufficient; Sam was encouraged to clarify his entries by writing the page number and problem numbers as well. The counselor also encouraged Sam to have his teacher initial his tracking system before leaving the class to ensure that what he wrote was accurate. On days that there was no homework, the agreement was that Sam would write "None" in the space for that class, but still obtain his teacher's initials.

In subsequent sessions, the counselor checked Sam's assignment notebook for the teacher's initials. On those days that Sam obtained all of the initials and wrote sufficient information to understand the assignment, the counselor praised his performance and, anticipating potential motivation issues, included a point system to earn occasional "homework passes" from his teachers. If Sam did not obtain all the initials or provide sufficient information, the counselor helped him track down the actual assignments using an online "homework hotline" provided by his school. At the outset, Sam only had an average of one assignment initialed in his planner, but after a month of consistent monitoring, Sam was able to get all initials on most days. Consequently, Sam's teachers reported fewer missing assignments.

In this example, the counselor used a "homework hotline" to verify the data in the assignment notebook, but in truth such tracking systems are often inaccurate or out of date. As a result, counselors might have to consider several other methods for checking these data. For example, school-based counselors might have access to an assignment list kept by special education teachers in their classrooms. Many special education teachers post a list of assignments given each day, and even if the student is not receiving special education services, these postings often provide information for all classes in the school. Alternatively, some teachers post their assignments weekly on the school web page, and counselors can print them prior to meetings with the student. In other situations, the counselor might encourage the student to contact another student from his class and ask for the assignment information.

In instances where students consistently fail to obtain teacher initials or check their tracking system against a reliable source, counselors might establish behavioral contingencies. In the example above, the counselor started with a point system toward "homework passes," but other counselors might try praise for a while and then add point systems only when necessary. If after two sessions without teacher's initials, for example, the counselor might consider this option. Similarly, if the student reports that classroom circumstances make it impossible to get teacher initials, the counselor might schedule a teacher consultation and use this time to create a mutually acceptable means for the counselor to get accurate information about class assignments.

Ideally, however, once such strategies are established and the student begins to have success tracking assignments, the counselor will fade his involvement in the intervention, turning over much of this responsibility to either the parents or the student. Generally, once the student attains 100% of initials and records assignments correctly for four consecutive sessions, the counselor might consider fading prompts and behavioral contingencies that may be in place until none remain. During this time, the counselor can continue checking the planner at every meeting and recording the data for tracking purposes, but specific efforts to ensure generalization of the behavior should begin as soon as possible. Once all behavioral contingencies have been faded out, the counselor might occasionally check the planner at random sessions to determine if tapering this intervention leads to a reduction in turning in assigned work. If the student continues to turn in completed assignments on time without this intervention, then the counselor may drop the requirement for initials in other classes, one at a time. When teacher initials are not required, the counselor must establish another method of determining the accuracy of assignments recorded.

Conclusion

In this chapter, we have discussed many of the academic interventions that were used within the CHP. Generally, we try to target the executive functioning deficits associated with ADHD, including memory, organization, and planning. Like many other academic interventions, we introduce study skills (e.g., flash cards) and mnemonic strategies (i.e., initial letter strategies) because these interventions are highly effective—not just for students with ADHD but for students in general. In addition, we have found three specific interventions that appear to be effective. First, we target note-taking strategies and offer feedback specific to note-taking performance. Note-taking interventions require coordination with teachers to ensure that what is discussed in the counseling session generalizes to the classroom, and feedback on class notes often requires the counselor to either obtain the teacher's master notes or to consult with the teacher to implement the intervention in the classroom. We return to the idea of teacher consultation later in this volume. Second, we target organization skills by constructing checklists and then recording student performance over time. Some common targets of intervention include binders, bookbags, and lockers. We find that without intervention, students become increasingly disorganized during the school year, eventually affecting academic performance (e.g., lost assignments). Third, we target assignment tracking, which similarly appears to deteriorate as the school year progresses. Students often overestimate their ability to remember assignments, so motivation to keep an accurate and consistent system is undermined. Like note-taking, interventions targeting assignment tracking often require close collaboration with teachers and may lend themselves to teacher consultation as well as direct service provision.

Module 4.1: Note-Taking Skills

Goal:

- The student will improve note-taking skills and classroom performance.

Materials:

1. Master notes from classroom teacher (requires regular teacher communication).
2. The student's notes from class.
3. Materials for a reward system (if needed)

	Elements	Description
□	*Introduce note-taking skills*	We generally begin by having students show and interpret their notes from a class. Students typically struggle with this activity, so we support them through the process by asking questions and praising any student strengths that may be apparent
□	*Discuss options for note-taking*	The counselor introduces an approach to note-taking (e.g., outline-style notes) that can improve or replace the student's current strategy, but that is consistent with classroom expectations. In general, note-taking requires students to make distinctions between main ideas and supporting details, so we discuss these concepts and have students attempt to identify each in a set of notes from class
□	*Practice note-taking skills*	The student listens to instruction and practices their note-taking techniques. The instructor pauses instruction at points to check student adherence to note-taking procedures and quality of recorded notes. The instructor uses a model for the notes during initial practice sessions and fades these over time *Note*. Note-taking training sessions can be done for a targeted student or within the context of small group or class setting.
□	*Monitor performance*	The counselor encourages the student to try the new note-taking strategy in class and then review their performance in subsequent sessions. The counselor will need to access to the teacher's master notes in order to assess performance, but if this is accomplished, the counselor can calculate an accuracy score based on the proportion of main ideas and supporting details correct. Alternatively, the counselor might request data on the student's test and quiz scores to provide another means of measuring effectiveness
□	*Encourage adolescent to self-monitor*	If success is realized over time (e.g., >80% accuracy in notes over several counselor check), counselors taper the frequency of checks while encouraging adolescent independence. For example, counselors might substitute note-taking checks entirely with feedback from teachers regarding test/quiz scores. If the counselor finds that the adolescent's performance falls off at any time, the intervention can be ramped up to weekly (or more) checks and a reward system might be introduced. Conversely, checks might be discontinued altogether if individualized report card goals are met (e.g., all B's or better)

Module 4.2: Organization Checklist

Goal:

- The student will improve physical organization of school-related materials (e.g., bookbag, binder) and independently monitor organization over time.

Materials:

1. Organization checklist (see example in Appendix C).
2. Evidence of previous academic performance.
3. Materials for a reward system (if needed)

	Elements	Description
□	*Introduce organization concepts*	The first session typically begins with the counselor asking the adolescent to describe (and show) her organization system. Secondary students typically keep binders and bookbags to transport materials between home and school, but we commonly find that these materials are highly unorganized and insufficient. We relate the organization system to the adolescent's current academic record (e.g., report cards, teacher ratings) and discuss how poor organization can negatively impact school performance. Typically, we will have previously established the adolescent's personal goals for academic performance (e.g., "What grades are *you* comfortable with?"), so discrepancies between actual performance and their own stated goals can be discussed (e.g., "It sounds like your strategy so far is keeping you short of your goal")
□	*Construct an organization checklist*	We shift into training and explain that *consistency* is the most important aspect of organization. Regardless of how an adolescent decides to organize herself, the outcome will depend mostly on how well the system is maintained over time. Counselors introduce the concept of an organization checklist and offer several suggestions for what might appear on such a list (see Appendix C), but allow and encourage adolescents to modify the list based on their specific preferences and needs. The counselor must judge whether the proposed modifications are appropriate and adequate for the system to be successful. In the first session, the organization system is set up to match the checklist exactly and counselors explain that the organization checklist will be used in subsequent sessions to assess how well the student has maintained the system. In general, we construct separate checklists for binders, bookbags, and lockers

□	*Monitor performance*	In all subsequent sessions, counselors record the adolescent's performance using the tracking sheet developed with the adolescent. Specifically, the number of organization targets met (e.g., "binder is free of loose paper") is recorded as a proportion of the total number of items on the checklist. For example, if the intervention targets nine specific requirements for the binder, the counselor records the number of requirements met over nine (e.g., three correct items out of nine equals 33 %). Note that the score on organization is based on the state of the organization systems at the time of the check—adolescents are allowed and encouraged to correct errors during the check, but the score recorded is based on what the counselor initially finds. We generally encourage organization checks to occur at least weekly
□	*Encourage adolescent to self-monitor*	If success is realized over time (e.g., 100 % accuracy for eight consecutive checks), counselors taper the frequency of checks while encouraging adolescent independence. For example, counselors might continue to meet with the adolescent on a regular schedule and have them fix any errors in their organization system independently, but flip a coin to determine if the counselor will also check the system against the checklists. If the counselor finds that the adolescent's performance falls off at any time, the intervention can be ramped up to weekly (or more) checks and a reward system might be introduced. Conversely, checks might be discontinued altogether if individualized report card goals are met (e.g., all B's or better)

Module 4.3: Assignment Tracking

Goal:

- The student will accurately track school assignments to improve timeliness of submitted schoolwork.

Materials:

1. Assignment tracking system (e.g., planner).
2. Evidence of previous academic performance.
3. Materials for a reward system (if needed)

	Elements	Description
□	*Introduce assignment tracking concepts*	The first session typically begins with the counselor asking the adolescent to describe her strategy for tracking assignments. Secondary students are typically encouraged by educators to keep "planners" or other systems to track assignments, but we commonly find that these systems are unused or misused. We compare the stated efforts against the adolescent's current academic record (e.g., report cards, teacher ratings) and discuss any discrepancies. Typically, we will have previously established the adolescent's personal goals for academic performance (e.g., "What grades are *you* comfortable with?"), so discrepancies between actual performance and their own stated goals can be discussed (e.g., "It sounds like your strategy so far is keeping you short of your goal")
□	*Assess current assignment tracking performance*	It is important to access the adolescent's current assignment tracking system to assess potential strengths and weaknesses. We find that students with disruptive behaviors often fail to record assignments at all, partly because they overestimate their ability to remember this information without a formal system. It is important at this step for counselors to learn about the teachers' expectations for assignment tracking, as many school districts are moving toward online systems
□	*Formalize an assignment tracking system*	Here, we shift into training and explain aspects of assignment tracking that are vital. We find that written systems outperform other options (e.g., electronic calendars) because written systems are easy for adults to check. In the CHP, we require that the assignment tracking system is written, but allow the possibility of altering the strategy over time based on student success

□	*Monitor performance*	Following the first session on assignment tracking and in all sessions thereafter, we record the adolescent's performance using a tracking sheet (see Appendix B). Specifically, the number of assignments the adolescent tracks with adequate information (i.e., due date, page numbers) is recorded as a proportion of the total number of assignments expected. For example, if the intervention targets the four core courses, the counselor records the number of assignments tracked over four (e.g., two assignments correctly recorded out of four equals 50 %). For days that assignments are not assigned in a class, adolescents are expected to write "none" in order to receive credit for tracking. Even if these checks only occur weekly, counselors work backwards in the tracking system to record a fraction for every school day. We generally encourage checks to occur at least weekly
□	*Ensure that information is accurate*	To ensure accuracy, counselors check the assignment tracking system against a reliable source of information regarding schoolwork. For example, online tracking systems or direct contact with teachers may allow counselor to verify student performance "on the fly," but if not, counselors plan regular times to compare the student's performance against a gold standard. Discrepancies between the student's tracking and the gold standard are discussed and changes are made to the tracking system to ensure accuracy, as needed. Such difficulties might require the addition of a reward system (e.g., earning special activities or privileges)
□	*Encourage adolescent to self-monitor*	If success is realized over time (e.g., 100 % accuracy for eight consecutive checks), counselors taper the frequency of checks while encouraging adolescent independence. For example, counselors might continue to meet with the adolescent on a regular schedule to discuss school-related issues, but flip a coin to determine if the assignment tracking system is checked as part of that discussion. If the counselor finds that the adolescent's performance falls off, the intervention can be ramped up to weekly (or more) checks and a reward system might be introduced. Conversely, checks might be discontinued altogether if individualized report card goals are met (e.g., all B's or better)

References

Barkley, R. A. (2006). Attention-Deficit Hyperactivity Disorder: A handbook for diagnosis and treatment (3rd edn.). New York: Guilford.

Erchul, W. P., & Martens, B. K. (2010). *School consultation: Conceptual and empirical bases of practice* (3rd ed.). New York: Springer Publishing.

Evans, S. W., Pelham, W., & Grudberg, M. V. (1995). The efficacy of note-taking to improve behavior and comprehension of adolescents with attention deficit hyperactivity disorder. *Exceptionality, 5,* 1–17.

Evans, S. W., Axelrod, J. L., & Langberg, J. (2004). Efficacy of a school-based treatment program for middle school youth with ADHD: Pilot data. *Behavior Modification, 28,* 528–547.

Evans, S. W., Serpell, Z. N., Schultz, B., & Pastor, D. (2007). Cumulative benefits of secondary school-based treatment of students with ADHD. *School Psychology Review, 36,* 256–273.

Evans, S. W., Schultz, B. K., White, L. C., Brady, C., Sibley, M. H., & Van Eck, K. (2009). A school-based organization intervention for young adolescents with attention-deficit hyperactivity disorder. *School Mental Health, 1,* 78–88.

Forness, S. R., Kavale, K. A., Blum, I. M., & Lloyd, J. W. (1997). Mega-analysis of meta-analyses: What works in special education and related services. *Teaching Exceptional Children, 29,* 4–10.

Kapalka, G. (2009). *Counseling boys and men with ADHD.* New York: Routledge.

Mastropieri, M. A., & Scruggs, T. E. (1998). Constructing more meaningful relationships in the classroom: Mnemonic research into practice. *Learning Disabilities Research & Practice, 13,* 138–145.

Miller, W. R., & Rollnick, S. (2002). Motivational interviewing: Preparing people for change (2nd edn.). New York: Guilford.

Nigg, J. (2006). *What causes ADHD? Understanding what goes wrong and why.* New York: Guilford.

Rafoth, M. A. (1999). *Inspiring independent learning: Successful classroom strategies.* Annapolis Junction: NEA Professional Library.

Rogers, C. R. (1961). *On becoming a person.* Boston, MA: Houghton Mifflin.

Willcutt, E. G., Doyle, A. E., Nigg, J. T., Faraone, S. V., & Pennington, B. F. (2005). Validity of the executive function theory of attention deficit hyperactivity disorder: A meta-analytic review. *Biological Psychiatry, 57,* 1336–1346.

Chapter 5
Social Interventions

...many young Americans from marginal and authoritarian backgrounds find temporary refuge in radical groups in which an otherwise unmanageable rebellion-and-confusion receives the stamp of universal righteousness within a black-and-white ideology. Some, of course, 'mean it,' but many are merely drifting into such association.
Erik Erikson, from *Identity: Youth and Crisis* (1968)

The Interpersonal Skills Group (ISG) has been a component of the after-school version of the Challenging Horizons Program (CHP) since the earliest pilot study in 1999. The ISG is designed to address the social impairments commonly associated with attention deficit hyperactivity disorder (ADHD), but unlike programs designed to *teach* social skills, the ISG targets social performance deficits for the reasons we discuss in Chap. 2. Thus, the ISG relies heavily on small group social activities and performance feedback from a trained counselor. In this chapter, we describe the ISG activities as conducted in the CHP in middle and high schools. In the after school settings, we typically have a 2:1 participant to counselor ratio, which may prove infeasible in other settings (e.g., social skills groups led by school counselors). We close this chapter by discussing how these interventions might be integrated into individual counseling for adolescents, based in part on research we have conducted in high schools. Readers are also reminded that the ISG component of the CHP has not been thoroughly studied as a standalone program, so we do not know the independent contribution these interventions make to the outcomes of the program as a whole. Thus, we consider these procedures as *possibly* efficacious, but more research is needed.

Helping students improve their social functioning can be a difficult challenge, but one that warrants attention because social impairment strongly predicts poor long-term outcomes. Students with ADHD tend to alienate themselves from peers with immature behavior, pestering, bossiness, apathy, or failed attempts at humor. Simply coaching adolescents to replace these behaviors with what adults deem to be "ap-

B. K. Schultz, S. W. Evans, *A Practical Guide to Implementing School-Based Interventions for Adolescents with ADHD*, DOI 10.1007/978-1-4939-2677-0_5

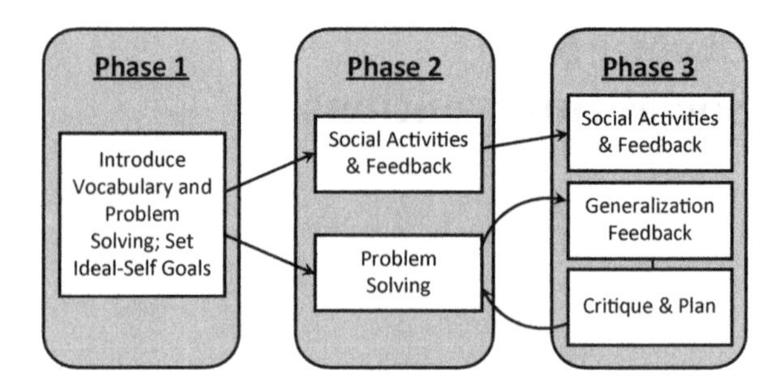

Fig. 5.1 The three phases of the interpersonal skills group

propriate" behavior is unlikely to lead to social success.[1] Rather, we focus on the connections between behavior and its consequences, based on definitions provided by adolescents themselves. When adolescents define and then identify the behavior–contingency connections in controlled social settings, we believe the experience can generalize to other settings where naturally occurring contingencies are less obvious.

To review our earlier discussion, there appear to be several reasons why adolescents with ADHD and other disruptive behaviors struggle with behavior–contingency connections. First, studies have demonstrated that disruptive youth are not as adept as their peers at recognizing cause and effect relationships in the context of social behavior. In order to learn from the social contingencies that shape social behavior, it is critically important that one recognizes the connections between reinforcement and punishment and the social behaviors that lead to them. Second, disruptive adolescents have difficulty recognizing the subtle behaviors of others that have social meaning. As a result, they often miss a large portion of the communication that occurs in social situations. Ostensibly, this problem can result from the student not attending to the cue, or because the adolescent impulsively responds in an ineffectual manner. Third, adolescents with disruptive behaviors typically have deficient problem-solving skills. Specifically, disruptive adolescents are often unable to generate feasible solutions to social problems, so this is a common target of intervention in programs for this population, including the CHP. Fourth, many students have difficulty regulating displays of emotion. Anger, distress, and frustration are often expressed to a degree that appears out of proportion to the actual situation.

ISG Overview

In the after-school program, the ISG curriculum is comprised of three "phases," including instruction, in-vivo activities with feedback, and skill generalization (see Fig. 5.1). During phase 1, the focus is teaching the terms and procedures of the ISG,

[1] We often point out that, as adults, counselors do not know how to be "cool" or "popular" in contemporary secondary schools, and any attempt to teach something that we do not understand ourselves is doomed to failure.

including our approach to social problem solving. During this first phase, students create social goals (i.e., *ideal-self* goals) that develop and grow for the remainder of the intervention period. During phase 2, students practice the problem-solving steps and participate in live social activities punctuated with feedback and coaching from their counselor, based on the ideal-self goals. When a student masters at least two ideal-self goals (defined by performance scores, described below), she moves into phase 3, which involves generalization activities along with continued problem-solving activities. Our goal in the final phase is to transfer new skills to settings outside of the program, which typically involves relationships with peers, family members, and teachers.

Counseling Strategy

In the ISG, the principal responsibility of counselors is to help students define and recognize the social consequences (both good and bad) of their actions and plan for more effective behaviors in the future. Thus, counselors give specific feedback on student social performance, both inside and outside of the ISG. Much of this work is a function of our understanding of social impairment, and we use this knowledge to guide our feedback and generalization efforts. Thus, it is critical that counselors refrain from lecturing, making judgment statements, or attempting to train specific social skills because these efforts are almost always ineffective. Instead, we encourage our counselors to use a solution-focused strategy that encourages students to define for themselves the behaviors that meet their goals, while avoiding or modifying behaviors that move them away from their goals. Below are some of the general counseling strategies we use to help adolescents target and meet specific goals.

Encourage Previously Successful Behaviors Even adolescents with serious social skill deficits occasionally have successes. One of the primary goals of the counselor is to help the adolescent focus on those instances and identify what specific behaviors led to success. A student who complains about his teacher in January probably has a history of coping with the teacher at previous times. The counselor might ask: "What was happening when things were better?" "What were you doing differently in September?" "What do you do on good days that you could also do on bad days?"

Challenge Self-Defeating Assumptions Occasionally, an adolescent's recollection of the past will be wrought with inaccuracies. In such instances, the counselor does not argue, but still challenges the faulty perceptions using questions such as, "What makes it seem that way?" "Is there any other evidence that this is true?" "Is this assumption consistent with the way the person treats you at other times?" Admittedly, this type of questioning is cognitive-behavioral in nature and can seem somewhat confrontational, but when used at opportune times, we find that this strategy can move the counseling session forward. Still, we warn new counselors not to over-rely on these strategies because the inherently challenging nature of such questions—signaling that the adolescent has a flawed understanding of their world—can backfire if used indelicately.

Prompt Questions About Others' Behavior When an adolescent talks about social events, important details are often missing or the description is unclear because the behavior–consequence connection is misunderstood. In such situations, counselors can ask: "I'm confused, what caused ____ to act like that?" "What makes ____ doubt you?" "That's strange! What made ____ get so upset?" "So what are they likely to do next?" The counselor's aim is to help adolescent clients think critically about social interactions, with a focus on previous successes and proactive planning for upcoming social events. In this way, the counselor switches the focus from problem to solution. CHP counselors are far more likely to give the client a homework assignment between sessions and then revisit progress at the next meeting, rather than delving into previous problems. We believe that praise for small successes on homework (e.g., "I'm impressed with what you were able to do!" "What does it say about you that you were able to do that?") is far more likely to motivate behavior change than is revisiting and reworking problems alone.

Phase 1

During phase 1 (usually two to three 30-min sessions), we conduct an interview to gather background information on each participant specific to social skills, and then we train participants on the vocabulary and problem-solving procedures that are required in the later phases. The first session begins with the counselors meeting with adolescents individually to complete the ISG interview (discussed below). During the rest of phase 1, the counselors present and explain the vocabulary and problem-solving steps. Participants are often encouraged to make flash cards to help them learn the terms (see Chap. 4). Once the participants have learned the terms, understood the problem-solving steps, and have demonstrated proficiency in an oral quiz, we start the process of helping each identify ideal-self goals. Participants choose two goals, typically in the form of desirable traits (e.g., "to be kind," "to be funny"), and operationally define these goals with behaviors they believe express the trait. As the goals are formulated, the tracking process begins in a designated ISG folder that contains all of the forms we use to track progress (discussed later). To protect confidentiality, these materials are kept with the counselor and stored in a locked cabinet when not in use.

ISG Interview

The ISG Interview is an extension of the Initial Appraisal (see Appendix A) intended to uncover social aspirations and goals. During the interview, the adolescent can write their responses to the questions on loose-leaf paper, but typically we encourage the adolescent to talk while we take notes. The goal of the interview is relationship-building and clarification, not judgment or teaching, so counselors rely heavily on open-ended questions and reflections throughout. We tell our counselors that this is not a time to teach, or judge, or tell your own stories, rather it is a time to listen and show interest. We find that adolescents generally enjoy this time and ultimately offer a lot of information that can inform the ISG process.

Because the questions we pose in the Initial Appraisal are intended to get the therapeutic relationship started, the actual process of the ISG interview can vary depending on how the adolescent answered those previous questions, but in general, we ask two additional questions:

1. Tell me about the time in your life that you were the most happy, most sad, most angry, most scared, and most proud.
2. If I could interview your family and friends, how would they describe you? What are some positive things they might say? What might they say that would not be so positive?

Several follow-up questions often present themselves depending on the adolescent's responses. For example, "Is it safe to say that you really like the way your teammates treat you on your wrestling team?" and "What makes your mom think you are rambunctious?"

ISG Vocabulary

Also in phase 1, it is important for adolescents to understand the basic terms for the ISG. These definitions are listed below in the order we recommend for instruction.

Ideal-Self The "ideal-self" is our image of what we would like other people to think about us. It is a list of adjectives that describe the person we would like to be. The image is ideal because it reflects who we strive to be and not necessarily who we are. The ideal-self can and will change over time as we modify and refine this image. In practice, the ideal-self goals will require enough specificity so that the constituent behaviors are observable (e.g., being "cool" means to stay calm in stressful situations and tell jokes that make others laugh); but at the outset, students most often start with broad adjectives, such as "nice" or "funny" (perhaps the two most commonly chosen goals). Operational definitions then follow in an iterative manner, shaped by experiences during the social activities within the program (see Creating Ideal-self Goals below).

Real-Self The "real-self" is what other people actually think of us. Like the ideal-self, it is a list of adjectives that describe how others perceive us, but often it contains descriptors we might not want people to assume about us (e.g., "disorganized," "lazy"). The real-self changes as we change our behavior, but at a much slower rate because others' impressions are subject to a *"reputation bias."* We purposely discuss the reputation bias with adolescents and explain that people form opinions of others based on past experiences and these are difficult to erase. To help others form new impressions, one must consistently demonstrate new behavior for a sustained period of time so that the old memories are replaced with new memories. We concede that this may not be "fair," but it is unfortunately how social impressions work.

Reinforcement Reinforcement follows a behavior and increases the likelihood that the person will exhibit the behavior again. For example, a teenager might get an allowance after cleaning her bedroom, increasing the likelihood she will clean it again.

Punishment Punishment follows a behavior that decreases the likelihood that the person will exhibit the behavior again. For example, if a teenager stays out past her curfew, she may lose the privilege of watching television.

Creating Ideal-Self Goals

In the after-school version of the CHP, where the ISG has been most closely studied, we help student participants set their own ideal-self goals after the basic vocabulary has been mastered. This can be a very difficult process. Developing a sense of who we are is a normal part of development in adolescence, but one that does not come easily. We typically begin by asking the students to think of someone they admire. This can be a real or fictional person and we ask each of them to describe why they like that person. The adjectives that the students generate are written on a board for follow-up discussion. Next, the counselors ask the students to describe behaviors exhibited by the person that are consistent with the adjectives. Questions such as, "If I were to meet this person, how would I know that they are *smart*?" can help facilitate this discussion. After this discussion, there is a list of characteristics that the students see as admirable and they are accompanied by behavioral definitions. It is at this point that students can be encouraged to choose two or three from the list that they would like others to attribute to them (i.e., ideal-self). Although this may be seen as an indirect path to ideal-self goals, we have found that students understand this concept much better when discussing these characteristics in relation to others, prior to discussing themselves.

Sometimes the students' early choices may seem inappropriate (e.g., "I want to be tough and mean"). Students may say, "I want people to fear me. It is how I can be respected by others." The job of the counselor is not to judge these goals, but to help the student define the goals in such a way that it is easy to know when it is achieved (e.g., "How can you tell if someone is mean? What do mean people do and how often do they do it?"). We encourage participants to practice these goals in phase 2 and give them feedback on whether they exhibit the identified behaviors. Students have almost always abandoned such goals on their own within a few practice sessions because they realize that they do not want to upset the other group participants. In practice, this may take several sessions, and even after reasonable goals are defined initially, many students will redefine and clarify these goals over time. In order to help participants evaluate their ideal-self goals, we reconvene the group and discuss the benefits and consequences of bringing the real and ideal-self together. Some questions we pose to the group include, "How can the ideal and real selves be brought close together? For example, what are some reasons that they may currently be far apart?" "Are there times when your ideal- and real-self are close together? If so, when and how?" By defining these terms and then reframing the goal as bringing the two concepts closer together, we make an abstract idea easier for adolescents to grasp.

Next, we discuss social situations and identify the reinforcing and punishing contingencies in each. For example, we might ask, "What methods do your teachers, parents, and friends use to punish or reward your behavior?" Contrived contingencies such as candy and time-out can be a good starting point for demonstrating the effects of contingencies; however, the discussion should primarily focus on *social contingencies,* which are invariably more subtle than contrived contingencies. Examples of behaviors from others that reinforce our social behaviors include attention, compliments, interest, offers to assist, and being sought out for conversation or social activities. Examples of punishment include ignoring, criticism, being left out of activities, laughing at (not with) someone, and ridicule. These and other subtle social contingencies form the behavioral feedback that adolescents with disruptive behaviors characteristically miss or fail to interpret correctly. Typically social contingencies get increasingly subtle as we move the discussion from interactions with adults (e.g., parents, teachers) to interactions with peers.

We then focus on how social contingencies relate to our own ideal- and real-self goals. Specifically, we point out that social contingencies are more salient when they reflect our ideal-selves. For example, if a student scores points in a game of basketball, his teammates are likely to compliment him. For a student whose ideal-self involves being seen as athletic, this positive interaction will probably increase the likelihood that the student will practice his basketball shot because he desires more of these compliments. In other words, knowing that one has gotten closer to her ideal-self is rewarding. Conversely, if a student places no value on being seen as athletic, compliments during a game of basketball may have little reinforcing value. So what one student finds very rewarding, another may hardly notice. Other examples that help students understand this concept include being complimented as "cute" or "pretty"—clearly these comments can be very rewarding for one person and potentially offensive for another. We find that this part of the group discussion often helps students to think of their ideal-self in behavioral terms.

When we return to individual work (group participants spread out around the room working independently), the goal is to identify behaviors that would make their real-self align with their ideal-self. Counselors can encourage this process by moving around the group offering guidance, suggestions, and feedback to the goals being prepared by the students. We encourage each student to identify at least four corresponding behaviors that contribute to other people believing that their ideal-self goal pertains to them. For example, being "friendly" may be defined by the following four behaviors: (1) greeting people you know, (2) offering help to others when possible, (3) starting conversations with others, and (4) smiling at people. Over time, this definition might change, but this represents a good starting point in most cases. If a student is reluctant to engage in this activity, counselors explain that it can be difficult to identify these behaviors. For students who really struggle at this stage, we offer to set their goals for them and the corresponding behaviors, but explain that we prefer when students do this for themselves. Such a prompt often works to get students motivated, but if the student agrees to let the counselor set her goals, we focus on the characteristics of people the student admires (e.g., "Think of a famous person you like and describe them to me." "For now, let's set these traits as your goals and see how it works—you can always go back and make changes.").

Problem Solving (i.e., "WILBUR")

Also in phase 1, students are taught a six-step model of problem solving that we refer to by the acronym "WILBUR." The method for instruction typically begins by providing a card that lists the six steps and encouraging students to use it for reference during the problem-solving activity; however, over time we remove the cards and coach students to remember the WILBUR acronym without prompts. The six steps of the problem-solving model are as follows (WILBUR acronym in bold):

1. **W**hat is my worry/concern?[2]
2. What would **I** like to happen?
3. **L**ist some ideas of things I could do to solve the worry/concern?
4. Which is the **B**est solution?
5. **U**se the solution.
6. **R**eview how well the solution worked.

In phase 1, it is only important that students memorize the steps, oftentimes through the use of examples. We do not use the problem-solving steps until Phase Two (discussed below).

Mastery Test

Before students are allowed to participate in phase 2, the group leader(s) individually asks each student to define all of the terms above during an oral quiz. In practice, we allow students to take the oral quiz as many times as needed to pass, but the group will remain focused on this material until all students have demonstrated "mastery," which we define as 90 % or better on the quiz. If some students complete this activity before others, the students who have finished may help other students study for their oral quiz or participate in small group activities until all students have demonstrated mastery. In general, we have found that all participants can pass the quiz by the end of the fourth 30-minute session, but we will make modifications to the procedures in cases that extend beyond this timeframe.

[2] Similar to Taffel (2005), we find that the word "problem" (i.e., What is my *problem*?) is off-putting for adolescents because it sounds accusatory. Hence, we try to use neutral terms such as "worry" or "concern."

Phase 2

Phase 2 consists of two main group activities. First, during 30-min group sessions, students practice the application of their ideal-self goals during in-vivo social activities.[3] Second, students practice the problem-solving procedures in individual sessions with their counselor, as applied to real social problems as they arise. Phase 2 involves coaching students as they practice modifying their behavior during social activities so it is consistent with their ideal-self goals. This phase is complete when students demonstrate mastery of at least two of their ideal-self goals, with mastery defined by counselor and student ratings of in-vivo social performances (discussed later). Once a student has mastered two ideal-self goals, she begins phase 3, which focuses on generalization of skills outside the program.

Social Activities and Feedback

We provide a group leader's guide for the social activities and feedback in module 5.1. The purpose of in-vivo activities is to help students recognize and respond appropriately to social cues and give them the opportunity to practice exhibiting behaviors consistent with their goals. Thus, the activities in this phase emphasize practice over counseling, so we provide brief, focused feedback only periodically while students spend as much time as possible in social activities. The social activities we use are developmentally appropriate pursuits that adolescents might realistically engage in with their peers during their free time, such as sports (e.g., soccer, basketball, four-square), board/card games, and group art projects. Generally, we provide very little setup for each activity other than to provide the necessary materials—participants must decide for themselves how the game will start, who will be on teams, and what rules they will follow.

Just prior to the activity, the students meet with their counselor to briefly review their ideal-self goals and the corresponding behaviors. Then during the activity, the counselor watches and listens closely for behaviors related to the student's ideal-self goals and records notes on the ISG Card, which is provided in Appendix D. These behaviors can be positive, negative, or neutral. In other words, the counselor records instances of the student exhibiting behaviors consistent with her ideal-self goals as well as behaviors counterproductive to the goals. Counselors also note the reaction of peers to the student's target behaviors.

Approximately every 10 minutes (or three times per session), the counselor takes students aside to individually review progress on each goal, using the scale on the ISG Card (−3 to +3). We begin by asking the student to rate themselves on this scale

[3] In our most recent application of the program, the ISG occurred twice each week and this schedule proved convenient. Alternative schedules may work just as well, but we have found that participants generally prefer the social activities to problem solving, and a session ratio of 3:1 appeared to keep most participants engaged. It also allows students ample time to attempt homework assignments stemming from the problem-solving group.

(e.g., "How do you think you did on your goal to be funny?"), and then the counselor provides a rating. If the student assesses their performance similarly to that of the counselor, we consider this an accurate self-appraisal, which is desirable even if the raw score is low. For example, if both the counselor and student agree that the performance was "−3" (strongly moving away from the goal), we offer praise for accuracy and briefly discuss how the student might achieve a "−2" or better. If the student and counselor rating are discrepant, the counselor provides a rationale for their rating (e.g., "I noticed that you only said one thing during the game and no one laughed, which is the opposite of how you defined funny"). The feedback is based entirely on the established definitions of the ideal-self goals worked out between the adolescents and their counselor. This way, the feedback can be presented in a matter-of-fact way, and the scale plays the role of the "bad guy" when the feedback is unfavorable, not the counselor. In other words, the rating is not a function of whether the counselor thought the student met a goal, but whether the behavior met the definitions provided previously by the student. Moreover, the counselor offers only very brief feedback tied to the adolescent's goals and ignores (to the degree possible) concerns not targeted by the student.

In the early sessions of ISG we find that, regardless of the ideal-self goal, students struggle to anticipate their counselor's ratings. We believe this is a product of the adolescent's difficulties with social cues, so as part of our feedback the counselor asks the student to identify specific behaviors that led to their self-rating (e.g., "What did you do to earn that score?"). Often students will respond to this question with "I don't know," and this may in fact be accurate! The counselor might highlight the reaction of peers as a means to focus on social cues in future activities and feedback sessions (e.g., "What did Tommy do when you took the cards?"). In any event, we try to limit feedback sessions to no more than 3 minutes, and then send the adolescent back into the social activity with a plan to earn a higher score next time (e.g., "What could you do differently in the next 10 minutes?"). This process is repeated throughout the ISG period so that each student is pulled out at least three times during the activity. Just like practice of most skills, repetition is important, with more repetitions and feedback being preferred.

Often students will target social goals that are difficult to rate during our activities. For example, a student may have a goal to be perceived as "athletic," but our planned activity might be to play a board game. In such instances, the counselor records N/A (not applicable), but over time we strive to define goals in such a way that some assessment can be made in most settings. In the case of athleticism, the student may actually mean that he wants to be seen as strategic and competitive, but still affable. If this is the case, he may choose to substitute another goal over time to ensure that ratings can be made during these activities. Students are asked how they would like others to perceive them in situations without any opportunity to be athletic and these can be the focus of some of the phase 2 sessions. Still, we find that it is best to let the student keep a goal even if it seems to be a poor choice rather than debate the appropriateness of the student's selection. Students can occasionally gain important insight into what personality characteristics they value by going through the trial-and-error process of identifying and then reworking ideal-self goals.

Changing Goals

It is common for a student to want to change his ideal-self goals or add new ones. In addition, some may wish to narrow or expand the behaviors that define the goals. During these discussions, we encourage counselors to use the WILBUR problem-solving model. We begin this discussion by asking the student why she wishes to make a change. In other words, what is the concern with the current wording of the goals? We provide a guide for our version of problem solving in module 5.2. It is important to note that throughout WILBUR, the counselor emphasizes that people only have control over their own behavior, so the adolescent cannot expect to directly change others' behaviors or problems. Sometimes our behavior can influence the behavior of others, but during the WILBUR discussion, counselors remain focused on behaviors or problems that the students can directly control. Therefore, problems such as "My teacher is an idiot!" are unworkable because we cannot control the teacher's behaviors (or supposed idiocy), we can only change how the student copes with the situation. So the counselor reframes unworkable problem statements into workable concerns or worries (e.g., "When you say that your teacher is an idiot, are you saying that he gets on your nerves?").

Each of the following steps is included in this activity:

Step 1: What is my worry/concern? In this step, the student defines the problem in terms that indicate how the problem leads to unwanted consequences. For example, if a student is upset with a teacher's discipline techniques, she is encouraged to state the problem in the first person, using an "I" statement, which often requires the counselor to reframe initial attempts. For example, the initial problem statement might be, "Mrs. Smith always gives me in-school suspension (ISS)," but this does not describe how it is a worry or concern for the student. The counselor might reframe this as, "My concern is that *I* frequently have to spend time in ISS." Given that the problem may be that the student wants to change goals, we try to ensure that adolescents discuss this concern in the first person (e.g., "I am unhappy with the goals I chose for ISG").

Step 2: What would I like to happen? The resolution statement generated in this step should define what would have to occur for the student to know that the concern had been resolved. The adolescent is encouraged to consider the potential impact of the resolution on the real-self and determine whether this resolution would bring real-self and ideal-self closer together or further apart. In the example above, the resolution statement might be, "I won't have to spend time in ISS anymore." Or even better, "I will return to my regular class schedule." When adolescents struggle with this step, we use the miracle question or some variation thereof (see Chap. 3).

Step 3: List some things I could do to solve the concern/worry. In this step, adolescents creatively generate ideas to solve the problem, but judgment and evaluation is withheld until the next step. The only criterion we impose is that potential solutions must reasonably lead to the resolution statement; otherwise, we try not to impose rules that might constrain the brainstorming process. If a student offers a troubled solution (e.g., "Bring a gun to school"[4]), we might write down the solution, but then ask for additional solutions. If multiple violent suggestions are offered, we might create a category we call "violent solutions" and then ask the adolescent for nonviolent solutions (e.g., "We have lots of violent solutions—what are some nonviolent solutions?"). When the student is stuck, the counselor might remind her that solutions generally fall into one of three categories: 1) ignore the problem; 2) ask someone for help; or 3) do something different (adapted from Greene and Ablon 2005). When adolescents are vague, we encourage them to describe the solution in as much detail as possible (e.g., "Who are you going to ask for help?" "When would you ask?"). Research suggests that adolescents with disruptive behaviors generally produce fewer solutions than their peers when discussing problems, so the overarching goal in this step is to achieve as many ideas as possible. The counselor writes all solutions on paper for the adolescent to see and keeps the focus on this step until a list of at least four solutions is generated.

Step 4: Which is the best solution? At this point, we evaluate the advantages and disadvantages of each of the potential solutions generated in the previous step. The group leader addresses each generated solution one at a time and encourages the adolescent to consider the social consequences of each. For example, the adolescent might be asked how implementing each solution would impact their real-self. What are the risks to their real-self? How do these risks compare to the risks associated with other solutions or with ignoring the problem? Adolescents evaluate these solutions and select one or some combination of ideas. Even when there are no good solutions, the student should select a "best" solution. Often the counselor asks the adolescent to vote on each solution using a thumbs-up/thumbs-down strategy (e.g., "Thumbs-up or thumbs-down: Would 'talking to the teacher' keep you out of ISS?"), and records the results on the paper.

Note that the counselor does not guide the adolescent to a solution nor judge their choice at this point. The only time a counselor should interfere with a chosen solution is if it would pose a safety risk for the student or someone else. In these situations, the group leader might focus on the potential consequences on the real-self as a means to get the student to consider consequences. Even so, adolescents will often choose options that the counselor predicts will fail, but we allow adolescents to make non-dangerous mistakes and then follow up in subsequent sessions.

Step 5: Use the solution. After the adolescent selects a solution, the counselor discusses a plan for implementation, which we refer to as "homework." Specifically, the counselor can discuss how the selected solution recommendation could be implemented, and then assign a timeframe for completion. Counselors might also role-play the solution with the student to ensure that the strategy selected is clearly understood. The counselor then saves the list of solutions that the adolescent generated for use in the follow-up sessions.

---

[4] Again, we are recalling an unserious suggestion once posed by an oppositional student. If this were a serious threat, we would obviously discuss this individually with the student and warn parents and school officials.

Step 6: Review how well the solution worked. After implementing the solution as homework, the student evaluates the extent to which the resolution statement was achieved. If the solution caused additional problems or if it did not achieve the desired goal, then the concern is revisited and the problem-solving process is repeated. If the student did not attempt the solution, the option is removed from the list and the student should return to Step 3 or 4 and try again using the original list of solutions saved by the counselor. In the CHP, an unused solution is a failed solution!

Phase 3

After mastering phases 1 and 2, the focus of the intervention shifts to generalization of the skills outside of the program. The schedule remains similar to phase 2, but every other session is replaced with two main tasks: (1) critique and plan and (2) generalization feedback. The critique and plan task involves critiquing a recent social interaction and planning a future interaction. As in phase 2, the student's behavior is evaluated in relation to their ideal-self goals. The generalization feedback task involves presenting the adolescent with ideal-self ratings provided by anonymous teachers (or other adults) regarding their behavior in the classroom and elsewhere. But unlike the activities of the previous phase, phase 3 requires advanced counseling skills and a strong therapeutic alliance to ensure that these elements work.

Critique and Plan

Selecting a Social Interaction Counselors begin by engaging the student in a conversation about examples of social interactions they have experienced in the past week. They identify interactions that have an impact on the relationship between the student and others, result in an emotional response, or involve a detailed sharing of ideas. Simply saying "hello" to a peer in the hallway would not be an acceptable social interaction for this activity. An extended telephone discussion with a friend, a conversation with a teacher after class, discussion at a lunch table, or an argument with a parent may be suitable examples. If a student brings up a social interaction that does not meet these criteria, counselors should acknowledge the interaction and encourage the student to continue thinking about other social interactions from the past week. The counselor should prompt the student for a social interaction that lasted 2 minutes or more and discussed something that was important to the student, or a conversation that made the student or the person he was interacting with angry, happy, sad, excited, or nervous. The counselor and student may create a list of social interactions that have occurred in the past week, and then select an interaction from this list.

Critique the Social Interaction Once the counselor and student have identified an appropriate social interaction, the student should provide a detailed explanation of the conversation or event and associated behavior that comprised the interaction. The counselor should thoroughly question for details about the context, reactions of people present, and how the interaction ended. The counselor should ask the student specific questions about details of the reactions of others and not accept global descriptions such as "it was fine." The counselor should prompt the student with questions such as, "What did your friends say?" or "What did your friends do in reaction to you?" Then the counselor and student review the ideal-self goals and behavioral definitions and the counselor should ask the student to estimate how the counselor would have rated the student in relation to the ideal-self goals using the −3 to +3 scale on the ISG card. Specifically, the counselor might ask the student to consider how her behavior corresponded to the behavioral definitions of the goals and the types of direct and indirect feedback the student received from the others in the interaction. Interpreting the reactions of others should be part of every discussion of the scoring of interactions. Reasons for differences between the counselor's and student's perceptions should be discussed, but agreement is not necessary. If a problem is identified during this discussion, the counselor should encourage the student to use the problem-solving steps (WILBUR) to help choose the best solution to the problem. Using the problem-solving steps is optional and may not need to occur if no problems are identified during this discussion.

Create a Plan for the Next Social Interaction After critiquing the student's behavior during the selected social interaction, the next step is to plan with the student a social interaction that is likely to take place during the next 48 hours. It is often helpful to plan an interaction with the people who were involved in the interaction critiqued above to allow the student the opportunity to correct or improve his real-self. The counselor asks the adolescent to describe how she plans to interact with the others in the upcoming social interaction, including specific behaviors, questions, and statements that the student will make (i.e., predicting that "I will be nice" is insufficient). The goal of this meeting is to evaluate these predictions in relation to the ideal-self goals prior to the activity, but not to necessarily script the entire interaction. Rather, the counselor asks the student how she will incorporate feedback from others to modify her plan and behavior during the interaction. If there is adequate time, the counselor might help the student practice through role-play, with the counselor providing a variety of responses to the student's behavior to help the student learn to make adjustments by reading the reactions of others and using the information to alter her behavior. Additionally, the counselor might ask the student to explain why the other person in the interaction might respond in various ways (e.g., may have misinterpreted what the student was saying, may view the relationship differently than the student thought he or she did). Before the planning session ends, the counselor and student discuss how this plan will influence the student's real-self, and make a plan to evaluate the interaction with the counselor during the next meeting.

Consider the following example of a critique and plan session: Beth's ideal-self goal is to be seen as "funny." When she comes to her meeting with her counselor, she talks about an encounter she had with one of her friends, Anna, in the hallway that same day. Beth was trying to be funny when she unzipped Anna's backpack, letting all of her books fall out of her backpack onto the floor. Anna did not think it was funny and is now angry at Beth. The counselor and Beth talk about how she knows whether behavior is perceived as funny and Anna's response was interpreted in relation to this. Beth notes that other kids laughed. The counselor asks Anna about which of the kids' perceptions of her is most important to her in determining her real-self. In other words, whose perception matters most: Anna's or the other kids? In addition, the other kids may have had other impressions of Beth in addition to funny, such as mean. The counselor asks Anna if there was any indication of this in the kids' reactions and discovers that one of the onlookers commented, "That was cold!" The counselor and Beth determine that her behavior of unzipping Anna's backpack really did not help her achieve her ideal-self goal because Anna got mad. Beth rates her behavior at a "−2," and says that although she was trying to be funny, no one thought her behavior was funny at all.

With the counselor's help, Beth decides that she will make Anna a card to apologize for her behavior. The Critique and Plan activity in this situation revolved around the apology card, discussing several aspects of that interaction to prepare for that discussion. The counselor asked, "Should you give her the card in person or leave it for her in her locker?" "Should you get a funny card or a blank card?" "What if Anna does not respond or react to the card. What then?" The point of this activity is to build on the phase 2 work in the ISG to eventually solve problems of social issues that arise in other settings. The counselor essentially plays the role of the inner-dialogue when navigating difficult social situations. It is vital that counselors model an honest, but not overly critical inner-dialogue. We want adolescents to be able to internalize these conversations so that the experience might benefit their social reasoning skills in the long-term.

Generalization Feedback

Generalization feedback uses anonymous information gathered from an adolescent's teachers (and possibly other adults) about her performance on ideal-self goals in settings outside of the program. We protect the identity of the adult who provides the feedback because when adolescents know who the individual is they often dismiss the information as flippant or vindictive.

Independent Appraisals Counselors start the generalization feedback by interviewing and collecting ratings from teachers, counselors, lunch monitors, or others who see the adolescent regularly. To protect confidentiality, we take two precautions. First, we provide the adults with a rating scale that includes the adolescent's ideal-self goals, but also randomly generated goals from a database of desirable personality traits. Thus, raters do not know which specific behaviors were chosen by the adolescent. Second, the counselor explains confidentiality concerns to the raters and requests that there is no discussion with others. When the ratings are collected, the counselor briefly asks the adult about specific events that influenced their ratings of the adolescent. The counselor is careful not to write anything on the form that she does not want the adolescent to see, so the adult's feedback is carefully worded to keep it anonymous. Critical feedback should be included, of course, but it needs to be framed as constructive criticism.

The Feedback Session When counselors present the adult's ratings to the adolescent, they begin by asking the adolescent to predict what the adult reported. Often the adolescent does not wager a guess, but sometimes the question prompts a discussion of events that might have otherwise gone unmentioned. For example, there might have been a recent argument between the student and a teacher that the counselor was unaware of, and that incident may have impacted the ratings. The counselor and student then review the goals and their operational definitions and then review the adult's feedback. The counselor asks the adolescent to consider this feedback in relation to her goals and identify the behaviors that may have led to the positive and negative impressions. Generally, we believe the counselor should not identify which teacher provided the feedback. If the student seems eager to know which teacher rated her, the counselor should ask why, but not offer the information (e.g., "I'm sorry, but the rules are I can't tell you. Who would you guess it is? What makes you think it is Mr. Ferguson?"). The student's agreements and disagreements with the feedback are explored, but the counselor refrains from judging or defending the accuracy of the adults' perceptions. The information is simply a reflection of the real-self as we have defined it in the CHP; regardless of whether the information is true, fair, or biased, it is the perception of one adult who knows this adolescent.

The discussion then shifts to how this information relates to the adolescent's ideal-self goals. If a concern or worry is identified, the counselor engages the adolescent in a discussion about what steps she could take in response to the feedback. Often in these cases, the counselor and adolescent choose to add behaviors to the operational definition of an ideal-self goal for clarification. In this way, new goals or modifications to current goals can result from this discussion. In any event, the students leave these meeting with a plan for closing the gap between their real- and ideal-self goals. If the adolescent discusses specific plans to discuss issues with the adults she suspects provided the feedback, then a Critique and Plan session can be completed prior to that discussion.

Consider the following example of generalization feedback: One of Demetrius' ideal-self goals is to be seen as smart, yet his teacher Mr. Smith sent Demetrius to the office because he was distracting the class by giving silly answers during classroom discussions. Demetrius' school counselor met with Mr. Smith, asked him to rate Demetrius across several positive personality traits,[5] and found that the ratings were mostly inconsistent with Demetrius' ideal-self goals. The counselor interviews Mr. Smith and records specific examples of this behavior, along with the reactions of other students.

[5] Again, we provide rating scales with the adolescent's ideal-self goals mixed in with randomly generated goals to provide some confidentiality. To the teacher, the form looks almost like any other rating scale.

Later, the counselor meets with Demetrius to give him feedback, stating that one of his teachers mentioned silly answers in class that distracts the other students, which led to low ratings (−2) on a measure of appearing "smart." The counselor asks, "What's going on with that?" In the ensuing discussion, Demetrius identifies behaviors that do not match his ideal-self goal, and talks about alternative behaviors that may have been more aligned with being seen as smart. The counselor and Demetrius then create a plan where Demetrius is going to work on only giving serious answers in his classes, even when he thinks he has something funny to say. Demetrius plans that he will answer at least two questions with serious answers the next day.

Counseling and Feedback during other CHP Activities

Although the generalization activities discussed so far offer the CHP staff an opportunity to assess behavior outside of the program, we have found that it is difficult to do this as frequently as we would like. Thus, we supplement these activities with additional observations we make during unstructured times. In other words, feedback on the student's social behavior is not limited to the ISG activities and can be given during all CHP activities, including when parents pick participants up or when participants talk with teachers after school. Counselors also use naturally occurring breaks in the CHP activities to give feedback to students about their social behavior in these settings. Naturally occurring breaks include water breaks during recreation and transition time between activities. Counselors take students aside individually to provide feedback similar to regular ISG sessions. Feedback sessions may or may not include formal ratings, but the conversation that occurs is similar to those that take place in the feedback sessions following ISG activities. The counselors begin the feedback process with open-ended questions (e.g., "How do you think you did in that situation?") and give the student time to evaluate herself using the ideal-self goals. If the student accurately assesses her performance (relative to the counselor's assessment), the counselor praises the adolescent's ability to accurately predict the counselor's rating. If the student does not accurately assess their performance, the counselor should share the rating they gave the student and provide examples of the student's behavior that led them to rate the student in that specific manner.

Consider the following example of providing feedback: Ryan is playing basketball with the rest of the group during the recreation period (a 30-minute activity during the after-school program). One of Ryan's ideal-self goals is to be seen as athletic. His operational definitions include participating in all sports activities, being a good sport, and helping others learn skills associated with sports. While warming up, Ashley is having trouble figuring out how to make a layup. Ryan notices Ashley is struggling, asks her if she would like some help, and shows her a new way to shoot a layup. The group splits into teams and begins a game of basketball. During the game, Ryan is mostly encouraging of his teammates, except for one time when he yells at one of his teammates, Justin, for missing an easy shot. Moments later, the counselors stop the game for a water break. Ryan's counselor pulls him aside after he gets water and asks Ryan how he thinks he is doing on his ideal-self goals. Ryan tells his counselor that he thinks he is doing great, and if he had to rate himself he would give himself a "+3." Ryan's counselor asks Ryan for specific examples that lead Ryan to rate himself so strongly. Ryan mentions helping Ashley with her layup. Ryan's counselor agrees with that observation, but points out that he later yelled at Justin for missing a shot. Ryan tells his counselor he forgot about that, and would try to only say positive things at his teammates when they returned to the game.

Counseling Challenges in the ISG

We have encountered many challenges when implementing the ISG. Below are some of the most common issues.

Adding or Modifying Ideal-Self Goals

It is important to note that during ISG discussions it is not unusual for the student to decide to modify her ideal-self goals or add a new one. Sometimes students discover that applying the same couple of ideal-self goals to every situation is not appropriate and some situations call for other goals. In these cases, we encourage CHP counselors to remain enthusiastic about the student's current goals, while avoiding any direct suggestion that goals should be changed. Instead, we ask the adolescent if goals should be changed when we note any of the following situations:

- The adolescent is unsure that the goal pertains to the activities and discussions in the ISG.
- The adolescent says that a goal is no longer appropriate for them.
- The adolescent directly asks to change or add goals (and the counselor agrees).

In these situations, the counselor *asks* if is time to modify goals or add a goal; however, it is important to note that some participants ask to change their goals as soon as they feel challenged. If the request for change appears to be an attempt to avoid difficult but necessary discussions, we want to be careful not to switch goals too early. But assuming that the counselor agrees with the participant, the reconsideration of ideal-self goals is framed as a valuable sign of growth. For example, counselors might say, "That's a good point. Sometimes students need to change goals as they mature." Or, "I'm glad that you realized this. Some goals may be appropriate for some situations and not others." The goal in these situations is to affirm the student's insights regarding the relevance and appropriateness of their goals, but without encouraging changes that are inconsistent with the best interests of the student's development. Often, conversations about goal changes offer a chance to use the WILBUR problem-solving steps. Then all decisions regarding goal replacements, additions, and deletions are recorded on a current list of goals kept by the counselor.

Data Collection

Consistent with other interventions in the CHP, we emphasize the importance of data collection. For this reason, we devised several forms for tracking outcomes in the ISG. For example, we use the ISG Card to record the counselor and participant's ratings during the social activities and feedback in the program. Counselors maintain an individualized ISG Card for each of their students that includes the date of the ISG session, a list of each of the student's ideal-self goals, and the operational definitions for each of these goals (typically, an electronic copy is created and then printed as needed). On the back of each ISG card is a space to record comments and next steps. In this section, counselors note the feedback they provided to the student and what the student identified as her next steps.

At the end of each ISG session, the student's average score for each goal is computed and recorded in the appropriate box on the ISG Mastery Tracking Form (see Appendix E). The form is meant to track all instances when the student has achieved an average score of 2 or 3 on any of her goals. Once this occurs on three consecutive sessions on a single goal, then we consider that the goal has been "mastered." The date that the student masters each goal is recorded on the bottom of the form. These same forms can be reused with minor modifications in the phase 3 generalization activities.

Individual Applications of the ISG

As mentioned at the beginning of the chapter, the ISG has been researched mostly in the context of the after-school version of the CHP. The counselor-to-student ratio in those settings is probably difficult to reproduce in most practice settings, so we have started to examine strategies for integrating ISG activities into individual counseling. In a high school-based study, we paired disruptive adolescents with paraprofessional "coaches" who worked part-time in the schools. As part of the intervention package, we infused some of the ISG activities into the individual sessions. Not all of the activities readily translate to individual sessions, but we have had success.

Consider the following transcription of an actual high school counseling session. The math teacher had recently complained about her math class and identified the adolescent as one of the more disruptive students in the class:

Coach: Tell me about your math class and what it's like in there.
Adolescent: Everybody comes in, and everybody starts to have class, and everybody gets notes. And, just, everybody goofs off.
C: And how do you fit in to that?
A: I goof off with them.
C: You contribute to it.
A: Yeah.
C: Do you instigate it?

A: Maybe every now and then, but I'm not normally the one to start it.
C: But it's affected how much work you've been able to do this [grading period].
A: Yeah.
C: Do you make a conscious choice to avoid the work, or how does it go?
A: Well, sometimes I'll be talking to someone while she [the teacher] is going over something and I don't get it because I wasn't paying attention. And, uh, I'll ask for help and she'll tell me that I should have been paying attention, which is my fault. So, I end up missing all of it, so I can't do the homework because I don't understand. She'll just say, "You need to pay attention."
C: How are you perceived in that class? You have friends in that class, how do they see you?
A: The clown, I guess.

Here, the coach shifts from adult judgments of the situation (including her own) to how the adolescent is perceived by his peers. The coach then reminds the adolescent of goals that he had set for himself in previous meetings. These goals, which included "being seen as a go-getter," are seemingly at odds with the adolescent's clown reputation in the classroom.

C: How would you rate yourself on being a "go-getter" in your math class? We'll use our scale, with positive three being the best you can be and negative three being the exact opposite of how you want to be seen. Zero is no evidence either way.
A: Uh…probably a zero. Right now I am going toward [the goal], but I haven't been…I've been slacking off a lot.
C: So you're saying there's no evidence either way?
A: Yeah.
C: How do you think your teacher sees you? How would she rate you?
A: Definitely not a hard worker.
C: So, a negative number?
A: Uh, maybe like a negative two, for work ethic.

The coach then asks the adolescent to rate himself on two other ideal-self goals, including "being sociable" and "being seen as happy." The adolescent rates himself highly on these goals.

A: [My classmates] always think I'm happy. And I am happy.
C: So [the rating for being happy] would be like a positive two or a positive three?
A: Yeah.
C: Okay…(brief pause for reflection) It's interesting that, in that class, you have to do one or the other [be either a "go-getter" or be "happy"]. Is that right?
A: Yeah, kinda' because, like, if I'm not cutting up, I'm working, and if I'm not working, I'm cutting up. And a lot of times I choose the bad one—cutting up.
C: Hmmm…Is there any way to reconcile those two things? How could you be, say, a one or a two on both of these things [being a "go-getter" and "happy"] at the same time? Is that possible?

A: I don't know. Maybe.
C: How could that happen?
A: Maybe, like, in between notes, cut up? But…I don't know, because once I get started on cutting up, it goes all class. And I can't really stop—I don't know why. Kinda' can't get back around to work.

At this point, it becomes obvious that the adolescent defines "being seen as happy" as indistinguishable from being a class clown. The counselor uses this information to discuss in more detail what "being seen as happy" means for this adolescent, and how the definition probably differs dramatically across peer and teacher perceptions.

Our example highlights the fact that the same principles of the ISG can be integrated into individual counseling, although the elements may not fit cleanly into 30-minute sessions like those that we have outlined in modules 5.1 and 5.2. Still, the combination of goal setting and scaling questions appears to be an effective way to address social performance deficits in a manner that protects the therapeutic alliance, while avoiding presumptions that adults can coach age-appropriate social competencies to adolescents. We find that encouraging adolescents to set goals for themselves, while not always easy (and usually requiring revisions), helps us to approach topics that may otherwise have been difficult to discuss. Of course, this is not to say that new classroom management strategies are not also in order—perhaps in consultation with the teacher—but from a counseling standpoint, we attempt to help adolescents work through the problem-solving process for themselves.

Conclusion

In this chapter, we have reviewed the ISG, which is a component of the CHP targeting the social performance deficits of adolescents with ADHD. We rely heavily on in-vivo group activities that force students to navigate difficult social interactions while providing frequent feedback based on the student's own stated goals. We rely somewhat on cognitive-behavioral strategies to achieve our goals—namely, having students discuss the discrepancy between their ideal- and real-self goals—by making these terms as concrete as we possibly can. In fact, we allow adolescents to struggle to define their social goals over time during repeated practice and performance feedback. It is not unusual for adolescent who have gone through this process to change their goals frequently, based on frustrations experienced in the group activities, but also through experiences outside the group. For these reasons, we include a problem-solving process to help structure that process. Our problem-solving model is similar to those used in other programs, and we find that it is useful in addressing the daily crises experienced by adolescents; in fact, we once had a parent ask us who "Wilbur" was because he overheard his daughter talking about "him" to her younger sibling. We also find that when adolescents are upset, having a problem-solving model to turn to often helps to deescalate the situation. In a high school study, a student barged into our meeting room to complain about an incident

Table 5.1 Common "Ideal-self" goals

Athletic	Competent	Happy	Mature	Smart
Brave	Competitive	Helpful	Nice	Thoughtful
Caring	Cooperative	Honest	Open-minded	Trustworthy
Calm	Friendly	Kind	Outgoing	Upbeat
Confident	Funny	Likeable	Responsible	Witty

that had just transpired with a teacher. He had thrown his books across the room and stormed out after cursing at the teacher. We used the WILBUR steps and found that the student calmed with time and, by the end, had even decided to apologize to the teacher, even if he were to be suspended for his behavior (he was).

Still, the greatest challenge when helping adolescents with social concerns is generalization beyond the treatment setting. To aid the transfer of skills, we have added the third phase of ISG, which relies on planning social activities outside the program and considering feedback from anonymous adults familiar with the adolescent (e.g., teachers). We have been surprised to find how rare it is for adolescents to correctly guess who provided the feedback, even when specific examples were provided, but encouraged to find how motivated adolescents generally are to discuss the feedback. However, as we mentioned at the start of this chapter, readers should be cautious when interpreting our results. The specific procedures of ISG have not been adequately tested in isolation, so we are not sure of the degree to which ISG contributes to our overall results. Similarly, we are uncertain how effective these procedures are as elements within strictly individual counseling sessions. Whenever possible, we encourage counselors to look for ways to address social performance deficits—such as those commonly seen among adolescents with ADHD—in context of actual social events (Table 5.1).

Module 5.1: Social Activities and Feedback

Goals:

- The adolescent will recognize when their behavior is consistent or inconsistent with their social goals.
- The adolescent's self-appraisals in social settings will match that of adults observing those same interactions.
- Both adolescent and adult ratings of the social performance will suggest mastery of social goals.

Materials:

1. ISG Card listing the adolescent's "ideal-self" goals
2. ISG Mastery Sheet
3. Any materials required to conduct a social activity (e.g., sports equipment, board games)

	Elements	Description
□	*Group leader chooses a social activity and gathers the necessary materials*	Prior to conducting the group, the group leader collects the materials (if any) required for a social activity. For example, if the social activity is a sport, such as soccer, the group leader provides a soccer ball, goals, and perhaps cones to delineate the field. We generally do not let group participants pick the activities because their choices are likely to be too comfortable—the point of the activity is to create unfamiliar and potentially challenging social situations (e.g., rules are unclear, teams are unfair)
□	*Remind group participants of their social goals*	Counselors meet briefly with each group participant to review "ideal-self" goals established in earlier sessions (described in this chapter). Group participants are asked how their ideal-self goals might apply to the chosen social activity (e.g., "How does someone appear "smart" when playing board games?")
□	*Start the activity and observe*	Once participants have briefly reviewed their goals, the counselors encourage the group to start the activity. To ensure that the activity includes realistic social problem solving, the counselors provide little, if any, instruction to get the group started. Group participants decide for themselves how the activity will work, including teams, rules, scoring, etc. Counselors only interrupt the activity if participants get physically aggressive or if verbal altercations suggest that physical aggression is imminent (e.g., cursing, racial slurs)

	Elements	Description
□	*Provide feedback*	After roughly 10 min, the counselors stop the activity and pull students aside to provide feedback on the ideal-self goals. The counselor starts by asking students to rate themselves on a scale from −3 to + 3, where −3 is moving strongly away from the goal and + 3 is moving strongly toward the goal. A score of 0 means that there is no evidence in either direction. The counselor records the adolescent's rating and asks for their rationale (e.g., "What did you *do* to earn that score?"). Counselors then explain their rating on the same scale, using specific examples from the observation as their rationale. The counselor's rating should be as "objective" as possible, based on the adolescent's own operational definition of their ideal-self goals, along with a brief rationale. Then the counselor asks how the score might be improved in the next session/future. This procedure is repeated for each active ideal-self goal and scores are recorded on the ISG Card
		Example: "Your performance seemed consistent with a −1 because although you tried two jokes during the game, I didn't hear anyone laugh. You said before that getting people to laugh out loud was important, so this seemed like you were moving away from that goal a little. Is there something you could differently that might make this group laugh and earn you a + 1 or higher?"
□	*Repeat*	After the feedback sessions, students are sent back to the social activity and the counselors continue to observe. Generally we offer three feedbacks in a 30-min session. Thus, feedbacks must be brief! We try to have all feedbacks completed in 3 min or less
□	*Follow-up*	Counselors generally save more detailed feedback for individual meetings outside of the Social Activities and Feedback sessions. We use this time to ask students how they think progress is going on their goals, based on the long-term trends recorded on the ISG Master Sheet. We also find that graphing these scores, with counselor ratings in one color and adolescents scores in another, helps to make progress more obvious

Module 5.2: Problem Solving

Goals:

- The adolescent will learn the WILBUR six-step process of problem solving.
- The adolescent will generate several solutions to everyday social problems encountered by adolescents.
- The adolescent will be able to apply WILBUR to actual problem scenarios provided during group activities.

Materials:

1. Cards for each participant listing the steps of WILBUR (early sessions only)
2. Paper and writing utensils

	Elements	Description
□	*Identify worries/concerns*	When worries or concerns are reported to the counselor, the adolescent is encouraged to discuss the events in detail as much as they can remember. Counselors use open-ended questions and uses the terms "worries" or "concerns" (rather than "problem") to avoid sounding judgmental
□	*A problem statement is constructed*	The counselor helps the adolescent select on main problem (several concerns might be discussed) to form a single problem statement (i.e., worry or concern). The counselor might say, "It sounds like the main issue here is _____."
□	*Adolescent is led through each step of the WILBUR problem-solving model*	The counselor then leads the adolescent through WILBUR (e.g., "What does *W* stand for?" "What is the concern in this example?"). In this session, the focus is mostly on the first four steps (with steps five and six discussed in a subsequent session)
□	*W—what is my concern/worry?*	The objective is to create an "I" statement that suggests ownership of the problem, rather than attributing the problem to others
□	*I—what would I like to happen?*	The objective is to imagine a desirable resolution and how things will look when the concern/worry is over. The "miracle question" and other solution-focused strategies can be helpful at this step
□	*L—list all possible solutions*	The objective is to brainstorm possible solutions that could lead to the desired resolution, while withholding judgment on the relative value of each suggestion until the next step. Rather, in this stage we praise the adolescent for generating as many solutions as possible (e.g., "Good job! You're coming up with a lot of clever solutions!")
□	*B—pick the best solution*	The objective is to choose a solution that is most preferred by the adolescent. At this stage, the counselor asks the adolescent how her solutions might impact her real-self as a means of weighing the likelihood of success. However, with the exception of solutions that could lead to harm, we allow adolescents to take the lead in this process (e.g., "What do you think? Would this solution work for you?")

	Elements	Description
☐	*U—use the solution*	The counselor helps the adolescent plan a homework assignment that requires the use the solution. The timeframe has to be clear: "By our next meeting, you have agreed to ___."
☐	*R—review*	In a subsequent session, the counselor follows up on the homework assignment and helps the adolescent assess her performance. Success is praised, and failed or unused solutions are replaced with other options. At this point, the participant might brainstorm new solutions not discussed previously, and these new ideas might replace a failed or unused solution

Chapter 6
Working with Families

I have never known any perfect families, any perfect children, or for that matter, any perfect couple. Nor do I expect to meet any.
Virginia Satir, from *Peoplemaking* (1972)

One of the most common strategies for helping families of young children with any behavior disorder is to teach parents new strategies to increase their child's desired behaviors and extinguish undesired behaviors. Such programs include "Parent Training" or "Parent Management Training," where the focus is primarily psychoeducational in nature: The therapist *teaches* the parents to build on prior successes or replace ineffective strategies for new strategies.[1] The underlying assumption is that parents inadvertently reward a child's behavior problems when they use ineffective strategies and that these problems can become increasingly worse with time. Research on child antisocial behavior generally supports this conclusion (Kaminski et al. 2008), but it is also clear that influence within the parent–child relationship is bidirectional, such that child behavior influences how parents manage their children. So rather than assuming that a child's behavior is simply a passive reflection of parenting practices, therapists understand that children are born with temperaments, and that these inborn traits affect parenting practices. Parents of a child with a difficult temperament, for example, may find themselves using more harsh or punitive discipline than they would otherwise prefer, partly because typical parenting practices seem insufficient.

Research on parenting programs as a stand-alone or adjunct family intervention has expanded since the 1960s and, in recent years, researchers have summarized these results in several meta-analyses. In general, parenting programs appear to be effective across for childhood behavior problems (Brestan and Eyberg 1998; Maughan et al. 2005; Serketich and Dumas 1996) among elementary school-age

[1] For simplicity, we will refer to this class of interventions as "parenting programs" throughout this chapter. Readers should be cautioned that similar interventions, such as functional family therapy or multisystemic therapy, fall under a different purview and are not the focus of this chapter.

B. K. Schultz, S. W. Evans, *A Practical Guide to Implementing School-Based Interventions for Adolescents with ADHD*, DOI 10.1007/978-1-4939-2677-0_6

children. For economically disadvantaged families and otherwise distressed parents, however, the benefits of parenting programs are often diminished (Lundahl et al. 2006; Reyno and McGrath 2006). Further, there is a general trend for parenting programs to be less effective for families of adolescents than for families of younger children. Some research suggests that this latter finding might be because adolescents generally exhibit more serious conduct problems than do children. When examined statistically, for example, the severity of the behavior problems is a better predictor of poor parenting program outcomes than is the child's age (Ruma et al. 1996). Taken together, these findings suggest that although parenting programs are a well-established and empirically supported treatment option for children with disruptive behaviors (Evans et al. 2014), families with multiple economic and interpersonal stressors, as well as families of adolescents, might require additional or even alternative interventions.

At the outset, then, it is important to acknowledge the potential strengths and weaknesses of parenting programs for families of adolescents. One potential advantage is that parenting programs can be cost-effective when offered to several parents in a group format, which is a common practice. However, research suggests that individual sessions are often more effective than group sessions when working with families from disadvantaged backgrounds (Lundahl et al. 2006), so it may prove beneficial for clinicians to consider such factors when deciding between group or individual sessions. Another potential advantage of parenting programs is that, in contrast to individual counseling for the adolescent, the parent is brought into the therapeutic process, thereby avoiding the "garage mechanic" phenomenon, where parents view the change process as occurring solely between the therapist and their child (see Chap. 2). Although the inclusion of parents offers a potential advantage, some family dynamics are so problematic that parents have a difficult time enacting meaningful or lasting change without more intensive intervention. For example, studies of violent adolescents in juvenile justice settings have shown that families benefit from a multisystemic approach to treatment that includes probation officers, social workers, physicians, behavior therapists, and families working collaboratively to address youth behavior (e.g., Henggeler et al. 2003). In addition, in a series of studies examining the benefits of a few types of family therapy with adolescents with attention deficit hyperactivity disorder (ADHD), Barkley et al. (1992, 2001) concluded that families, and specifically parents, may not be an effective target for producing improvement with these youth. In contrast, we believe that parenting programs *alone* are insufficient for meeting the needs of adolescents with ADHD or conduct problems.

In this chapter, we describe a parenting program that we have used with families of adolescents with ADHD who participated in the Challenging Horizons Program. Much of the material used in the program was drawn from, or influenced by, several sources (e.g., Robin and Foster 1989; Langberg 2011), culminating in an approach that is consistent with other parenting programs. However, throughout our work with parents we focus on a common area of concern for adolescents with ADHD—homework compliance—and use this as a "running example" of all the elements of behavior contracting. In other words, the goal of the program is to teach parents an effective strategy for behavior contracting with their teens, and we use homework compliance to exemplify the main concepts. Each family's behavior contract is tailored to meet their specific needs, but when discussed in small groups, the example of homework compliance demonstrates the stages of contracting: planning, introduction, implementation, monitoring, and renegotiation. Our running example also points out how behavior contracts evolve over time, and how parents might anticipate and troubleshoot common difficulties. As discussed in Chap. 2, the impairments associated with ADHD are pervasive, and it is unlikely that short-term interventions will lead to large-scale improvements. Rather, effective intervention for ADHD often requires long-term interventions, and this calls for interventionists to prepare families for such an investment of time.

Not all families will enter the parenting program with concerns around homework compliance, and we acknowledge this at the outset of the parenting program. In our experience, some families report that teachers have reduced academic expectations outside of the classroom, sometimes to the point that homework is expressly prohibited in a written plan. In other cases, parents have openly admitted that after years of frustration around academic issues, they have opted to back away from expecting their child to do any homework at all. But the goal of our parenting program is not to achieve homework compliance, per se; rather, the goal is for parents to engage their child in a behavior contract around a specific area of concern, using principles of contingency management. We have chosen to approach this goal through a presentation of the "Homework Management Plan" (HMP)—a program we created to address homework compliance—using both a short, user-friendly manual and video vignettes.[2] In our studies of the intervention, however, parents have successfully used these same materials to target compliance with chores, improved sibling relationships, and even setting a timeframe for college planning. Below, we describe the HMP drawing directly from the materials we share with parents, modified only slightly for our intended audience of practitioners. Even though the basic concepts may already be familiar to our readers, we present the concepts similarly to how we explain them to parents, so as to provide somewhat of a script for practitioners when working with families.

The Homework Management Plan

The HMP is a strategy for parents to help their children and adolescents finish their homework assignments. Homework problems can happen in any family, but especially among families of children with ADHD and other learning problems. Problems with homework often result in arguments between parents and their children, leading to frustration in the home. The goal of the HMP is to help parents make a plan with their child(ren) that will increase the likelihood that homework is completed, with less family conflict.

[2] For our purposes here, we will describe the examples in the video as needed to make our points clear to readers.

Is Homework Really Worth the Trouble?

When children refuse or struggle with homework, parents often ask themselves, "Why should my child have homework after spending more than 6 hours at school?" This is a good question, and one that we hear in some form or another from many parents. Parents are often surprised to learn that the research on homework suggests that it is effective, especially as students enter middle and high school. Students who do homework earn better grades and higher test scores than students who do not do homework. So, in general, it appears that homework is worth the trouble.

However, it is important to note that not all homework assignments are created equal. It turns out that homework is most effective when (1) the directions are clear, (2) students are given options (e.g., homework is a choice between two equal assignments), and (3) it is graded and feedback is given. In addition, it appears that students benefit when homework assignments vary in format. In other words, assignments that change between practice (i.e., worksheets), preparation (i.e., reading ahead in textbook), and extension tasks (i.e., applying classroom skills to new situations) are likely to keep a student's interest and be most effective.

Sometimes parents find that their child's homework is not graded, the directions are unclear, there are no options, and the format never changes. In such cases, parents might speak with their child's teacher about possible changes; but of course, children should never be aware when their parents question homework assignments! When children are aware that their parents and teachers disagree, motivation can become an issue. In the end, this will make it more difficult for parents to get their children to be successful in school and will likely lead to more frustration at home. In general, we encourage parents to meet directly with teachers to discuss homework concerns if any arise; otherwise, children may become overly dependent on their parents to help them cope with or escape frustrating situations.

Getting Started with the HMP

To understand the HMP strategy, it is important for parents to know how to help children and adolescents change their behavior. In terms of homework, parents often find that their child is very disorganized. For example, they forget to write down their assignments or bring home the materials they need to complete their work. In other cases, children bring home everything they need, but they do not understand the assignment or forget the directions. Adolescents might also refuse or "balk" when it comes to their homework, despite their parents' pleading, lecturing, and assistance. Our goal with the HMP is to offer parents new ways of responding in these situations.

To change a child's behavior, we encourage parents to think in terms of rewards and punishments. Rewarding and punishing consequences clearly vary for each child, and what may be a reward for one (e.g., ride to the library) could be seen as a punishment by another. Ideally, parents will rely on both rewards and punishments to shape their child's behavior, but we often find that parents rely too heavily on one or the other. It seems that parents of children with problem behaviors focus too much on the unwanted behavior and, as a result, become "punishment focused." In other words, some parents try to change behavior mostly through punishments alone. Parents might clean out their child's bedroom of all games and toys, and withhold rewards for increasingly longer times. Yet these efforts still do not change their child's behavior for the better. In fact, as we have discussed in previous chapters, it often makes things worse. Consequences can also fail to change a child's behavior in a desirable direction when the rules are not clear or the consequences for behavior are not immediate and consistent. Consider the following conversation between a mother and her son:

Mother*:* When you get a chance tonight, I need you to clean your room

Son *(playing a videogame):* Okay, in a minute … I need to save my game at the next level-up

A half-hour passes and the son is still playing his game

Mother *(getting frustrated):* You still haven't cleaned your room! Do it now or you're in big trouble!

Son*:* Okay, okay, I'll do it! Gosh!

Son slowly goes to his room. Mom comes in 15 min later to check on his progress and finds him on his computer

Mom *(angry):* I told you to clean your room and you haven't done a thing! Your clothes are all over the floor and your bed is a mess! Why don't you ever do what I ask?

Son*:* I put away my shoes and my jacket, and now I'm cleaning out my MP3 player!

In this scenario, the mother's request to "clean your room" is not very specific. The son claims that by "clean," his mother is concerned about his shoes and jacket. Then, without clear directions, the son is distracted by his MP3 player and begins "cleaning" that instead. Now imagine this same scenario had the mother said, "You'll have access to your computer tonight after your clothes are in the hamper and your bed is made." If her demands were specific and the consequences were clear, the son would be more likely to respond in the way his mother intended. Similar to other behavior contracting strategies (e.g., Anastopoulus and Farley 2003), the HMP helps families by making behavioral expectations clear, consistent, and very specific.

Planning

Parents need two things prior to starting a behavior contract like the HMP. First, parents need a "reward menu," which is a list of rewards that will be available to their child each night after specific homework goals are met. Second, parents need to anticipate problems by considering what is keeping their child from being successful currently. We will explore these two concerns below.

Creating the Reward Menu The reward menu is a necessary step in the HMP. Without clear and immediate rewards, many children will not see the benefit in doing homework. As we often explain to parents, it would be nice if all children were excited by the chance of getting an "A" the following day (or even later), but the reality is that many children are not motivated by grades—especially children with a history of failure. Likewise, many children are unmotivated by gifts or money when the next report card comes out 3 months later. Such rewards are simply too far in the future to make a difference today. Unfortunately, parents, teachers, and counselors sometimes over-rely on long-term rewards and end up believing that children are "lazy" and "do not care" because the child does not respond to the adults' efforts.

To be more effective, parents need rewards that can be provided nightly and that are easy to either give or withhold. In other words, parents have to ask themselves, "What would my child be willing to work for *each night*?" Of course, families vary in what they can offer to their children, so parents must ask themselves: "What rewards can I *realistically* and *comfortably* offer my child *each night*?" For example, a child may be highly motivated by earning $100 each night for doing homework, but most parents cannot realistically offer that reward (nor would we recommend it). A child may be highly motivated by playing board games with her whole family until midnight each night, but most parents cannot keep such a promise every night of the week—not to mention the problems the next morning when the family has lost sleep! Thus, we encourage parents to think about what would be required of them to provide a potential reward, and then weigh that against their energy level on their *worst typical night*. All parents have bad days, and all parents have limited energy. In order to be consistent, parents should pick rewards they can realistically offer under "bad-day, low-energy conditions." The mistake many parents make is to promise a highly motivating reward, only to find that they cannot provide it consistently. For example, some parents have offered their child special desserts (e.g., homemade ice cream), but then have a bad day and either forget to pick up the supplies after work or simply lack the energy to follow through. Such inconsistency can ruin parents' attempts to keep a behavior contract.

Here are some examples of realistic and motivating rewards parents have used on a daily basis with young adolescents:

Minutes of videogame time	Minutes of basketball with dad
Minutes of phone time	Points toward a gift card
Minutes of TV remote time (child determines what family watches on television)	Points toward a "get-out-of-chores" card (child gets time off from chores)
Minutes at a friend's house	Craft supplies (e.g., beads and paints)
Friend gets to come over	Board games with parent(s)/sibling(s)
Minutes of computer time	Access to parents' hobby supplies

Notice that some of the rewards on this list are tangible (e.g., beads), others are points toward long-term rewards, and still others are activities or special privileges. In general, activity and privilege rewards are preferable because they are relatively easier to give and withhold. For example, if the reward is 30 minutes of computer time, it is easy for parents to know when the reward started and stopped, and just as easy to withhold (e.g., "We'll log onto the computer *after* you do 30 minutes of homework").

It is important for parents to consider how they will withhold rewards when their child does not do homework. If parents cannot withhold a reward—for any reason—the child will not feel a need to *earn* it. Further, if parents do not have easy ways to withhold the reward, they may not have the energy to enforce the rule on bad days. Here are some general ideas for how to withhold common rewards:

Reward type	How to withhold
Activities with friends	Withhold transportation
	Disallow guests at the house
Activities with parents	Parent does not participate (and does not "give in")
Cell phone	Use "pay-as-you-go" cell phone plan and only purchase minutes or text messaging based on compliance with behavior contract
	Keep phone/charger in locked cabinet
Computers/Internet	Create secret password to log onto computer
	Disconnect modem
Videogames	Put luggage lock through one hole on the power cord plug (Olympia et al. 1992)

Of course, praise is the easiest reward parents can offer and, as a result, is the most preferable. However, we assume in the HMP that children need more than just praise to do their homework. Someday praise alone will be enough, but probably not yet! Until then, parents are likely to be most successful when they use praise along with rewards. Thus, the reward menu requires careful planning, and we encourage parents to come up with at least four or five items to include on the list (with the child's input in most instances).

Preparing for Success The other thing parents should do before starting the HMP is to try to anticipate the likely roadblocks to success. Parents should ask themselves, "What is keeping my child from doing more homework?" Or, "What is keeping my child from doing *higher quality* homework?" It is not always easy to know the answer(s), but in general, parents can get a better sense of the problems by considering the following:

- *When* is the best time for homework: Immediately after school or later?
- *How* much homework time is realistic each night before my child gets too tired?
- *Where* is the best place for homework?
- *Who* is available to monitor the homework?

The HMP strategy is designed to help families clarify expectations, but each family is different and each family will have their own answers to these questions. In short, we assume that parents are the experts when it comes to their children. Parents can predict what is likely to work and what is likely to fail, based on their past experiences. If a parent knows that their child completes more homework at the kitchen table than in front of her computer, then one rule may be to have homework consistently done at the kitchen table.

To get children to follow the rules, they should be encouraged to explore and negotiate solutions to the problems. We have found that children who feel invested in the contract are more likely to follow through than those who are not invited to negotiate the terms. Hence, the HMP strategy involves a process of parent–child negotiations that lead to a behavior contract.

Step One: Establishing the Rules

When working with parents, we concede that there are several things that parents simply cannot control. For example, parents cannot control what their child brings home from school. Parents cannot control whether their child writes down the correct assignments, or that other means of checking assignments are always accurate (e.g., “Homework Hotlines”). Moreover, parents cannot be certain what their child is supposed to do for homework each evening. Because these things are out the parents’ control, it is important to accept these limitations and work around them. Thus, we encourage parents to focus their energy on the things they can control. For example, parents can encourage their child(ren) to spend time on homework each evening. As a result, time spent on homework is the focus of the HMP: Parents plan the rules about homework time, even before they discuss the HMP with their child.

When Should Homework Happen? In an example we share with parents, we discuss a situation where a young teenage daughter brings home a poor report card. When the father points out that he has not seen the daughter do homework at home, she explains that she does her homework “on the bus” or “in the morning.” We then ask the parent(s) how they might respond in this situation. Through such examples, we introduce some solution-focused strategies, similar to those discussed in Chap. 3. For example, the father might calmly say, “That doesn’t appear to be working because you’re not getting it done on time.” He bases this on the teacher comments on the report card, and then uses this information to set the stage for the negotiation that will lead to a behavior contract.

We emphasize the importance of parents planning basic expectations prior to introducing the behavior contract. One of the most important decisions for parents to make is when their child will start homework. Parents might consider the pros and cons of having their child start their homework immediately after school, or later in the evening, or even in the mornings. We encourage parents to think about which times are likely to work best before having this discussion with their child, but allowing the child some freedom of choice can give her the feeling of participation and investment. When the adolescent argues against change we coach the parent to explain, "That hasn't been working in the past," but to keep encouraging the adolescent to think about other possible solutions. Even if the adolescent is unable to offer a viable and acceptable option, we still encourage parents to include their input as much as possible.

How Much Homework Time Should Be Required? Again, the answer to this question will be different for different families, but in general we encourage parents to base this decision on how much time their child spends on homework already, and how this has helped or hurt their grades. For example, if a child rarely spends time on homework and is receiving poor grades, then a starting goal of 15 or 30 min is a step in the right direction. Even though it is unlikely that 15 or 30 min will be enough for most children, it is enough to start the process of change. Behavior contracting like that in the HMP is a long-term plan and not a quick fix. Besides, children who rarely do homework are unlikely to suddenly accept 2 hours of homework. Such drastic changes are unrealistic and likely to fail.

In other cases, children spend several hours on homework but are unproductive. They sit in front of their books and papers for hours but get very little done. In these cases, we encourage parents to actually *reduce* the amount of time spent on homework. When a child spends too much time on homework, the quality of the work suffers. This is the principle of "diminishing returns"—the quality of work in the second hour is far less than the quality of work in the first hour. This can occur even when breaks are taken. In these cases, the goal may be to improve the quality and efficiency of work in a shorter timeframe. We will return to this idea later, but generally we encourage families to limit the timeframe to less than an hour when first starting the HMP. Again, 1 hour of homework will not seem like enough for some children, especially when they are frequently off-task, but it is enough to start the process of change.

In another example we share with parents, a father asks his daughter how much she thinks is reasonable to spend each evening on homework and then they negotiate a time that is acceptable to both. Again, we point out that before this discussion, it is important for the parenting team (i.e., both spouses and caregivers) to agree on the minimum amount of time they are going to require the child to spend on homework each night. Then, when negotiating a time with the child, parents can ask for an hour or even more of homework and allow their child to "negotiate down" (see Step Two for more details). This gives the child a sense of participation and investment, and increases the likelihood that she will follow through. Parents should also plan to find homework time that will allow at least one adult to be available to monitor homework time and offer assistance as needed (this is likely to vary throughout the week). In order for the HMP to be effective, it is vital that an adult actively monitors the adolescent's compliance with the contract.

Step Two: Negotiating Rules and Goals

By this point, the parents have established basic rules around homework time. Parents know when they want homework to occur, how long they want their child to work, which nights of the week they want homework to occur, and who will be available to monitor the homework. Moreover, parents agree on these terms. Now it is time to consider what happens when these rules are followed and when they are not. When the rules of the HMP are followed, children will receive rewards from the rewards menu for one night. Thus, it is important that the reward menu is planned in advance and the items on the list are realistic and exciting for the child.

When the rules of the HMP are not followed, rewards are withheld for one night. We find that the rules around homework start time and length are most often challenged because the adolescent either forgets to bring home the required materials or they will forget what assignments are due. Because the HMP targets time—a facet of the agreement that parents can control—adolescents are required to work on *something* during homework time, even if it is not actual homework. In other words, parents give the child something to do in these instances, including reading a newspaper article or reading ahead in a textbook; but whatever the task, we strongly recommend that the child writes a brief summary of this work for the parent to read. In fact, parents may even read the adolescent's written summary and then throw it away to point out the waste of time created when assignments are not correctly tracked or materials are left at school. This will make it more likely that the child will bring home what they need the next time. If the child does the task that the parent assigns and fills the entire homework time, then rewards are given as usual. If not, the rewards are withheld for one night. If the child refuses at first but then changes her mind, rewards are withheld until the homework time is completed.

Notice that rewards are not withheld for longer than one night. Parents are often surprised by this aspect of the plan, but the reason is so adolescents have a fresh chance of being successful with the HMP each day. When rewards are withheld for more than one night, the adolescent may feel that she has no reason to do her homework the following night—the lingering punishment erases the potentially motivating aspect of a reward menu.

The last rule of the HMP is that during homework time, an adult will occasionally check-in to see how things are going. As mentioned earlier, children oftentimes sit in front of their work but do nothing. The occasional check is to see if the adolescent is actively doing something, such as reading or writing. When the adolescent is clearly not working during these checks, the parent should *add* some homework time. Generally, we recommend that parents add five additional minutes each time the child is caught off-task for more than a brief moment. However, these checks should not be used too often so that the additional time does not exceed fifteen extra minutes total. Rather, parents should only add extra minutes when the off-task behavior is clear—such as when the parent finds the child doodling. If this problem occurs frequently, we recommend that a parent briefly help the child get back on track but still extend the time.

It is also important that the homework time is not interrupted. This means that if the child gets up and leaves the homework area, the clock should be stopped and not started again until she returns. As a result, some parents use timers or stopwatches to help track time. Parents who can anticipate this problem should carefully plan ways to track time. In another example we share with parents, a father explains these rules to his daughter and that her rewards will be withheld if she does not follow the rules. The daughter's privileges, such as videogames, telephone, computer, and television, are withheld until the homework time is met. If she refuses to work for the homework time, the father's response is disappointment—not anger. In the example, when the daughter asks what will happen if she skips her homework time, the father says, "That's fine. I would rather you do your 30 minutes. I think that will help you get better grades. But if you decide that you do not want your rewards, you can choose to do that." Many parents find this approach difficult, but it is important that adolescents be allowed to experience failure before they can experience success. In our experience, well-chosen rewards will assure that the adolescent does not choose to skip their homework too often. Still, adolescents will sometimes test their parents on this rule to see what their reaction will be. We emphasize that under no circumstances should the parent give up and give the rewards when faced with this challenge! Giving up can actually reward misbehavior and, as a result, the adolescent is more likely to refuse homework again in the future. Thus, parents should be ready to withhold the rewards whenever faced with defiance.

Establishing Goals We encourage and coach parents to help their child to identify specific long-term goals that will decide whether she is successful or not. In an example we present to parents, a father says that if his daughter is able to earn *C*s or better on her next report card, then the homework time (30 min) will stay the same. However, if her grades fall below *C*s, they will increase the amount of time she is to spend on homework each night, by 15 minutes. Goals like these will vary from family to family. In some families, a goal of all *C*s or better is realistic, but we have worked with families where a more realistic goal is to set a goal that the child receives no more than two *D*s. In still other families, it made sense that the child should make a goal of all *B*s or better. As a general rule of thumb, setting a goal of all *C*s or better means that—if the goal is met—children will easily pass their classes and will be unlikely to fall behind their peers.

Step Three: Troubleshooting

Up to this point in the HMP, we have discussed ways to establish a homework time, set goals, and negotiate the rules. Next, we explore different situations parents might encounter as they go through this process.

Conflicts with Other Activities In an example we share with parents, a son asks to have nights off from the HMP when he has other activities (e.g., soccer games). It is very important that the HMP be as consistent as possible, so there should be no breaks. Instead, the homework time may need to be changed on some nights, depending on the child's schedule. In this specific example, the parent makes an arrangement with the son to get homework done prior to special activities.

Not Meeting the Long-Term Goal Parents may find that their child does not meet their long-term goals in the HMP. For example, an adolescent might receive one *D* in Science and several *A*s and *B*s on her report card after setting a goal to get all *C*s or better. Many parents would be tempted to ignore the *D* because the other grades are strong. However, it is important to stay consistent with the original goal. The parent might say, "Remember that contract we signed? Our goal was *C*s or better in every class. We are going to have to increase your study time this next grading period to get that Science grade up." As described earlier, we encourage parents to increase homework time by 15 minutes when the long-term goal is not met.

Homework Time Cannot Be Monitored by an Adult Often, children will suggest that homework is done during times that the parent(s) cannot monitor. For example, adolescents might suggest that they will do homework immediately after school during a time when neither parent is home. Again, homework time should always be negotiated for a time when at least one adult is available to make sure the child is actually working on schoolwork. It would be nice if parents could trust their child(ren) to do their schoolwork on their own, but we assume in the HMP that children are struggling with homework prior to beginning the plan. Whether the child is 12 or 17, if she has not been doing homework on her own up to this point, the parent should not rely on her to start now.

Child Starts Homework Time Too Late in the Evening Other adolescents may want to start homework late in the evening. Although we encourage parents to give their child choices when setting a homework time, it is generally better to start homework earlier in the evening rather than later. When homework time starts late, rewards will not be as meaningful, especially if the child has had access to other enjoyable activities beforehand. When an earlier homework time is set, the parent can begin withholding rewards at that point until the time is completed, making the rewards potentially more salient.

Adolescent Works Very Slowly During the Homework Time This is a concern that comes up for many parents that may be related to deficits associated with ADHD (e.g., Sluggish Cognitive Tempo). In cases where children sit in front of their homework and accomplish little, we encourage parents to give rewards based on *how much* homework is completed. For example, if a child has several worksheets to complete but only finishes one during her homework time, the parent may only reward her with 10 of the 30 minutes of videogame time she would normally receive (i.e., roughly the same fraction of the total assignments she completed). Thus, the homework time becomes a "beat-the-clock game" where the more that is done in the timeframe, the better the reward. Sometimes parents find that it helps to sit with their child for the first part of homework time in order to improve how much she actually completes. Parental assistance may help this situation, but we encourage parents to find ways to remove themselves from homework over time. Instead, we encourage parents to base the rewards on how much the child finishes during *independent* work. It is important to note that this approach requires parents to know their child's assignments, which is not always possible, so this strategy would not be feasible in many situations.

Adolescent Loses Interest in the Rewards Sometimes adolescents decide that they are no longer want the rewards that were written into the behavior contract.

Parents should be wary of these claims because adolescents sometimes hope that by saying, "I don't care," their parents will give up trying to enforce the plan. In truth, the "I don't care" stratagem often works—especially with peers and some adults—because it allows adolescents to escape frustrating situations. When this problem occurs in the HMP, we encourage parents to stick to the plan anyway. If the adolescent says "I don't care" to losing their rewards, the parent can respond, "I'm sorry you feel that way, but I understand you had a bad day. You can try again tomorrow night." If the adolescent does not return to a previous level of success with the plan within a week, the parent should think about making the rewards more appealing, or find new rewards to add to the menu (see Case Example Three, below). For example, if the reward is videogame time, we encourage parents to consider buying or renting a new and popular videogame. Then that evening, the parent can say, "Have you heard about that new game ____? I stopped by the store today and picked up a copy. I'd really like to play it with you, but remember that contract? You'll need to do your homework first." However, parents should be careful. It is better to get the reward first and then mention it to the adolescent, rather than having the adolescent direct the parent to get things for them. Sometimes adolescents will attempt to manipulate their parents by asking for new things frequently. In these cases, parents should consider new rewards that are more activity- or privilege-based, such as basketball time with dad or visitation time with friends.

Step Four: Writing the Contract

Using the ideas and plans discussed so far, parents can write the HMP into a behavior contract. A behavior contract can be a very effective strategy in ensuring that the agreements between parents and children are followed. We have included a sample contract in Fig. 6.1, along with a blank copy for parents to use in Appendix F. Our contract format can be changed to reflect the specific concerns of each family, but we strongly discourage parents from adding too many components to their contracts. One mistake that many parents make is to try to use the behavior contract to solve every problem all at once. It is best to keep the contract simple—especially when it is first written. When parents add too many "moving parts," the contract becomes very difficult to enforce consistently. We explain that it is better to start small and then add new expectations at later negotiation meetings.

No two behavior contracts are ever exactly alike because all families are different. In our contract form, several guidelines have already been laid out for parents. These guidelines include:

- A clear and reasonable goal, such as specific report card grades
- The time when the homework will be completed and monitored
- A reasonable amount of time to work on homework
- How to handle special occasions, such as snow days and holidays
- What to do when no homework is assigned or brought home

Guidelines:

1. My goal for the next report card is: *No grades less than a C*
2. I will work on my homework *Sun - Thur* at this time: *7:00pm*
3. I will work on my homework for this amount of time each day: *30 minutes*
4. What will happen if I'm not working during homework time? *Add 5 minutes*
5. I understand that even if I do not have homework, I will use the homework time to study for tests and quizzes, or as an alternative: *Mom or Dad will give me an assignment to do*

Additional Terms: *When homework time is completed, I will have access to the computer and Playstation for 2 hours, not to go past 10:30*

By signing this contract, I *Bobby Person* (print name) understand the terms that are described above. This agreement will start today and will be renegotiated when I receive my next report card / mid-term report, and changes will depend on how I am doing at that time.

Student Signature: ____________________ Date: __________

Parent Signature: ____________________ Date: __________

Fig. 6.1 Homework contract sample

In order to make the contract "official," parents and their child sign and date the contract at the bottom. Children should be told that their signatures do not necessarily mean that they agree to the terms, it just means that they understand what the contract says. In situations where children refuse to sign the contract, parents should sign anyway and explain that even if the child does not agree to follow the plan, they will.

Once the contract is signed, it is important for the agreement to start immediately. Many parents make the mistake of waiting to start the contact until the following day or even the following week, but children often try to renegotiate the contract during that time. Instead, we encourage parents to start the contract right after it is signed so that children are clear about the expectations. An immediate start also sends the message that the parent is serious about making the change.

Case Examples

Throughout this chapter, we have described the HMP and highlighted several problems that parents often make when starting it. Below are three stories based on the experiences of actual families that have tried the HMP, ran into difficulties, and then made changes that led to success. It is important to note that most families will experience difficulties when making any change in the expectations placed on their children. In fact, it is probably most realistic to expect things to get worse before they get better, which is something we share with families openly. Consider the following experiences of parents who have tried the HMP (names and other identifying details are changed to protect confidentiality).

Case Example One Susan, a single-mother of 11-year old Allie, became increasingly concerned by Allie's oppositional behavior at home. Whenever they discussed schoolwork, Allie became quickly upset and argued that everything was fine at school and that she had nothing to work on in the evening because she got it all done in study hall. Susan was a very organized person with a highly responsible office job, so she was flabbergasted when she peeked in Allie's bookbag one day and found trash, old food items, and an assignment tracker with nothing written in it. At the mid-point in the school year, Allie's grades crashed down to D's and F's, which was very inconsistent with her previous A/B average in elementary school. Susan became worried that Allie would fail Sixth Grade if things did not change. The family tried the HMP and, in consultation with a psychologist, Susan planned a behavior contract to target 45 min of homework each evening.

After her initial meeting with Allie to set up the contract, Susan met with the psychologist and reported that Allie refused to sign it. The psychologist and Susan reviewed the plan and two problems were clear. First, Susan wrote most of the plan prior to meeting with Allie. Second, Susan was excited about the contract and decided to add in several expectations outside of homework, including the completion of household chores and the avoidance of "arguments" and "temper tantrums." In her attempt to tackle all of these problems, Susan had scribbled notes in the margins of the HMP contract, with additional notes on the back of the page.

The psychologist encouraged Susan to sit down with Allie again and to renegotiate the contract "from scratch." While it is preferable to wait until the scheduled time for the first renegotiation, it was clear in this case that the starting contract was unlikely to work. For example, by writing most of the contract in advance, Susan had left Allie out of the negotiation process. Susan felt that "negotiation" with Allie undermined her parental authority, but in truth, structured negotiations with children can effectively model how adults solve disagreements without arguments and hurt feelings. The negotiation is also an important component to earning the child's trust and willingness to participate. The psychologist reminded Susan that just because she was "negotiating" with Allie did not mean she was going to agree to everything Allie wanted. The psychologist also encouraged Susan to simplify the plan by removing expectations for chores and "good behavior" outside of homework. In their discussion, the psychologist asked what would happen if homework was completed but the chores were not, and Susan responded honestly, "I hadn't thought about that." The psychologist pointed out that it is important to keep the first contract as simple as possible (refer to sample contract in Fig. 6.1), and then expand to other areas if needed, based on results.

Susan agreed to follow the psychologist's recommendations and later that evening she renegotiated the contract with Allie. Although Allie still refused to sign, Susan signed and said that she would follow her part of the agreement even if Allie did not. The next few nights, Allie complained that she had no homework and Susan responded by either assigning a writing assignment (which Allie refused to do, even though she lost her privileges as a result) or encouraging Allie to study for her upcoming tests and quizzes. After three nights, Allie reluctantly spent the time studying for quizzes to ensure that she received her privileges. Over time, the arguments and frustrations around homework compliance diminished and Allie's grades improved.

Case Example Two Mike and Terry are the parents of Mark, a 14-year old high school freshman. Mark had taken stimulant medication for ADHD throughout most of elementary and middle school, but now that he has entered high school he has requested to try the school year without medication. Mark's pediatrician supported the decision,[3] provided that the change did not result in dramatically lower grades. Mark has a strong academic record, with no less than C's through middle school, and he hopes to go to college following graduation. Mike and Terry agree to let Mark stop taking his medication, as long as he agrees to do 15 min of homework each night, and initially he seems very excited to sign the HMP.

After the second grading period, Mark's grades slip and he receives an "F" in two of his courses. Naturally, Mike and Terry are upset and set up a time to renegotiate the homework agreement with Mark. Mark goes to see his school counselor to discuss his disappointing report card and, in their discussion, Mark comes up with the idea to see a tutor each week rather than make changes to either the amount of homework he does each night or to restart his medication. The school counselor encourages Mark to discuss this with his parents at the renegotiation as a possible solution.

That evening, Mark enters the renegotiation meeting visibly defensive. He argues vehemently with his parents that he should not have to do more homework or take medications, and that tutoring is the only option he will agree to. He also tells his parents that the school counselor agrees with him, which surprises and frustrates his parents. Mike and Terry feel undermined by the school counselor's input. Caught off guard, Mark's parents agree to let him try tutoring. In the following days, Mark does not follow through with asking his teacher about tutoring, and

[3] All decisions regarding medications should be done in consultation with a qualified physician.

after a week his parents grow tired of asking. Ultimately, no change is made to the homework contract, despite the F's.

The school counselor meets with Mark the following week and realizes that Mark is headed toward failure again because he did not make any changes. She calls the family to discuss the situation but finds that the parents are frustrated with her for encouraging Mark to "argue his case." After this confusion is clarified, it is clear that Mark has effectively sidestepped the renegotiation process by pitting his parents and school counselor against one another. The counselor encourages Mark's parents to meet with Mark again and to use the mid-term grade report as evidence that immediate change is needed.

That evening the family meets again, and this time Mark's parents offer him two options: (1) Mark either agrees to increase homework time to 30 min per night, or (2) he meets with his pediatrician to discuss a low dose of medication. The tutoring option is taken off the table because Mark did not follow through when given the chance. Mark reluctantly agrees to 30 min of homework each night and the contract is signed. Eventually, Mark recovers in the two classes he had failed and finishes out the school year with passing grades.

Case Example Three Deandrea's daughter Kamlyn, a tenth grader, was struggling in most of her classes. Kamlyn had a history of being very resistant to her mother's attempts to help her with organization or homework, despite earning low grades since elementary school. Deandrea discussed these concerns with the school psychologist, who recommended the HMP. Deandrea's biggest concern involved her ability to withhold privileges from Kamlyn when she refuses to finish her homework time. After thinking about the problem for a while, Deandrea set up a homework plan that was rewarded with special privileges, such as visits to her cousin's house (who lives a block away).

Two weeks after the start of the new homework plan, Deandrea met with the school psychologist and admitted that she gave up with the plan after only a few nights. Kamlyn was more resistant than Deandrea had anticipated, and on the first night Kamlyn refused to do any homework. After 30 min of pleading, Deandrea gave in and allowed Kamlyn to go to her cousin's house to avoid further arguing. The next night, the same thing happened again, but Deandrea decided that she would not give in again. After 45 min of arguing, Kamlyn seemed ready to do her homework, but when her mother was occupied with dinner, Kamlyn walked to her cousin's house.

In her conversation with the school psychologist, Deandrea admitted that she actually wanted Kamlyn and her cousin spent time together because this was one of the few social activities that Kamlyn enjoyed. By putting these visits on the reward menu, Deandrea had set herself up to withhold a privilege that she was not ready—or able—to withhold. Deandrea re-examined the reward menu and decided that access to the Internet and Kamlyn's cell phone were easier to withhold than the visits to her cousin's house. Working with the school psychologist, she found a way to put a password on the computer, and made a plan to lock up Kamlyn's cell phone each morning before school. Then in the evenings, Deandrea was able to easily control access to both rewards.

Following these changes to the plan, Kamlyn refused to sign the contract because she did not want to lose access to her cell phone. Still, Deandrea signed the plan and agreed to “keep up my side of the agreement.” That night, Kamlyn refused to do any homework and Deandrea replied calmly, “I’m sorry to hear that, but you won’t have access to the computer or your cell phone tonight. Let’s try again tomorrow.” Kamlyn argued that this was unfair, but Deandrea walked away and attended to other concerns. After a while, Kamlyn returned and asked if she did the homework if she could get her phone back. Deandrea agreed and Kamlyn read over her notes from class for the time. In the following days, Kamlyn continued to complain that the new plan was “stupid,” but would then give in later when Deandrea’s response was calm and consistent. At one point Kamlyn refused to turn over her cell phone in the morning prior to school, but when Deandrea explained that she would have to cut off the cell phone plan, Kamlyn reluctantly gave her the phone. Slowly the nightly protests improved and Kamlyn finished her homework on most nights. When Kamlyn followed the HMP for an entire week with few complaints, Deandrea surprised her by adding new features to her cell phone, thereby making the phone even *more* desirable. Over time, Kamlyn became more consistent with her homework and the number of missing assignments dropped dramatically. As a result, Kamlyn’s grades improved in her math and English classes.

Conclusion

In this chapter, we have reviewed a behavior contracting strategy we have successfully used with parents of adolescents with ADHD and conduct problems. Specifically, we focus on homework compliance as a starting point because this issue is a very common complaint that, when explored, exposes related issues with communication and limit setting. The goal is to construct a behavior contract that clearly spells out the parents’ expectations and the contingences—both rewards and punishments—that will be used in response to the adolescent’s behavior. In cases where homework is not a concern (e.g., the school has removed the expectation that the adolescents will complete homework), we then find another concern that can benefit from behavioral contracting. We find that the process of constructing a contract helps parents to understand how they might be more effective when addressing their child’s problem behaviors, especially if there has been a long history of difficulties.

We realize that parent training strategies such as the one we discuss in this chapter are rare in schools. School counselors and psychologists do not often have the chance to work with parents outside of brief IEP meetings or disciplinary actions. To effectively enact the strategies we describe may require changes in the roles that school mental health professionals play in schools. Often these roles are defined by school administrators. We argue that school mental health professionals are most beneficial to their schools when they are actively engaged in practices that work and, based on the literature on interventions for ADHD and related disorders, parent outreach and training should be a large component of the job description.

References

Anastopoulos, A. F., & Farley, S. E. (2003). A cognitive-behavioral training program for parents of children with attention-deficit/hyperactivity disorder. In A. E. Kazdin & J. R. Weisz (Eds.), *Evidence-based psychotherapies for children and adolescents* (pp. 187–203). New York: Guilford Press.

Barkley, R. A., Guevremont, D. C., Anastopoulos, A. D., & Fletcher, K. E. (1992). A comparison of three family therapy programs for treating family conflicts in adolescents with attention-deficit hyperactivity disorder. *Journal of Consulting and Clinical Psychology, 60,* 450–462.

Barkley, R. A., Edwards, G., Laneri, M., Fletcher, K., & Metevia, L. (2001). The efficacy of problem-solving communication training alone, behavior management training alone, and their combination for parent–adolescent conflict in teenagers with ADHD and ODD. *Journal of Consulting and Clinical Psychology, 69,* 926–941.

Brestan, E. V., & Eyberg, S. M. (1998). Effective psychosocial treatments of conduct-disordered children and adolescents: 29 years, 82 studies, and 5,272 kids. *Journal of Clinical Child Psychology, 27,* 180–189.

Evans, S. W., Owens, J. S., & Bunford, N. (2014). Evidence-based psychosocial treatments for children and adolescents with attention-deficit/hyperactivity disorder. *Journal of Clinical Child and Adolescent Psychology, 43,* 527–551.

Henggeler, S. W., Rowland, M. D., Halliday-Boykins, C., Sheidow, A. J., Ward, D. M., Randall, J., & Edwards, J. (2003). One-year follow-up of multisystemic therapy as an alternative to the hospitalization of youths in psychiatric crisis *Journal of the American Academy of Child and Adolescent Psychiatry, 42,* 543–551.

Kaminski, J. W., Valle, L. A., Filene, J. H., & Boyle, C. L. (2008). A meta-analytic review of components associated with parent training program effectiveness. *Journal of Abnormal Child Psychology, 36*(4), 567–589.

Langberg, J. M. (2011). *Homework, organization, and planning skills manual.* Washington, DC: National Association of School Psychologists.

Lundahl, B., Risser, H. J., & Lovejoy, M. C. (2006). A meta-analysis of parent training: Moderators and follow-up effects. *Clinical Psychology Review, 26,* 86–104.

Maughan, D. R., Christiansen, E., Jenson, W. R., Olympia, D., & Clark, E. (2005). Behavioral parent training as a treatment for externalizing behaviors and disruptive behavior disorders: A meta-analysis. *School Psychology Review, 34,* 267–286.

Reyno, S. M., & McGrath, P. J. (2006). Predictors of parent training efficacy for child externalizing behavior problems—a meta-analytic review. *Journal of Child Psychology and Psychiatry, 47,* 99–111.

Robin, A. L., & Foster, S. L. (1989). *Negotiating parent adolescent conflict: A behavioral family systems approach.* New York: Guilford Press.

Ruma, P. R., Burke, R. V., & Thompson, R. V. (1996). Group parent training: Is it effective for children of all ages? *Behavior Therapy, 27,* 159–169.

Satir, V. (1972). *Peoplemaking.* Palo Alto: Science and Behavior Books.

Serketich, W. J., & Dumas, J. E. (1996). The effectiveness of behavioral parent training to modify antisocial behavior in children: A meta-analysis. *Behavior Therapy, 27,* 171–186.

Chapter 7
School Consultation

Men live in a community in virtue of the things which they have in common; and communication is the way in which they come to possess things in common. What they must have in common in order to form a community or society are aims, beliefs, aspirations, knowledge—a common understanding—as the sociologists say. Such things cannot be passed physically from one to another, like bricks... The communication which ensures participation in a common understanding is one which secures similar emotional and intellectual dispositions—like ways of responding to expectations and requirements.
John Dewey, from *Democracy and Education* (1916)

Practitioners can find success when working directly with adolescents and their families in the manner we have laid out in the previous chapters; however, it has been our experience that comprehensive intervention requires the practitioner to collaborate directly with educators. For community-based practitioners who do not already have a relationship with school professionals, the initial school-entry process can be daunting. We are familiar with many failed attempts at community-school collaboration due to a wide variety of reasons, but mostly it seems that communication breaks down due to some form of mutual distrust, or when community-based practitioners unwittingly transgress school conventions. Educators might also ignore recommendations provided by community providers, for example, when the suggestions seem unversed in educational or institutional practices.[1] School-based mental-health professionals have an obvious advantage, of course, but successful teacher consultation always requires that the consultant effectively communicates with teachers and demonstrates a valuable expertise in behavior management. Part

[1] In one instance, a community-based practitioner recommended that an adolescent attempting to quit smoking be allowed to chew gum in his classes. Although such a recommendation might be perfectly reasonable in other settings, the psychologist had clearly not weighed the implication of allowing 1 student in a class of 30 such liberties, particularly when the purpose was to replace an undesirable behavior.

B. K. Schultz, S. W. Evans, *A Practical Guide to Implementing School-Based Interventions for Adolescents with ADHD*, DOI 10.1007/978-1-4939-2677-0_7

of this involves learning about the school system (if needed), garnering the support of the building administrators, identifying the *key opinion leaders* in the schools (see Atkins et al. 2003), and respecting the overwhelming challenges that teachers face in the classroom daily.

What assistance can consultants offer teachers? In our experience, there is much that teachers can learn when it comes to student behavior problems. Teacher training programs rarely provide more than one class on behavior management (State et al. 2011), leaving teachers to learn these skills "on the job." Common attempts to train in-service teachers, including conferences and workshops, largely fail to change classroom practices (Joyce and Showers 2002). The result is that teachers feel unprepared to address disruptive student behaviors. Surveys of in-service teachers have found that only one-third feel very well prepared to address the needs of students with disabilities in general (Parsad et al. 2001), and roughly one-half (52 %) identify classroom behavior management as the area of greatest need (Coalition for Psychology in Schools and Education 2006). The focus of this chapter is on the basic techniques of behavioral consultation in secondary schools, based on our experiences in the mentoring version of the Challenging Horizons Program (CHP). School consultation that aims to change systemic processes or classroom curricula are beyond the scope of this chapter; instead, we assume that practitioners are working directly with a target student and have the written permission of the primary caregiver to collaborate with their child's teachers. We begin by briefly reviewing best practice parameters for behavioral consultation and then describe our specific approach in the CHP.

Behavioral Consultation in Schools

All models of behavioral consultation (including CHP consultation) employ a strategy of indirect service provision whereby behavioral consultants (BCs), by definition, rarely provide direct services to students. Instead, a triadic relationship is forged between the BC and the school professional, or *consultee,* who then provides direct services to the student (see Fig. 7.1; Kratochwill et al. 2002, p. 583). The goal of behavioral consultation in schools is, as its name would imply, to improve student behavior, but there is also an attempt to strengthen the behavior management skills of the consultee. Hence, school-based BCs have two clients—the student and the consultee—thereby defining success as improvement in student behavior, teacher response, or (ideally) both. Of course, there are other stakeholders outside of the triadic relationship of consultation, including parents, school administrators, and the wider community, who have additional criteria for success. For example, a parent might be genuinely pleased to hear that her son's classroom behavior had improved but is perhaps more interested in seeing his grades improve. Among school administrators, the most salient indicators of success often involve decreased office referrals and suspensions. BCs can expect to find many definitions for success, depending on the stakeholder.

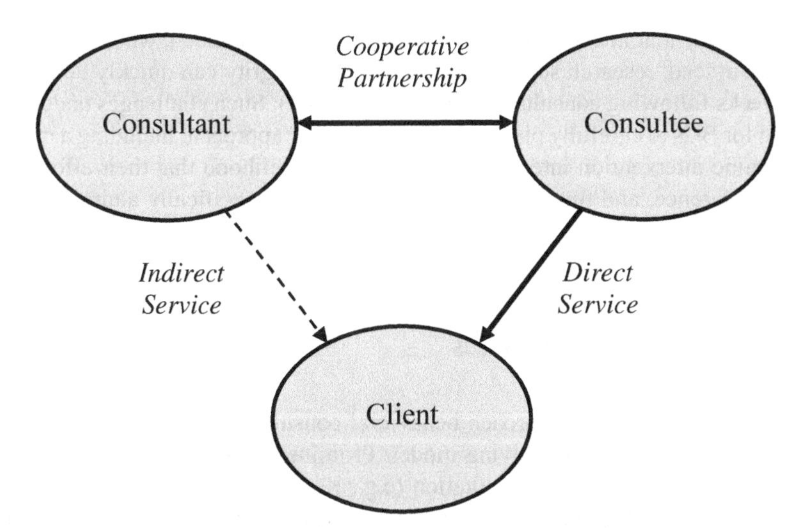

Fig. 7.1 Triadic relationship of consultation

Advantages of Behavior Consultation As a service delivery model, school consultation offers several advantages over direct service provision, including (a) efficiency, (b) improved teacher efficacy, and (c) treatment acceptability. First, consultation efficiently provides teachers with the information necessary to implement behavioral interventions to a wide range of students (Frank and Kratochwill 2010). Teachers who receive consultative services are likely to develop skills and resources that are reusable with other students in the future, possibly before more intense interventions are needed (Kratochwill et al. 2002). Second, the capacity of teachers to intervene in behavior problems can increase following direct consultation with a consultant (Sterling-Turner et al. 2002). Such findings support the underlying logic of consultation, although many questions exist as to how best to maintain quality interventions over time (see Challenges below). Third, teachers generally value behavioral consultation and express a desire for consultants to increase the time they devote to consultation (Gilman and Gabriel 2004). Indeed, school psychologists appear to be increasingly using consultative strategies to address student needs (Reschly 2000), which suggests that school-based professionals find consultation beneficial.

Challenges of School Consultation Despite the potential advantages cited above, there have been dissenting voices in the literature. For example, Witt et al. (1996) found little evidence to support the effectiveness of behavioral consultation and concluded that this was due to poor treatment integrity. In other words, consultation does not guarantee that consultees implement interventions as intended (Moncher and Prinz 1991). Typical approaches to behavioral consultation are overly reliant on "discussions with teacher consultees, rather than objective assessment of actual behavior changes." Without objective measures of child or teacher behavior, a BC might conclude that interventions were implemented as intended, when in fact they were not. Indeed, research suggests that treatment integrity can quickly deteriorate in the weeks following consultation (Noell et al. 2002). Such challenges underscore the need for BCs to carefully plan and implement their approach, including a method to determine intervention integrity, to increase the likelihood that their efforts will make a difference, and the CHP consultation strategy specifically addresses these concerns.

The Problem-Solving Process

There are several ways to approach behavioral consultation, but perhaps the most widely used is the problem-solving model. Prominent authors in the field across many areas of school-based consultation (e.g., Kovaleski 2002; Rosenfield 2002; Zins and Erchul 2002) advocate a problem-solving approach because it is flexible enough to account for the unique challenges of each individual child (Reschly 2004). In short, the problem-solving consultative process incorporates five basic steps:

1. Form the consultative relationship
2. Identify the problem
3. Select an intervention
4. Implement an intervention
5. Evaluate outcomes (Kratochwill et al. 2002)

In keeping with the relevant literature, we employ a problem-solving approach to consultation in the CHP. What follows is a description of each stage of consultation, using actual examples from previous CHP experiences.

Step One: Forging the Consultative Relationship

In practice, the consultant–consultee relationship is the sine qua non of consultation, as change begins with, and expands from, these interactions. Recognizing this, school consultants have traditionally valued a cooperative, nonhierarchical relationship with consultees. In this fashion, consultants and consultees become partners in the consultative process (Allen and Graden 2002). There is mutual recognition that each participant is a professional in their respective domain; consultants are experts in mental health and consultees are experts in schools and education. Accordingly, consultees are free to accept or reject consultant suggestions based on their appraisal of school or classroom variables. Such nonhierarchical cooperation is thought to foster mutual respect and commitment, while avoiding feelings of coercion among consultees (Zins and Erchul 2002).

Although some authors describe the consultant–consultee relationships as collaborative in nature (e.g., Kratochwill et al. 2002), others suggest that the consultant–consultee relationship differs from true collaboration in that consultants exert unequal *influence* within these interactions (e.g., Erchul and Martens 2002). In any event, it is important to note that consultation does not resemble supervision. Consultants report that their influence derives primarily from their credibility, including the relevance of the information they provide and their perceived expertise, rather than from hierarchical pressures or consequences for noncooperation (Erchul et al. 2001). For this reason, Zins and Erchul (2002) describe the consultant–consultee relationship as a cooperative partnership, where consultants guide the process while consultees provide much of the background information about the student and their needs (p. 627).

Forging relationships with educators is vital to the success of consultation, but doing so is not always straightforward. In the CHP, we establish rapport with teachers by developing a sense of shared commitment, emphasizing the voluntary nature of teacher participation, and avoiding potential disagreements around controversial mental health labels (e.g., attention deficit hyperactivity disorder, ADHD).

Communicate a Shared Commitment Our relationship with participating teachers *ideally* begins with brief trainings at the participating schools.[2] During these trainings, we provide teachers with the relevant resources and present an overview of current literature on adolescents with ADHD. Research suggests that the consultative relationship benefits when consultees are knowledgeable about the interventions the BC might suggest. For instance, Vereb and DiPerna (2004) found that the more teachers know about ADHD and its treatment, the more likely they were to find evidence-based interventions acceptable. Moreover, the initial group trainings allow the CHP consultant to empathize with teacher concerns, which helps to establish an environment of shared commitment. When consultants share stories of students losing important belongings, having disorganized possessions, misreading social cues, and so forth, educators can easily identify with the experiences.

Emphasize Treatment Feasibility Our experience consulting with schools has been that of university-based researchers. When introducing our research projects in schools, it is not uncommon for teachers to have concerns about the potential workload of participation. To alleviate such concerns, we generally emphasize that *feasibility* is of paramount concern, and that we will only target interventions that are realistic for teachers to accomplish. To this end, we purposely use tentative language when introducing new ideas (Zins and Erchul 2002). For example, the BC might offer the caveat: "*I'm not sure if this intervention strategy will work, given your time constraints and other concerns. Can we give it a try and then meet again next week to talk about how it went?*" In our previous experiences in the CHP, this

---

[2] We use the term "ideally" here because school sites will vary in their ability to allot time for training. Typically, schools provide their teachers with "in-service" trainings at the beginning of each school year and we strive to participate in these meetings whenever possible. When this is not possible, consultants will need to provide an overview of the program and answer teacher questions individually during the first stages of consultation.

strategy was largely effective. The point is to highlight how the CHP was designed to implement strategies that have been shown to be realistic in school settings. Moreover, CHP consultants invite school consultees to help make such determinations, rather than trying to convince school professionals that our interventions are universally viable and effective.

Avoid Mental Health Labels Unfortunately, public perceptions of ADHD and other conditions do not always match clinical realities, and many treat ADHD in particular in a cavalier manner. ADHD has become a modern euphemism to explain away the most trivial instances of forgetfulness, restlessness, and social miscue, and CHP consultants might find that school-based professionals have these same biases. To lessen semantic debates fueled by the gap between professional and public opinions, it is prudent to avoid controversial labels whenever possible. Instead, whenever the topic is raised, CHP consultants readily admit the limitations of the label and then shift focus onto the student's *impairment*. Even when school professionals question a diagnosis, they still recognize the social and academic challenges children face. For example, children with ADHD are at greater risk of alcohol abuse (Molina et al. 2007), substance abuse (Molina and Pelham 2003), and school dropout (Kent et al. 2011) than their non-ADHD peers. By forecasting the student's long-term performance, the BC and consultee can often achieve consensus and focus their efforts on reducing the likelihood of unwanted outcomes rather than debating labels. Consider the following conversation between a CHP consultant and consultee:

Consultant: I'll admit, I'm not a big fan of the label [ADHD]. But if you think about the challenges they [students with ADHD] are facing now, and the kinds of pitfalls they'll face as they get older, I think we can probably agree that this group is especially at-risk for making very poor choices.

Consultee: I can see Ricky getting sucked into the peer pressure around drugs and alcohol—he can't say no to anyone now.

Consultant: And the research is consistent with that observation. So to me, the ADHD label can be useful, insofar as it helps us identify children at risk for poor outcomes; so we can work now to prevent problems down the road.

Notice that the consultant reframes ADHD as *at-risk*. In general, this strategy helps to avoid any biases that a teacher may have toward the ADHD label, and refocuses the consultation on the functional impairments that are the subject of step two.

Step Two: Identifying the Problem

Problems addressed by the BC are often defined by discrepancies between students' observed and required levels of behavioral performance (Kratochwill et al. 2002), but BCs and consultees do not always agree on which discrepancies require intervention and which to prioritize. As a result, it is important to define problems in observable and measurable terms (Zins and Erchul 2002). Such objective terms help to

(a) unify the various perspectives on the behavior, and (b) identify ways to measure the problem over time. For example, teachers working with a previous CHP participant were concerned about his frequent "meltdowns." Although the teachers were clear on what this meant, it was important to define a meltdown by its component behaviors. As it turned out, this student's meltdowns included tearfulness, abusive language, and physical aggression toward peers. With a little effort, the BC was able to record and track these behaviors using an agreed-upon definition, which is essential for the remainder of the problem-solving process. It is important to note that educators generally do not have an extensive background in behavior tracking and data collection, so concepts such as observable and measurable—which seem second nature to behavioral therapists—may require some explanation. Mostly this can be done through paraphrasing and reframing the concerns shared by the consultee (e.g., "*It sounds like the most disruptive part of the meltdown involves verbally abusive behavior, and we can define that as verbalizations that would typically annoy an adult. How often would you say that his behavior crosses that line during a typical meltdown?*").

Traditionally, consultants encourage consultees to take a lead in identifying which student behaviors to prioritize, based on an assumption of *ecological validity*. In other words, consultants have traditionally relied on teachers to define target behaviors, presumably because their impressions of students are authoritative. Others have questioned this assumption (e.g., Witt et al. 1996) and argued that it may be more accurate to assume consultees will at times need help in identifying *keystone* behaviors (Allen and Graden 2002, p. 571). Keystone behaviors are the underlying issues or antecedents that contribute to, or cause, the identified problem behavior. Conceptually, when keystone behaviors are addressed, positive change occurs across multiple behavioral domains. For example, an adolescent with ADHD might argue with his teachers over test and quiz scores, and teachers might readily identify the student's argumentativeness as a target for intervention. Argumentativeness would seem a straightforward behavioral concern, but these behaviors might actually stem from frustration the student feels because of his poor study skills. By learning effective study strategies, the student might experience success on tests, thus improving his grades and reducing the confrontations with teachers. CHP consultants generally follow the consultee's lead when identifying problem behavior, but listen carefully for clues that might point to keystone behaviors. In some cases, consultants meet with the student and ask for their impression of the problem as another means of listening for keystone behaviors. By design, CHP interventions generally target the most common keystone behaviors for adolescents with ADHD, based on our previous experiences; however, we anticipate that consultants will occasionally encounter new behaviors that will require some customization of our interventions in order to meet students' individual needs.

Identify Keystone Behaviors Identifying keystone behaviors can be difficult for educators in secondary schools because they typically see students during one class period per day. From these short observations, it can be difficult for educators to identify "themes" that emerge around a set of problem behaviors. For example, teachers of one student participating in the CHP reported that the child exhibited frequent off-task behaviors in class during direct instruction (i.e., class lectures). Teachers described the creative ways the student found to sit in his chair and how his constant shifting and squirming distracted his classmates. The teacher expected students to take notes during periods of direct instruction, but this student never actually took notes. When the consultant analyzed the situation with the teacher, he discovered that the desired behavior (note taking) was actually *discouraged* for this student. A well-intentioned but counterproductive 504 Plan[3] stipulated that this student received copies of the notes from his teachers. Together, the consultant and consultee devised a plan to have this student take notes in class and then compare his notes to those that his teachers provided after class. In this way, the student still received the class note accommodation, but only after he attempted to take notes independently. To motivate the student, the teacher provided classroom privileges for improvements in note taking, and this led to a reduction in off-task disruptions and a modest improvement in grades. Had the disruptive behavior been the primary target of interventions instead of the class note-taking activity, our outcomes might have been more limited.

Consider Contextual Factors When recommending interventions, it is important for BC's to consider the context and purpose of the target behavior. The CHP consultant approaches behavior problems from an eco-behavioral framework: We assume at the outset that problems cannot be attributed solely to the individual student, but must be considered in the context of environmental factors (Allen and Graden 2002). However, this poses a potential conflict in consultation because teachers may perceive a consultant's focus on classroom factors to be an indictment of their classroom management. The consultation literature highlights the importance of assessing the classroom environment, while simultaneously advocating a nonhierarchical, cooperative relationship between consultant and consultee (e.g., Zins and Erchul 2002). To achieve both aims, the CHP consultant attributes the need for change to special conditions created by students who are "at-risk." For example, the CHP consultant might explain to a teacher that, "*Most students will respond well to the dynamic classroom environment you've created, but at-risk students often respond best to strategies that match their concrete style of thinking. Are there ways that we can make the rules and expectations more clear and consistent for Ben?*" In this example, the consultant reframes changes in the teacher's practices as matching the student's individual needs, rather than condemning the teacher's classroom management style.

In addition to the contextual factors present at the time of the consultation, there are contextual factors related to the time of year that affect the ability of the BC to identify target behaviors. Many students with ADHD perform well during the first quarter to half of the school year, but then experience a performance "crash" during the second half of the year (Evans et al. 2005). The "crash" phenomenon

[3] A 504 Plan is a type of intervention plan that students with disabilities can receive when their disabilities impede their ability to benefit from typical classroom environments. Most commonly, 504 Plans outline classroom accommodations, such as additional time on tests, prioritized seating, and the use of electronic calculators.

can provide a challenging situation for the BC because parents and teachers often underestimate a child's academic impairment until late in the school year when performance rapidly deteriorates, thereby making intervention difficult. Although a proactive, preventive approach would suggest that efforts begin at a point in the school year when students are exhibiting minimal to moderate impairment, this might not occur because many educators try interventions only after impairment is widely recognized (Gilman and Gabriel 2004). The CHP consultant warns about this pattern and relies on prior experiences to provide examples. Still, even with encouragement to be proactive, the consultant might find that many consultees will opt to use one or two interventions early in the school year and then expand only after students exhibit severe problems. Proactive strategies might prevent, diminish, or delay these declines, so it is important for the consultant to encourage a proactive intervention strategy even when students are performing satisfactorily.

Previous studies of the CHP have demonstrated that this strategy helps to prevent the academic crash students with ADHD often experience. Schultz et al. (2009) conducted a survival analysis examining how long CHP participants were able to maintain a grade point average (GPA) above failing (1.0) during their sixth and seventh grade years when compared to a group of students with ADHD who did not receive the CHP. Results suggest that the students who did not receive the CHP were significantly more likely to experience failing grading periods than were CHP participants, even after statistically controlling for the influence of student intelligence (IQ). By the end of both school years, the cumulative percentage of CHP participants who consistently maintained a passing GPA remained above 70%, while passing rates in the nonintervention group fell as low as 48%. Thus, it appears that one of the main benefits of the CHP is prevention of failing report cards, and it is important to convey such expectations to consultees rather than unrealistically suggesting that the CHP will consistently help "C" students become "A" students.

Step Three: Selecting an Intervention

Once consultees define a problem behavior and understand the context, it is a common recommendation to collect baseline data before formally introducing an intervention. In the CHP, formal baseline measures—such as a series of classroom observations or teacher ratings over time—may not be feasible. We have found, for example, that the consultative relationship can suffer when consultees are required to painstakingly collect data for a small subset of students. Such uneven attention to students coupled with the added workload has the potential to breed discontent, so CHP consultants delicately balance the need for valid assessment data and the need to maintain rapport. For these reasons, CHP consultants typically turn to global performance indicators (i.e., universal measures), including report cards, grade books, and school attendance records, or teacher report, as proxy baseline measures.

Using universal measures (or other agreed-upon measures) as a starting point, the BC and consultee brainstorm potential intervention options. It is important for the consultee's suggestions and insights to be valued throughout this process (Kratochwill et al. 2002), and in the CHP this is accomplished in part by giving the consultee ownership over the intervention planning process. Thus, in the CHP, we enter the consultative relationship with a predefined set of interventions, but we have purposely simplified these interventions down to core elements that appear necessary for the intervention to work. For example, an intervention designed to improve assignment tracking skills (discussed in Chap. 3) includes three core elements:

- The student keeps a written system for documenting academic assignments.
- A consultee checks this system for accuracy and legibility at least weekly.
- The consultee rewards successful tracking or helps the student correct problems.

The CHP consultant uses these core elements to communicate the minimal implementation criteria to consultees, thereby allowing teachers the flexibility to modify the details to fit their schedules, resources, and other practical considerations. This promotes teacher engagement in the selection process, while still adhering to evidence-based techniques. Some researchers refer to this strategy as "flexibility within integrity," meaning that the interventionist is free to modify the intervention to meet their situation, while still using the components that are vital to the success of the intervention (Kendallet al. 2008).

Step Four: Implementing an Intervention

After identifying a problem and choosing an intervention, the consultative process moves into the implementation phase. At this point, CHP consultants and consultees set a timeframe for implementation and plan to meet at regular intervals to review progress. Generally, the consultant does not actively participate in the actual implementation of the intervention unless such assistance is required (e.g., the consultee requests a live demonstration of the intervention; the consultee–student relationship is strained). As mentioned above, one advantage of consultation over direct service models is that the mental health professional provides services to many adolescents through the intermediation of the consultee. Thus, CHP consultants generally encourage consultees to implement the interventions independently, and then follow-up in the next step of the process.

Step Five: Evaluating Outcomes

The final step of consultation is determining whether the student's behavior falls within an acceptable range following the intervention (Kratochwill et al. 2002). At this stage, the BC and consultee revisit the definition of the target behavior and collect data to compare to the baseline data or another agreed-upon benchmark. One of the most important aspects of this step is assuring that the intervention is implemented as intended (i.e., treatment integrity). However, ensuring adequate levels of treatment integrity is difficult, especially in the dynamic environments of secondary schools. To ensure accurate implementation, it is important to collect data that directly answer this question.

Noell and colleagues (2005) compared several techniques of consultation and assessed their impact on treatment integrity. It appeared that the most effective consultative strategy was "performance feedback," which involved frequent follow-up meetings to graph treatment integrity and behavioral outcomes. Performance feedback procedures require the BC to track indicators of intervention quality. For example, in a behavior report card intervention, the actual reports that go home to parents can be collected, evaluated, and then summarized for consultees. This approach to achieving treatment integrity appears to promote accountability (Noell et al. 2002). In actual practice, however, performance feedback strategies are often difficult to implement. In the Noell and colleagues (2005) study, for example, the ratio of BCs to consultees was roughly 1:7. In the CHP studies to date, the ratios have exceeded 1:10. In order for performance feedback to work in actual practice, CHP consultants use a specific strategy of performance feedback, which we describe later in this chapter.

In consultation, it is important to encourage high expectations, but to bring those expectations within a range that is realistic and attainable. Our goal as CHP consultants is to achieve optimal functioning *relative to the student's individual capabilities*. Thus, we define academic goals relative to the first grading period, which is typically the strongest time of the year for students with ADHD. In effect, this defines success as a lack of a crash, but such goals can prove uninspiring for many consultees. Nevertheless, levels of achievement and classroom behavior better than the first few weeks of school rarely occur for youth with ADHD and become increasingly unlikely as the school year continues.

It is important for the CHP consultant to keep measures of change relevant to consultees. For example, changes in behavior ratings scales (even those completed by the consultee) are not nearly as compelling as data based on daily school activities. Although teachers may appreciate the fact that scores on a rating scale of social functioning have improved, for example, they may be enthusiastic only when there is a reduction in classroom disturbance, an increase in attendance, or an improvement in homework completion. For this reason, we attempt to collect data relative to practical functioning issues that confront teachers daily.

Building a Mentorship

Our experiences in the CHP have led to some practical insights into behavioral consultation for secondary teachers, but we also recognize that many areas need improvement. For example, we were able to establish rapport with most teachers in our previous studies by emphasizing a sense of shared commitment, valuing teacher feedback, and avoiding the controversial ADHD label wherever possible. We have also found it useful to identify one teacher volunteer to take a lead in working with each student participant, who we refer to as the *mentor* (Note: we will use the term "mentor" throughout the remainder of this chapter to refer to the primary consultee for each student). However, once the consultation process began, we often ran into difficulties. In one instance, a mentor expressed concern that his rating scale data could affect the parent's decisions about medications, which made him uncomfortable. Despite our assurances, he chose to discontinue his participation in the program, making it necessary for us to find another mentor. So although we cannot claim a perfect satisfaction rate among all teachers who have participated in the CHP, we continually search for ways to meet the needs and expectations of mentors to the degree possible.

We designed the interview to be informative while maintaining an effective relationship with the mentor. As we stated above, the consultative relationship is the most important component of the process, so it is important to protect this relationship throughout the problem identification and intervention stages. Later, we also discuss common challenges and several strategies for addressing those challenges.

Interviewing the Mentor

For each student participant, CHP consultants will conduct an interview with the students' identified mentor. The goals of the interview are to (a) obtain the teacher's perspective on the student's most problematic behaviors, areas of impaired functioning, and strengths that may compensate for these problem areas, and (b) identify the CHP intervention/s that will best address these problems. We have compiled several example questions in Appendix G, but consultants are not limited to these questions. Consultants might also ask about the teacher's classroom rules, her behavior management plans, and what behavioral interventions she already uses to motivate children toward appropriate behavior. The consultant might also ask about an existing school-wide behavior system—if one exists—and use this system as a foundation for individual interventions for CHP participants. Further, consultants should not enter into new consultative relationships assuming that the mentor lacks usable skills; in fact, consultants may encounter "master teachers" who have very effective classroom management skills that can be integrated into the interventions. Whenever possible, we praise teachers for the interventions that they have taken the initiative to implement prior to consultation.

Toward the end of the interview, CHP consultants should summarize the entire discussion and begin to segue toward intervention planning. For example, the consultant might summarize the interview in the following manner:

> Let me see if I can summarize what we've said so far… It sounds like you have several concerns when it comes to Bobby, and some of what you've done so far has been helpful, but not 100 % successful. Of all the things that we have discussed, I'm most impressed with your classroom management strategy; and I share your concern that, for whatever reason, Bobby hasn't adapted to the classroom the way other students have. Specifically, it sounds like Bobby's tendency to complain about classroom expectations is perhaps the *most* troubling and disruptive behavior. Is that a fair assessment?

The summary is an important stage in the initial interview because many mentors will use this time to "vent" frustrations relative to the student. Although some venting is to be expected, the conversation can disintegrate into endless complaining if the consultant fails to paraphrase and shift gears to problem solving. Ultimately, an attempt must be made to identify a single behavior (i.e., keystone behavior) that might be targeted by an intervention. But of course, the consultant offers guesses, and invites the mentor to either agree or disagree by asking, "*Is that a fair assessment?*" In situations where the mentor struggles to identify one key area of concern, the consultant might offer the following analogy:

> Sometimes students enter the classroom with so many concerns that it can be nearly impossible to think of just one or two areas to address with an intervention. But, just as astronomers use telescopes to focus on one star at a time, we might learn a lot about how to help Bobby by focusing in on just one or two of his needs. So, if we were to select just one or two things, where do you think we should start?

If the consultant is unable to help the teacher identify behavior(s) to address in an intervention, the consultant can wait until their next consultation meeting and track student performance (i.e., gather additional baseline data) between sessions. Consultants do not have to have a full commitment from the mentor at the initial meeting, but the consultant should encourage the mentor to consider interventions for the child as early as possible.

Common Challenges

Through our experiences, we have identified a list of concerns commonly voiced by teachers, as well as challenging situations that frequently emerge in the context of a school-based consultation. Below we provide a list of common challenges we have encountered:

1. The teacher is unfamiliar with the recommended intervention.
2. The teacher reports that he/she has previously tried the intervention and is skeptical about its effectiveness.
3. The teacher expresses that s/he does not want to do the intervention.
4. The teacher wants to use an intervention that is not on the CHP-recommended list.
5. The teacher reports that the intervention takes too much time.
6. The teacher believes her intervention is effective, when other indicators (a graph of student behaviors; parent report) suggest it could be improved.
7. The teacher does not have the data/tracking sheet completed at the agreed upon consultation session.
8. The student–teacher relationship is highly negative, such that it is negatively impacting the potential success of the intervention.
9. The teacher wants to use the consultation session to vent rather than problem solve.
10. The teacher/classroom lacks foundational skills required for a CHP intervention.

It is beyond the scope of this chapter to go through all possible challenges that a CHP consultant might encounter, but there are general strategies and "process comments" that consultants can use to move beyond common roadblocks. In most instances, the process is the same, only the context differs. In Box 7.1, we provide specific strategies to work around some of the more common roadblocks. The purpose of our examples is not to pre-program CHP consultants with scripted talking points. Rather, our goal is to underscore the manner in which consultants convey warmth, empathy, and cooperation through their words and tone. Note that in each of our examples, the consultant shows collegial respect for the teacher consultee, and does not use her position to coerce or chide the teacher into cooperation. The consultant's responses act to validate teacher concerns, define and reinforce the cooperative partnership, encourage the teacher to openly express their concerns, convey confidence in the likelihood of success, and propose feasible steps toward a common goal.

Box 7.1: Common Difficulties in Consultation

In Chapter 7, Box 7.1, please delete the current text (too lengthy) and replace with the following: "In recent years, researchers and practitioners have increasingly noted the challenges involved in school consultation. In fact, some have started to apply motivational interviewing principles to school consultation in the hope of improving the likelihood of success (e. g., Herman et al. 2014). A review of those developments is beyond the scope of this book, but we have developed several practical strategies for use by CHP consultants. For example, when teachers express skepticism that psychosocial interventions can be effective, we reflect those concerns and then focus on the teacher's motivation for moving forward. Consider the following reflections:

> It can be frustrating when students break the rules this often.
> It sounds like you have invested a lot of time already and nothing seems to work.

By reflecting these concerns, we communicate warmth and empathy (i.e., common factors). Then our goal is to shift toward possible exceptions to the rules or the potential benefits for overcoming the challenges. For example:

> It feels like things have gone off the rails and you would be interested in learning new ways to get things going again.
> Are there things that worked in the past that we might be able to repurpose for the challenges we have now?

Similarly, if the concerns revolve around time constraints (a very common concern in schools), we start by reflecting those concerns:

> You are pulled in a lot of different directions.
> Focusing this much time and effort on one student can seem taxing in the short term.

Then we emphasize the issue of feasibility (discussed earlier):

> I'd like us to work together to see if we can come up with something that is truly feasible, given your time constraints.

Perhaps we can find efficient interventions to prevent worse problems later down the road.
Our goal will be to find ways to taper your involvement over time, while we slowly increase our expectations for this student.

Readers who are interested in learning more about motivational strategies in school consultation can refer to Herman and colleagues (2014).

Introducing CHP Interventions

CHP consultants guide teacher mentors toward interventions that are most likely to be effective, given the student's behavioral needs and the context. In general, the CHP employs many of the same academic and social interventions that are discussed in the previous chapters; however, consultants and mentors individualize these interventions to match each student's specific needs, with the resources and abilities of the mentor in mind. For these reasons, we will not revisit the interventions already discussed (e.g., organization tracking, assignment notebook monitoring) because we assume most readers can anticipate how these interventions can be modified in a consultative setting. Instead, we will focus on an aspect of consultation that is perhaps the single most important component to ensure treatment integrity: performance feedback. We have devised a very specific strategy for performance feedback, and we will turn our attention to that aspect now.

Performance Feedback

Performance feedback is a vital part of the consultation process, both to measure treatment outcomes and to ensure treatment integrity. It is important to note that our strategy for performance feedback in the CHP requires consultants to collect data from mentors on a regular basis, and then review those data at specific times. As mentioned above, other data collected in the CHP comes from the universal measures of school functioning (e.g., report cards, disciplinary referrals, and attendance records), but those data are often difficult to interpret[4] and insufficient to

[4] For example, administrators from one school that participated in the CHP used a flowchart of escalating consequences for behavior problems, starting with in-school detentions and culminating with out-of-school suspension or even expulsion. Although this strategy discouraged most students from repeat rule violations, many students with ADHD quickly moved through the flowchart and ultimately received suspensions for relatively minor infractions. In one instance, a CHP participant received an out-of-school suspension for possessing the *materials* needed to shoot spitballs, not for actually shooting spitballs. In comparison, behavioral referrals at another school resulted in academic probation. Under this system, students gradually lost privileges in response to behavior problems. In one instance, a student in the CHP was removed from his sports team—one of his

inform mentor performance. As a result, consultants focus their feedback primarily on the "permanent products" created during the CHP interventions, rather than the distal outcomes. Of course, a long-term outcome like a reduction in disciplinary referrals is a desirable outcome and may be reason to compliment the mentor, but the CHP consultants focus mainly on student and mentor performance at a session-by-session, "molecular" level. Achieving this level of behavior tracking will require training and ongoing coaching.

Although competing definitions of performance feedback can be found in the consultation literature, the core element appears to be an ongoing training strategy (i.e., learn, work, and learn), where brief didactic instruction is paired with experiential exercises and follow-up collaboration. In this way, performance feedback differs from typical approaches to teacher training, which are most often didactic, short in duration, and lacking in follow-up support services (Mullens et al. 1996; USDOE 1999), and inconsistent with what is known about adult skill acquisition (Blank et al. 2008; Mullens et al. 1996; Stuart et al. 2004; USDOE 1999). We argue that ongoing school consultation offers an exceptional mechanism for active professional development. Indeed, Han and Weiss's (2005) review of factors affecting teachers' intervention implementation found that ongoing feedback designed to enhance skills taught in training was strongly associated with intervention integrity, sustainability, and student outcomes.

Research on Performance Feedback

Over the last 15 years, several multiple-baseline studies have examined the impact of performance feedback on teacher adherence to a recommended procedure. Despite some inconsistencies, these studies provide compelling data that performance feedback produces higher levels of teacher adherence relative to either baseline conditions or an alternative strategy (e.g., Codding et al. 2005; Noell et al. 1997; 2014; Solomon et al. 2012; Witt et al. 1997). For example, one study found that among three teachers, the average adherence rates during baseline was less than 5%, followed by rates between 9 and 37% during standard consultation, followed by rates between 60 and 83% once performance feedback was added (Jones et al. 1997). Four other studies, including one randomized group design, demonstrated that when teachers were provided with performance feedback, integrity increased above 80% and student performance increased during this time (Noell et al. 1997, 2005; Witt et al. 1997). These studies demonstrate that the use of performance feedback enhances teacher's intervention integrity when offered on a daily schedule (e.g., Noell et al. 1997), weekly schedule (Mortenson and Witt 1998), bi-weekly schedule (Codding et al. 2005), and in a response-dependent schedule (Gilbertson et al. 2007). Further, some studies suggest that integrity declines once performance feedback was removed (Noell et al. 1997), while others offer some optimism that

few positive connections with the school—following an incident of horseplay that got out of control. In short, we have found that responses to behavioral referrals are not always valid or reliable outcome measures.

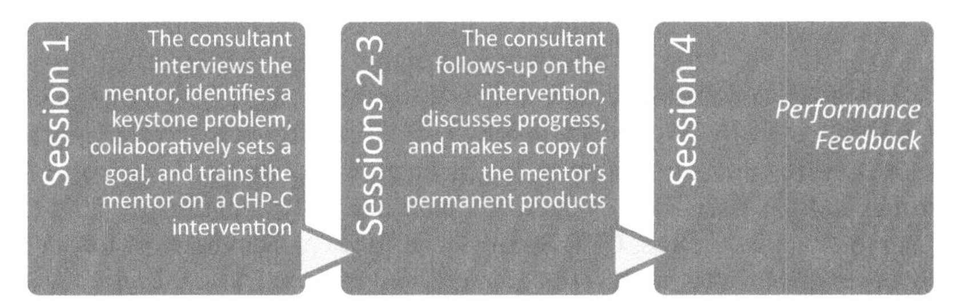

Fig. 7.2 Example timeline of consultative process

teacher integrity is maintained longer following performance feedback conditions relative to training-only conditions (Coddington et al. 1995; Witt et al. 1997). However, across all studies, data points for evaluating maintenance are limited.

Implementing Performance Feedback

In the CHP, consultants collect "permanent product" data from mentors, and these data form the basis of the performance feedback. Specifically, this involves copying data from the mentor's intervention tracking sheets, which are the same as those provided in the Appendices (e.g., "Organization Intervention Monitoring Record" in Appendix C). Data collection is a regular component of all consultation meetings, both before and during the implementation of an intervention. We have found that mentors vary in the degree of follow-through with interventions, so at times, the consultant may record that student–mentor sessions either did not occur or did not involve intervention tracking. Whenever the mentor and student meet, the expectation is that some form of permanent product will result, and the CHP consultants record these data during the subsequent consultation sessions.

The timeline of consultation leading up to the implementation of an intervention varies, depending on several factors. If, for example, a mentor is already using an intervention that is consistent with the CHP, the consultant could conceivably use the first consultation session to build a relationship, complete the initial interview, and get a commitment from the mentor to adopt effective tracking records. In this scenario, the consultant would review progress and record the permanent products as provided by the mentor in the second and third consultation sessions. Then, in the fourth session, performance feedback would begin (see Fig. 7.2). However, we find that in most cases, performance feedback starts much later because mentors struggle with initiating interventions. We encourage our consultants to take cues from the mentor and, if needed, divide the early steps of consultation across several sessions to ensure mentor understanding and "buy in." Another factor that might delay the start of performance feedback sessions is the amount of data collected by the mentor over time. If, for example, the mentor meets with the student once per week and only collects one datum at each meeting, the consultant would wait to initiate performance feedback until enough data are available to graph trends (see discussion of the "4–4 Rule" in the "Prepare Mentors for Special Feedback Sessions with Students" section below).

Performance feedback typically involves a four-step process including: (a) review of data, (b) praise for correct implementation, (c) discussion of corrective feedback, and (d) discussion of questions or concerns (Codding et al. 2005). In addition to these usual steps, CHP consultants also (e) prepare mentors for special feedback sessions with students. To accomplish all of these tasks, the CHP consultant will want to establish a consistent structure and routine for each performance feedback session. Prior to each performance feedback session, consultants review the student's progress data, prepare graphs (where applicable), and prepare discussion points (see Module 7.1). During the session, consultants take notes using the feedback template provided in Appendix H.

Review of Data Consultants begin the session by reviewing the student progress data. CHP consultants use line graphs to display these data along with a trend line to help determine if the student appears to be making progress. Typically, we construct these graphs for teachers and then present them in the feedback sessions, but some teachers prefer to use their own tracking software as the intervention progresses. Either way, our focus is on the most recent data and how these data points affect the trend.

Praise for Correct Implementation In cases of success (i.e., positive trend line), the consultant is enthusiastic, praises the teacher's efforts, and expresses curiosity about the factors that contributed to the success. In addition, consultants and mentors brainstorm ways to expand on this success. Consider the following interaction between a CHP consultant and a mentor:

Consultant: Wow! It looks like Skylar met her bookbag organization goal three meetings in a row—each time you checked her performance was 100 %. That's exciting.

Consultee: Yes, I am glad to see she's finally making progress.

Consultant: I know she had a slow start with this intervention. What do you think helped her make this change this past week?

Consultee: I don't really know. I assumed it was that her mom was giving her medication regularly. But you know, at the beginning of the week, she also showed me a picture of the rabbits that she was showing at the fair, and I was able to talk with her about this because my son used to show rabbits when he was younger. It was the first time that I've had a positive interaction with Skylar in a long time. I felt like she was more positive to me this week and I had a more positive outlook about her too. It was like that interaction set the tone for us for the week.

Consultant: Hmm. That's interesting. It sounds like it was a good experience for her. How did that positive tone[5] have an impact on the intervention?

[5] The consultant is reflecting the teacher's language here when she uses the word "tone." In general, it is better to use the teacher's language when describing changes, rather than offering value judgments.

Consultee: Well, I think I was a little more gentle in how I gave her feedback about her organization, and I think she was more accepting of that feedback. She really didn't argue with me this week.

Consultant: I wonder if we can capitalize on this situation? Do you think there is something that you can do to continue this positive tone between the two of you?

Consultee: Well, I guess I can try to find an opportunity to connect with her once before class someday.

Consultant: You know, I think that would great. Perhaps we'll find that by spending some free time discussing non-academic things, you might see improvements in her classroom performance.[6]

Sometimes we are interested in specific thresholds of behavioral performance, such as when students achieve 70 % more items correct on an organization checklist, rather than trends over time. When such threshold-based goals are met on eight or more consecutive checks, the consultant and mentor might discuss increasing the criteria for success as a means of moving the student toward normal levels of performance (e.g., from 70 % success on a checklist to 80 %). Such decisions are made on a case-by-case basis, but our goal in consultation is to keep increasing student expectations until performance is consistent with same-age peers.

Discussion of Corrective Feedback After discussing areas of success, consultants identify areas in need of improvement. For example, a student who achieved success on his organization goal may not perform well on a second goal targeting assignment tracking. In such instances, the consultant might express concern for the lack of progress, query about the factors that may have contributed to the pattern, and brainstorm with the mentor efforts to reverse the trend in the upcoming weeks. Consider the following consultant–mentor dialogue:

Consultant: Unfortunately, it looks like Skylar did not do so well on her goal to track assignments. What do you make of this?

Consultee: Well, even though she was in better mood when interacting with me, I still don't think she was connected to the class activities. So at the end of class when I remind students what the upcoming assignments are, she looked lost and was staring out the window.

Consultant: Hmm. Do you think that Skylar is aware of the goal for her assignment tracking? Like if she walked in now, do you think she would know what the target is?

Consultee: You know I wonder about that because I overheard Mrs. Wilson, the music teacher, asking her about her report card, and she described keeping better track of her assignments, but she was really vague about it. I actually corrected her and said "Remember, Skylar, you're supposed to track at least 50 % of the core classes in order to earn points. I didn't know if she was embarrassed or

[6] Some research supports this prediction. In the parent–child interaction therapy literature, for example, it has been shown that when adult–child relationships improve, there is a positive impact on child behavior. Further, adult discipline strategies are often more effective when there is a positive parent–child relationship.

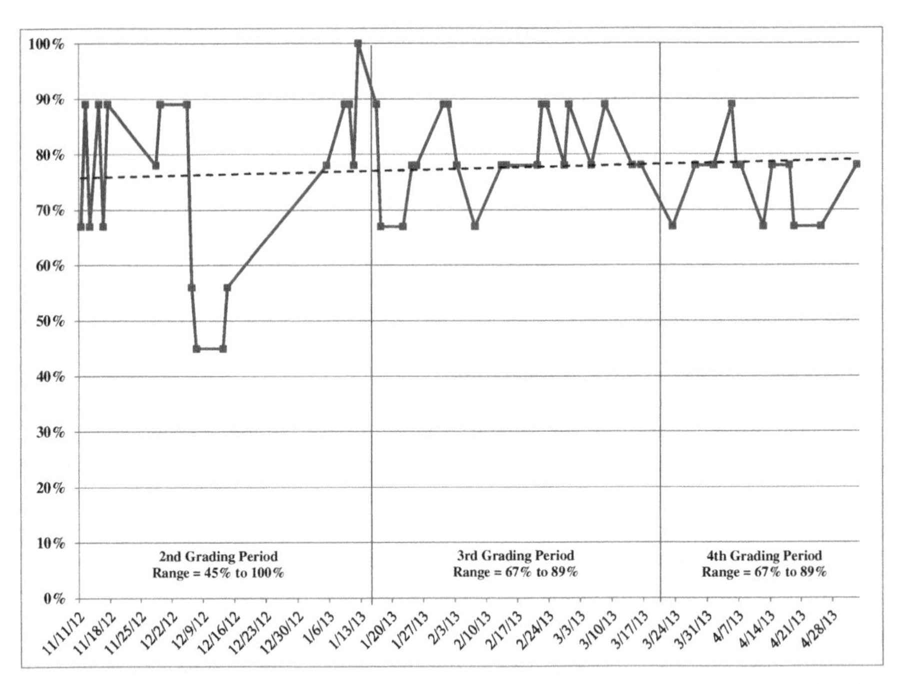

Fig. 7.3 Example of organization intervention graph. (Note: These are actual organization data collected from a middle school student. The *y*-axis represents the percentage of criteria met on a checklist measuring binder organization)

whether she really didn't know. You know, that's just Skylar. You never know if she's connected or not.

Consultant: I see. It does sound difficult to 'get through' to Skylar. Do you think it would be helpful to review her goals with her and plan some sort of cue that you'll give her in class? Would that motivate her to work toward this goal?

Consultee: I don't know. In the past, I would've said "no" because she's typically so moody toward me. But, if we stay in this good zone, she might accept that from me.

Consultant: Should we give it a try? Perhaps, as the individual work time starts you could subtly talk to her at her desk, remind her of the goal. You could just walk over and point to the assignment tracker without saying anything.

Consultee: I suppose I can try it. At least on the days that I don't think she'll snarl at me!

A line graph generated in the CHP is depicted in Fig. 7.3. The consultant might present the graph to the mentor and ask, "*This is what Skylar's progress on her organization goal has looked like over time. What do you think this says about her progress so far?*" If the CHP consultant has access to a computer during the session, he or she can add the most recent data and present the graph on the computer screen. If not, the consultant can draw in the latest data points on a hard copy.[7] In any event, the consultant shows the mentor the graph and then discusses what the graph suggests about intervention progress. In the CHP, we add an additional element that may not be shared in other programs. Once the mentor sees the graph, we encourage her to share the graph with the student at their next meeting. In our most recent study of the program, we then invited mentors to audio record that session with students so that we might also assess intervention competency or the quality of the mentor's interpersonal approach with the student. The audio recording component might prove infeasible in many settings, but we would still encourage consultants to request that the performance feedback graphs are shown to students to also get their reaction. To ensure that the graphs are easily understood by both mentors and students, we suggest tracking the following data:

CHP intervention	What to graph
1. Assignment tracking	Percentage of assignments (recorded correctly/initialed) over time
2. Organization skills	Percentage of checklist items met over time
3. Daily report card	Ratings for all behavioral targets over time
4. Study skills	Performance on relevant tests/quizzes over time
5. Note taking skills	Percentage of (main/supporting ideas) recorded correctly over time

CHP Challenging Horizons Program

In most cases, the mentor's tracking records will provide the data needed to produce a graph, with the exception of study skills. When mentors implement study skills interventions (see Chap. 4), the tracking sheets require the mentor to record examples of the study skills taught to the students, but these qualitative data do not lend themselves to graphing. As an alternative, the consultant might encourage the mentor to track the student's performance on relevant tests and quizzes following the initiation of this intervention, with the *x*-axis representing time (e.g., dates) and the *y*-axis representing either the letter grade or overall percentage.

Discussion of Questions and Concerns In the CHP, the consultant will provide performance feedback primarily from the permanent product data, as provided by the mentor, and any universal measures that may be readily available (e.g., report cards and disciplinary referrals). In other situations, consultants might directly observe teachers as they implement interventions and provide feedback on the implementation behaviors observed; however, this is difficult in secondary schools because consistent classroom observation is time and resource intensive. Typically, direct observation only occurs when mentors directly request this type of assistance. For example, mentors have requested that the consultant demonstrate an intervention with the student. In the absence of such observations, CHP consultants base

[7] To ensure that the graph has adequate space for hand-drawn lines, the consultant can add in the date of the planned performance feedback session into the spreadsheet before printing a hardcopy. When done correctly, the software will leave space for the consultant to extend the trend lines during the feedback session, using the most recent data.

their performance feedback on the permanent products, but we also encourage mentors to self-assess their implementation beyond what can be gleaned from the permanent products.[8] For example, we might simply ask, "How do you think it is going? Are you finding it easy to keep this intervention going?"

We also ask about other issues that may have come up since the start of the intervention. Keeping in mind the concept of *flexibility within integrity,* consultants and mentors may choose to bring up critical issues at the start of a consultation session, as these critical issues likely have bearing on the student and teacher data. However, consultants are careful in the management of the consultation time, so that teacher venting or crisis issues do not repeatedly detract from accomplishing the review of student data, teacher data, and the data-driven decision-making process. The latter activities are crucial to improving a student's behavior, so it is important to limit the amount of time that is spent in unproductive activities.

Prepare Mentors for Special Feedback Sessions with Students The last step of the performance feedback session is to encourage mentors to schedule a special session with students to view the graphs. These special mentor–student sessions typically take longer than a normal mentoring session because the expectation is that mentors will go through at least one intervention and then spend time talking about the student's overall progress. Mentors may need to schedule these meetings at special times, given the slightly longer timeframe. CHP consultants encourage the mentor to follow the same steps taken in the performance feedback session, which is to review the data, talk about successes and nonsuccesses, and then discuss questions and concerns. Students may want to change or drop goals, for example, and mentors can table these discussions for these longer feedback sessions. In other words, when students request changes, the mentor can ask them to wait until the next feedback meeting. However, the consultant will need to prepare mentors to alter or modify goals at these sessions, when warranted. In the CHP, mentors are encouraged to keep interventions and contingencies consistent until it is clear from the data that the student is not moving toward their goal. As a guiding principle, CHP consultants follow the "4–4 Rule": If a trend line suggests no or diminishing progress after four data points, then change is warranted;[9] otherwise, each goal is reassessed at four data point intervals from that point forward, looking back over the previous four data points.

In most instances, progress will require that teachers implement reward systems at some point in the school year. Given that most secondary teachers are unfamiliar with developmentally appropriate point systems for secondary students, we use what we call the "4–4 Rule." The 4–4 Rule helps us to determine if and when to modify interventions and reinforcement plans. In the CHP, all interventions are ini-

[8] As part of this study, research assistants will conduct direct observations during the latter part of the school year, but these data will not be provided to the consultants or mentors because this level of data tracking is inconsistent with typical school consultation practices.

[9] Note that for goals targeting threshold performances (e.g., >80% performance on a checklist), we might modify this rule to mean that for four consecutive checks, the goals are met.

tially rewarded through teacher praise alone, but other types of rewards are implemented as needed. Mentors and consultants begin by graphing the first four data points following the implementation of an intervention. These initial data tell us how well the student is responding to praise alone. If a student appears successful on this first graph, verbal praise is continued and no changes are made. If the student continues to meet high standards after two consecutive feedback sessions (i.e., eight data points), we consider the goal "mastered" (although we do not necessarily discontinue). However, if after four data points a student's performance plateaus or declines, a point system may be implemented. The points are accrued over time depending on intervention performance and can be "spent" on tangible or activity rewards during meetings with the mentors. Items on the reward menu are chosen by the student to the degree possible, but consultants and mentors prioritize rewards that are feasible in the school setting. For example, a reward of 15 min of basketball with the mentor is both inexpensive and easy to administer (in most cases).

The 4–4 Rule also means that progress is reevaluated and graphs are reconstructed every four sessions thereafter. If the student is making progress or maintaining satisfactory performance relative to predetermined thresholds, no modifications are made. However, if it appears that there is no progress, a point system is started or, if a point system is already in place, the reward menu is revisited (e.g., mystery motivators might be added). Alternatively, the counselor and mentor might consider intermediate, short-term goals, or to target additional problem areas. In other words, when trend lines plateau or decline, mentors might modify, add, or discontinue goals in the special feedback session with students.

When goal changes appear warranted, we typically present several potential modifications to the student and ask them to choose one. We find that this option works like "no-choice choices," because all of the alternatives that mentors offer are potentially useful. For example, a mentor might alter an organization goal by offering a privilege reward instead of only praise. The "no-choice" aspect of the change is a menu of feasible privileges for the student to consider. The second option is to add another goal, perhaps to expand on previous success. For example, once a student starts to master a binder organization goal as evidenced by eight or more consecutive checks, the mentor might include the locker in these checks. Conceivably, a student could improve organization in one area by storing materials in another area, so such goal expansion may be advisable. Alternatively, a mentor might add a goal to include note-taking strategies along with a study skills intervention as a means of reinforcing or supporting the first goal. The third option is to discontinue a goal. Typically, this last option is used in situations where the student has mastered a goal, as demonstrated by eight or more continuous data points above a predetermined threshold for success. In such cases, we often encourage mentors to "informally" monitor progress after the goal is discontinued by conducting random checks, so that goals do not disappear entirely.

Conclusion

In this chapter, we review the mentoring model of the CHP. The CHP is consistent with other approaches to behavior consultation, but we have geared our procedures to address the chronic nature of ADHD and related disorders. Typically, this means that we start consultation early in the school year and continue through the end of the school year, but our consultation sessions might taper off or interventions might shift to informal monitoring based on student performance. Perhaps the most unique aspect of the CHP consultation is our approach to performance feedback, which is repeated after every four student–mentor sessions (assuming consistent data collection), and includes a follow-up session between the mentor and student where students react to the performance graphs.

In our most recent study of the CHP we found that these procedures are feasible and acceptable for teachers, but we are still evaluating our outcomes at the time of this writing. Although we are confident that the CHP is beneficial for a meaningful proportion of students per previous research (Evans et al. 2007; Schultz et al. 2009), we are still curious to understand when consultation is most effective and under what conditions. We hope to discover the answers to these questions in the coming years as we analyze our most recent dataset and conduct additional effectiveness trials. In the meantime, we encourage readers interested in the CHP to focus mostly on what we have learned about performance feedback procedures in secondary schools. Based on our experiences and the relevant literature, it appears that without a strong and systematic approach to performance feedback, consultants will find that intervention quality suffers. However, when interventions are delivered with integrity, school consultation can offer a feasible and cost-effective means of delivering CHP-style interventions in secondary school settings.

Module 7.1: Performance Feedback

Goals:

- The mentor (i.e., consultee) will accurately assess student performance on interventions.
- The mentor will share the performance feedback graph with the student and record their interpretations.

Materials:

1. Graph(s) of permanent product data from all interventions currently underway.

	Elements	Description
□	*Review of data*	The consultant begins by asking teachers to describe the student's performance on the intervention(s) implemented through consultation. The consultant then shows the consultee the most recent graph of the permanent product data (e.g., organization checklist performance) provided by the mentor and invites an interpretation. For example, the consultant might ask, "What does this graph say about ___'s progress?"
□	*Praise for correct implementation*	The consultant praises the mentor for data collection, regardless of whether the student is progressing on the goals or not. The consultant also praises the mentor for the work conducted during their sessions with the students that generated the data
□	*Corrective feedback*	Consultants also discuss potential problems that may be obvious from the data. For example, if data are collected only rarely (e.g., once every 3 weeks), the consultant then problem-solves around these issues and discusses possible ways to improve the intervention process. The nature of this feedback will vary depending on the problems uncovered, but the goal for consultants is to ensure that potential roadblocks are openly discussed and realistic solutions are considered. Consultants might offer to directly assist in data collection, where possible, or to sit in on future mentor–student meetings to provide feedback on the process
□	*Preparing for student feedback*	In the CHP, we encourage mentors to keep copies of the graphs discussed in the performance feedback sessions to share with students in special follow-up sessions. Consultants coach mentors to ask specific questions including: *What does this graph say about your performance?* *What are some things that have gone well for you?* *What are some things that you could do better?* An option is to record or observe the follow-up session between mentors and students to assess intervention competency

References

Allen, S.J., & Graden, J.L. (2002). Best practices in collaborative problem solving for intervention design. In A. Thomas & J. Grimes (Eds.), *Best practices in school psychology IV* (pp. 565–582) Bethesda: National Association of School Psychologists.

Atkins, M.S., Graczyk, P.A., Frazier, S.L., Abdul-Adil, J. (2003). Toward a new model for promoting urban children's mental health: Accessible, effective, and sustainable school-based mental health services. *School Psychology Review, 32,* 504–513.

Blank, R. K., de las Alas, N., & Smith, C. (2008). *Does teacher professional development have effects on teaching and learning? analysis of evaluation findings from programs for mathematics and science teachers in 14 states.* Washington, DC: The Council of Chief State School Officers.

Coalition for Psychology in Schools and Education. (2006, August). *Report on the teacher needs survey.* Washington, D.C.: American Psychological Association. Center for Psychology in Schools and Education.

Codding, R. S., Feinberg, A. B., Dunn, E. K., & Pace, G. M. (2005). Effects of immediate performance feedback on implementation of behavior support plans. *Journal of Applied Behavior Analysis, 38,* 205–219.

Erchul, W. P., Raven, B. H., & Whichard, S. M. (2001). School psychologist and teacher perceptions of social power in consultation. *Journal of School Psychology, 39,* 483–497.

Erchul, W. P., & Martens, B. K. (2002). School consultation: Conceptual and empirical bases of practice (2nd edn.). New York: Kluwer. Academic/Plenum.

Evans, S.W., Langberg, J., Raggi, V., Allen, J., & Buvinger, E. (2005). Development of a school-based treatment program for middle school youth with ADHD. *Journal of Attention Disorders, 9,* 343–353.

Evans, S. W., Serpell, Z. N., Schultz, B., & Pastor, D. (2007). Cumulative benefits of secondary school-based treatment of students with ADHD. *School Psychology Review, 36,* 256–273.

Frank, J. L., & Kratchwill, T. R. (2010). School-based problem-solving consultation: Plotting a new course for evidence-based research and practice in consultation. In W. P. Erchul & S. M. Sheridan (Eds.), *Handbook of research in school consultation* (pp. 13–30). New York: Routledge.

Gilbertson, D., Witt, J. C., Singletary, L. L., & VanDerHeyden, A. (2007). Supporting teacher use of interventions: Effects of response dependent performance feedback on teacher implementation of a math intervention. *Journal of Behavioral Education, 16,* 311–326.

Gilman, R., & Gabriel, S. (2004). Perceptions of school psychological services by education professionals: Results from a multi-state survey pilot study. *School Psychology Review, 33,* 271–286.

Han, S., & Weiss, B. (2005). Sustainability of teacher implementation of school-based mental health programs. *Journal of Abnormal Child Psychology, 33,* 665–679.

Herman, K. C., Reinke, W. M., Frey, A., & Shepard, S. A. (2014). *Motivational interviewing in schools: Strategies for engaging parents, teachers, and students.* New York: Springer.

Jones, K. M., Wickstrom, K. F., & Friman, P.C. (1997). The effects of observational feedback on treatment integrity in school-based behavioral consultation. *School Psychology Quarterly, 12,* 316–326.

Kendall, P.C., Gosch, E., Furr, J.M. & Sood, E. (2008). Flexibility within fidelity. *Journal of the American Academy of Child and Adolescent Psychiatry, 47,* 987–993.

Kent, K. M., Pelham, W. E., Molina, B. S. G., Sibley, M. H., Waschbusch, D. A., Yu, J., Karch, K. M., et al. (2011). The academic experience of male high school students with ADHD. *Journal of Abnormal Child Psychology, 39*(3), 451–462.

Kovaleski, J.F. (2002). Best practices in operating pre-referral intervention teams. In A. Thomas & J. Grimes (Eds.), *Best practices in school psychology IV* (pp. 645–655). Bethesda, MD: National Association of School Psychologists.

Kratochwill, T.R., Elliott, S.N., & Callan-Stoiber, K. (2002). Best practices in school-based problem-solving consultation. In A. Thomas & J. Grimes (Eds.), *Best practices in school psychology IV* (pp. 583–608). Bethesda: National Association of School Psychologists.

Molina, B., & Pelham, W.E. (2003). Childhood predictors of adolescent substance abuse in a longitudinal study of children with ADHD. *Journal of Abnormal Psychology, 112,* 497–503.

Molina, B. S. G., Pelham, W. E., Gnagy, E. M., Thompson, A. L., & Marshal, M. P. (2007). Attention-deficit/hyperactivity disorder risk for heavy drinking and alcohol use disorder is age specific. *Alcoholism: Clinical and Experimental Research, 31*(4), 1–12.

Moncher, F.J., & Prinz, R.J. (1991). Treatment integrity in outcome studies. *Clinical Psychology Review, 11,* 247–266.

Mortenson, B. P., & Witt, J. C. (1998). The use of weekly performance feedback to increase teacher implementation of a prereferral academic intervention. *School Psychology Review, 27,* 613–627.

Mullens, J., Leighton, M., Laguarda, K., & O'Brien, E. (1996). *Student learning, teaching quality, and professional development: theoretical linkages, current measurement, and recommendations for future data collection (NCES 96—28). U.S. Department of Education.* Washington, DC: National Center for Education Statistics Working Paper.

Noell, G., Witt, J., Gilbertson, D., Ranier, D., & Freeland, J. (1997). Increasing teacher intervention implementation in general education settings through consultation and performance feedback. *School Psychology Quarterly, 12,* 77–88.

Noell, G.H., Duhon, G.J., Gatti, S.L., & Connell, J.E. (2002). Consultation, follow-up, and implementation of behavior management interventions in general education. *School Psychology Review, 31,* 217–234.

Noell, G.H., Witt, J.C., Slider, N.J., Connell, J.E., Gatti, S.L., Williams, K.L., et al. (2005). Treatment implementation following behavioral consultation in schools: A comparison of three follow-up strategies. *School Psychology Review, 34,* 87–106.

Noell, G. H., Gansle, K. A., Mevers, J. L., Knox, R. M., Mintz, J. C., & Dahir, A. (2014). Improving treatment plan implementation in schools: A meta-analysis of single subject design studies. *Journal of Behavioral Education, 23,* 168–191.

Parsad, B., Lewis, L., Farris, E., & Greene, B. (2001). *Teacher preparation and professional development: 2000.* Washington, DC: National Center for Education Statistics. Available at http://nces.ed.gov/pubs2001/2001088.pdf.

Reschly, D.J. (2000). The present and future status of school psychology in the United States. *School Psychology Review, 29,* 507–522.

Reschly, D.J. (2004). Commentary: Paradigm shift, outcomes criteria, and behavioral interventions: Where we've been, where we are, and where we need to go. *School Psychology Review, 33,* 408–416.

Rosenfield, S. (2002). Best practices in instructional consultation. In A. Thomas & J. Grimes (Eds.), *Best practices in school psychology IV* (pp. 609–623)Bethesda: National Association of School Psychologists.

Schultz, B. K., Evans, S. W., & Serpell, Z. N. (2009). Preventing academic failure among middle school students with ADHD: A survival analysis. *School Psychology Review, 38,* 14–27.

Schultz, B. K., Evans, S. W., & Langberg, J. (2014, February). *Interventions for adolescents with ADHD: Results of a clinical trial.* Paper presented at the annual meeting of the National Association of School Psychologists, Washington, DC.

Solomon, B.G., Klein, S.A., & Politylo, B.C. (2012). The effect of performance feedback on teachers' treatment integrity: A meta-analysis of the single-case literature. *School Psychology Review, 41,* 160–175.

State, T. M., Kern, K., Starosta, K. M., & Mukherjee, A. D. (2011). Elementary pre-service teacher preparation in the area of social, emotional, and behavioral problems. *School Mental Health, 3,* 13–23.

Sterling-Turner, H.E., Watson, T.S., & Moore, J.W. (2002). The effects of direct training and treatment integrity on treatment outcomes in school consultation. *School Psychology Quarterly, 17,* 47–77.

Stuart, G., Tondora, J., & Hoge, M. (2004). Evidence-based teaching practice: Implications for behavioral health. *Administration and Policy in Mental Health, 32,* 107–130.

U.S. Department of Education (USDOE), National Center for Education Statistics. (1999). *Teacher quality: A Report on the preparation and qualifications of public school teachers* (NCES 1999-080). Washington, DC: U.S. Department of Education (USDOE), National Center for Education Statistics.

Vereb, R.L., & DiPerna, J.C. (2004). Teachers' knowledge of ADHD, treatments for ADHD, and treatment acceptability: An initial investigation. *School Psychology Review, 33,* 421–428.

Witt, J.C., Gresham, F.M., & Noell, G.H. (1996). What's behavioral about behavioral consultation? *Journal of Educational and Psychological Consultation, 4,* 327–344.

Witt, J. C., Noell, G. H., LaFleur, L. H., & Mortenson, B. P. (1997). Teacher use of interventions in general education settings: Measurement and analysis of the independent variable. *Journal of Applied Behavior Analysis, 30*(4), 693–696.

Zins, J.E., & Erchul, W.P. (2002). Best practices in school consultation. In A. Thomas & J. Grimes (Eds.), *Best practices in school psychology IV* (pp. 625–643). Bethesda: National Association of School Psychologists.

Chapter 8
Afterword

At the beginning of each chapter in this book, we have offered a quote from influential theorists in science and psychology to underscore the perennial nature of our topics. Indeed, concerns around childhood behavior problems seem surprisingly similar over time, even as our theories and interventions evolve. In many ways this is discouraging. In spite of our "advances," practice looks similar to how it did 30 years ago when I (SWE) was a special education teacher. Contrast this state of affairs with other fields and industries. For example, I doubt many would argue that the telecommunications industry now appears similar to how it was 30 years ago. Telecommunications professionals go to great lengths to keep up with the latest advances in technology and, as a result, their products and services are far more effective than they were in the past. Yet many practitioners in mental health and education are mostly unaware of the latest advances in their fields and, unfortunately, some researchers are unaware of the key challenges faced by practitioners. Mental health practitioners and researchers alike are required to attend continuing education opportunities, but there are few, if any, incentives to stay current beyond the minimum number of required credits. Furthermore, there are many providers of continuing education programs who claim that the interventions and assessments covered in their training are "evidence-based," when this is not necessarily the case.

It is our contention that a key missing ingredient in our field is meaningful quality assurance. If a telecommunications professional failed to stay current with new technologies, for example, their knowledge would become quickly (and obviously) outdated. Although there are forms of quality assurance in education, classroom practices remain largely unchanged because our measures are insufficient to provide timely and informative feedback. For example, student test results have become the primary variable by which the quality of instruction is measured. Unfortunately, students' test performance is a function of many child and family characteristics that are beyond the control of the teacher. As a result, exceptional teaching may yield small student gains in some classrooms and poor instruction may yield large gains in others. Recent efforts have been made to measure teachers' performance in the classroom using observations by administrators. Although this may represent a step

B. K. Schultz, S. W. Evans, *A Practical Guide to Implementing School-Based Interventions for Adolescents with ADHD,* DOI 10.1007/978-1-4939-2677-0_8

in the right direction, it is unclear if most of the administrators are familiar with best practices and whether observations can be done frequently enough to obtain a valid representation of an instructor's teaching.

The quality assurance approaches for teachers are certainly problematic, but may represent more progress than has been accomplished in many community mental health clinics. In these settings, clinicians are often held most accountable for the number of billable hours. When the quality of services is addressed, it is often based on self report by clinicians with little to no verification of the relationship between services provided and best practices. Similar to the education system, it is also unclear if those in supervisory roles maintain knowledge of best practices. One notable exception to this is the quality assurance systems put in place by the Veteran's Administration (VA). Clinicians receive extensive training on best practices and recordings of sessions in practice are often compared to those standards. Of course the VA is a unique setting, but it provides one example of how we may advance quality assurance across the field.

But in comparison to the quality assurance challenges of education and community mental health, the field of school mental health is in much greater need of improvement. One of the major hurdles to quality assurance for school mental health professionals is that they are often supervised by an administrator and not a person trained in the field. In fact, there may be nobody in a school district that is aware of best practices, so it should not be surprising that most of these professionals are engaged in administrative tasks rather than service provision. For example, student scheduling and sharing information about post-high school training opportunities with students do not require people with a master's degree to competently perform, yet these are common responsibilities of school counselors. Still, administrators often justify school mental health positions to the boards of education based on the emotional and behavioral needs of their students. We argue that if addressing the emotional and behavioral needs of students was a real priority, quality assurance, training, and supervision related to meeting these needs would become an important part of school district practice and policy.

We do not intend for our concerns around quality assurance to be read as criticism of educators, clinicians, or school mental health professionals. In fact, given the current state of practice, it is incredible how many professionals in these fields keep up with the literature and modify their practices based on what they learn. Furthermore, it is hard to imagine an industry such as telecommunications (or others) making progress with such poor quality assurance programs—not to mention poor financial incentives—as those that exist in education and mental health. Still, it is clear that the development of feasible and acceptable quality assurance programs for education and mental health are sorely needed.

A model quality assurance program for the school mental health services was developed in Ontario, Canada and may prove to be an effective step forward in other countries. The Hamilton-Wentworth District developed a program called "School Mental Health ASSIST" that includes professionals who work to promote evidence-based school mental health practices within their district (see http://www.hwdsb.on.ca/wp-content/uploads/2012/11/Mental-Health-Assist.pdf). The origins of these services are described in a book chapter by a leading pioneer in our field and current director of the program (Short et al. 2007). Further development and evaluations of efforts like this one may lead to large gains in the quality of services that students with emotional and behavioral problems receive in our schools. In fact, we believe that advances in this area may be one of the greatest advances and much needed steps in the field.

Future Directions for the Challenging Horizons Program (CHP)

Throughout this book we have attempted to describe the CHP so that professionals could implement the basic components and understand the supporting research. Of course, new findings are emerging every day. At the time of this writing, we just completed a large study of many of the practices described in this book and are confident that our findings will help us to identify ways to improve our procedures. In particular, we hope to uncover ways to meaningfully predict which services will work for which students. For instance, it appears that families differentially engage in the after-school program versus the school consultation version, perhaps depending on resources or student needs (Schultz et al. 2014). In the future, we hope to conduct an adaptive study (e.g., randomly assigning participants to conditions based on previous performance) to answer such questions definitively.

We also hope to find ways to integrate the CHP interventions into the regular school day. Although we have confidence in the after-school version of the CHP, for example, we readily acknowledge that many school districts could not afford to deliver services similar to how we have in our research studies. That said, the after-school version of the CHP has provided an invaluable incubator for intervention design and testing over the past 15 years, allowing us to identify effective practices that may be disseminated in other ways. For this reason, we are shifting our focus to alternative delivery models. One promising strategy that we hope to explore to a greater degree has been to integrate the CHP interventions into a regularly scheduled study halls or resource rooms that students with the attention deficit hyperactivity disorder (ADHD) attend daily. We have conducted 2-year-long studies on this model of the CHP with encouraging results. If feasible, such models could ensure a high dose of intervention with minimal cost, while circumventing the barriers that prevent many families from seeking community mental health services.

We are also exploring new technologies to disseminate the CHP interventions. For example, online videoconferencing software offers an option for consulting with teachers in remote locations. Specifically, videoconferencing allows consultants and consultees to meet online and simultaneously manipulate electronic documents. We believe these options lend themselves well to performance feedback within consultation, particularly in the collection and graphing of student performance over time. Online videoconferencing also offers a flexible way to adjust for the common need to reschedule meetings on short notice, without incurring unnecessary travel costs. Currently we are pilot testing videoconferencing procedures in a rural middle school in North Carolina and hope to expand this research into more schools in the near future.

Of course it is impossible to anticipate all of the potential directions the CHP research and practice could go in the future. In any event, we sincerely hope that our work advances the discussion on interventions for adolescents with ADHD and leads to effective school-based interventions on a broad scale. The stakes for adolescents with ADHD are high, but outcomes are clearly improved when practitioners adhere to the principles outlined herein.

References

Short, K. H., Evans, S. W., Woehrle, T. S., & Ridolfi, C. M. (2007). E-BEST: Bridging the science and practice divide in school-based mental health. In S. W. Evans, M. Weist, & Z. Serpell (Eds.), *Advances in School-Based Mental Health Interventions: Best Practices and Program Models (Vol. 2)*. New York: Civic Research Institute.

Schultz, B. K., Evans, S. W., & Langberg, J. (2014, February). Interventions for adolescents with ADHD: Results of a clinical trial. Paper presented at the annual meeting of the National Association of School Psychologists, Washington, DC.

Appendices

Appendix A: Initial Appraisal Form

Student Name ____________________ Date Completed _______________

Age ________ Birthdate ________ Grade________

List the names and ages of all of the child's siblings

Names	Ages	Living at home? (yes or no – if no indicate where living)

List the names of all parents, step-parents, and other care-takers

Names	Relationship to child	Living at home? (yes or no – if no indicate where living)

B. K. Schultz, S. W. Evans, *A Practical Guide to Implementing School-Based Interventions for Adolescents with ADHD*, DOI 10.1007/978-1-4939-2677-0

List and describe any clubs, teams, or organizations that the child participates in now or has participated in during the last year.

What are the child's three favorite things to do?

How does the child spend unstructured time? Be specific, what did he/she do last weekend or yesterday evening?

Who are the child's two best friends and when was the last time he/she spent time with them outside of school?

What are the child's best and worst subjects? Why?

List the child's current teachers and the subjects that they teach.

What is the child's schedule?

Why does the child believe that he is involved in CHP?

Does s/he have any goals that you can help him/her with?

Main Findings

1	
2	
3	
4	
5	

Appendix B: Assignment Notebook Tracking Intervention Record

Instructions: Record the number of assignments and teacher initials obtained each day, over the number expected.

Date																					
# teacher signatures obtained																					
# teacher signatures expected																					
# assignments written correctly																					
# assignments expected																					
Date																					
# teacher signatures obtained																					
# teacher signatures expected																					
# assignments written correctly																					
# assignments expected																					
Date																					
# teacher signatures obtained																					
# teacher signatures expected																					
# assignments written correctly																					
# assignments expected																					

Appendix C: Organization Intervention Monitoring Record

Get organized! Be able to find your assignments and turn them in! Be able to locate your notes to study for tests! Open your binder and go down the checklist: for each item, write a Y (for yes) if you meet the question *fully* or an N (for no) if you do not meet the question fully. When finished checking divide the number of Y's recorded by 11 and record this in the last space as the percentage of your binder that's organized.

BINDER									
Is your assignment notebook secured by three rings so that it is the first thing you see when you open your binder?									
Is there a folder for each class you are taking *attached by three rings*? (1. Math, 2. Science, 3. English/Reading, 4. Social Studies, 5. P.E./Health, 6. other extracurricular courses)									
Are the notes from each subject organized from *oldest to newest* behind the subject folder and *secured by the three-rings* in the binder?									
Is there a pocket for papers your parents need to see, and only these papers are in it?									
Are all the papers that are in the binder school related? (no drawings, scrap paper, etc.)									
Is the Homework Folder attached by three rings behind your assignment notebook?									
Is your binder free of loose papers (are all papers secured in folder pockets or attached by three rings)?									
Within each subject folder: Are all non-homework papers for that subject in the right pocket of the folder?									
Are all papers in the correct section of the binder? (no papers in the wrong section)									
What percent of your binder is organized? Divide the number of Y's by 9 and then multiply by 100.									

Appendix C: Organization Intervention Monitoring Record (Continued)

Don't forget your bookbag and locker! Organize them too! Open your bookbag and locker and go down the checklist: for each item, write a Y (for yes) if you meet the question *fully* or an N (for no) if you do not meet the question fully. When finished checking, divide the number of Y's recorded by 4 for the bookbag and record this in the last space as the percentage of your bookbag that's organized. Repeat this for the locker and divide the number of Ys by 3 and record.

BOOKBAG										
Do you have the books you need to complete tomorrow's homework?										
You don't have books in your book bag that you don't need to complete homework due in the next 3 days or long-term assignments?										
Is your bookbag free from unnecessary clothing?										
Is your bookbag free from loose papers and objects (pens, toys, magazines, etc)?										
Percentage of criteria met (# of Ys/4)*100										
LOCKER										
Are the books neatly stacked (or shelved) with the spines facing out so that you can easily grab one in between classes or after school?										
Is your locker free of loose objects (papers, pencils, pens, toys, magazines, trash, etc.)?										
Is you locker free from unnecessary clothing?										
Percentage of criteria met (# of Ys/3)*100										

Appendix D: ISG Card

Client & Counselor Ratings

Student ID: ____________________

Date: ____________________

Counselor: ____________________

Activity Codes (*Circle One*)	
CBG	Play cards or board games
WLK	Go for a walk in small groups
SPT	Play a sport
CFT	Make a craft
IG	Interactive Game
PFE	Prepare food and eat

Ratings should indicate the degree with which the student portrayed each ideal-self goal according to the scale below. After the last feedback, transfer average ratings to mastery form (Appendix E).

Behavior is opposite of goal — *No Evidence* — *Behavior matches the desired goal*

Very Much **-3**	Some **-2**	A Little **-1**	**0**	A Little **+1**	Some **+2**	Very Much **+3**		Not Applicable **N/A**

Ideal Self Goals	Feedback 1	Feedback 2	Feedback 3	Feedback 4	AVG. SCORES
#1:	Kid / Staff				Kid / Staff
#2:	Kid / Staff				Kid / Staff
#3:	Kid / Staff				Kid / Staff

Note. Clients are asked for their self-ratings and these are recorded in the small boxes within each cell before the counselor shares his/her ratings, which are recorded in the large boxes within each cell.

Appendix E: ISG Master Tracking Form

Instruction At the end of each ISG session, record the date. Then compute the student's average score for each goal and record in the appropriate box. If the student has achieved a staff AND student score greater than or equal to 2 for any of his/her goals, record "Y" in the corresponding box. If the student has not achieved a staff AND student score of greater than or equal to 2, then record "N" in the corresponding box. Once three consecutive "Y's" have been obtained for a single goal, then the student has mastered this goal. Please record the date that the student masters each goal. The student can proceed to phase three of the intervention once he/she has mastered one goal.

Student's ID: ________________ Counselor's name: ____________________

	Average Ideal Self Goal #1		**Average Ideal Self Goal #2**		**Average Ideal Self Goal #3**		**Achieved 2 or 3 on Goal #1 (Y/N)**	**Achieved 2 or 3 on Goal #2 (Y/N)**	**Achieved 2 or 3 on Goal #3 (Y/N)**
Date	Student	Staff	Student	Staff	Student	Staff			

Mastery reached for Goal #1: ______

Mastery reached for Goal #2: ______

Mastery reached for Goal #3: ______

Appendix F: Behavior Contract for Homework Management

1. My goal for the next report card is: ______________________________

2. I will work on my homework ______________ at this time: ____________

3. I will work on my homework for this amount of time each day: ____________

4. What will happen if I'm not working during homework time? ____________

5. I understand that even if I do not have homework, I will use the homework time to study for tests and quizzes, or as an alternative: ____________________

Additional Terms: ____

____

____

____

____

____

By signing this contract, I ______________ (print name) understand the terms that are described above. This agreement will start today and will be renegotiated when I receive my next report card / mid-term report, and changes will depend on how I am doing at that time.

Student Signature: ______________________ Date: ________

Parent Signature: ______________________ Date: ________

Appendix G: Common Interview Questions for Consultees

1. What are this child's strengths? What are this child's weaknesses?
2. What are some things you are doing now that help this student work up to potential?
3. Describe one area where this student could improve. (GET SPECIFIC EXAMPLES by asking, "*What does he do that makes you describe him/that way*?")
4. When does problem behavior occur? During what time of day is it most problematic?
5. Where does the problem behavior usually take place (e.g., classroom, gym, hallway, bus)? What are the characteristics of that setting (e.g., individual seat work, group task, number of other students and adult's present, seating arrangement)?
6. How often does the problem behavior occur (i.e., frequency)?
7. How long does the problem behavior last (i.e., duration)?
8. What is usually happening just before the problem behavior begins (antecedents, triggers)? (e.g., Is the student interacting with a peer, being reprimanded, being told to do or not to do something, a transition)
9. How do you typically respond to the problem behavior?
10. What are the consequences associated with the problem behavior (e.g., student is removed from task, reprimanded, punished, ignored, sent to office, threatened by consequences, denied privileges, parent is called, note is sent home)?
11. How do other students react to the problem behavior (e.g., leave student alone, criticize student, laugh at student?
12. What are some positive strategies that have been helpful in reducing the problem behavior?

Appendix H: Consultation and Performance Feedback Template

Challenging Horizons Program

Teacher: Child ID: Date of Consultation:

Consultant:
****
******

Intervention:

Summary of Student Progress since Last Consultation Session:

1. Areas of Student success:

2. Areas of Student non-success:

3. Review Graphs for each intervention (attach copies to this document)

4. Problem Solving Ideas (if applicable):

5. Action Steps:

A Practical Guide to Implementing School-Based Interventions for Adolescents with ADHD

Brandon K. Schultz, Steven W. Evans

This innovative volume details counseling interventions for secondary students with attention deficit hyperactivity disorder (ADHD) and its associated academic and conduct problems, particularly focusing on youth at risk for developing serious disruptive behaviors. It addresses the continuing debate over counseling for youths with ADHD by identifying key elements common to reputable therapies and suggesting a framework for their successful implementation. The core of the book discusses the Challenging Horizons Program (CHP), a behavior- and solutions-focused approach to counseling adolescents with ADHD that has been studied extensively for more than 15 years. Based on the quality of research, the CHP has been included in the National Registry of Evidence-based Programs and Practices maintained by the US Substance Abuse and Mental Health Services Administration (SAMHSA). Excerpts from actual sessions illustrate typical therapist-client interactions in the CHP, and sample modules from the program's treatment literature expand the book's descriptions of effective hands on interventions.

Counseling skills featured in this book include:

- Bridging the research-into-practice divide.
- Establishing a therapeutic alliance with students with ADHD.
- Developing and implementing interventions for memory, organization, and planning.
- Enhancing young clients' social skills.
- Enlisting family members in the intervention process.
- Working directly with teachers to improve student behaviors.

A Practical Guide to Implementing School-Based Interventions for Adolescents with ADHD is an essential resource for researchers, clinicians and related professionals, and graduate students in such disciplines as school and clinical child psychology, social work, educational psychology, psychotherapy and counseling, and learning and instruction.

B. K. Schultz, S. W. Evans, *A Practical Guide to Implementing School-Based Interventions for Adolescents with ADHD*, DOI 10.1007/978-1-4939-2677-0

Index

B. K. Schultz, S. W. Evans, *A Practical Guide to Implementing School-Based Interventions for Adolescents with ADHD*, DOI 10.1007/978-1-4939-2677-0

CPSIA information can be obtained at www.ICGtesting.com
Printed in the USA
LVOW01*1742021015

456708LV00010B/101/P

9 781493 926763